Popular Singing and Style

Popular Singing and Style

2nd Edition

DONNA SOTO-MORETTINI

BLOOMSBURY
LONDON • NEW DELHI • NEW YORK • SYDNEY

Bloomsbury Methuen Drama
An imprint of Bloomsbury Publishing Plc

50 Bedford Square
London
WC1B 3DP
UK

1385 Broadway
New York
NY 10018
USA

www.bloomsbury.com

Bloomsbury is a registered trade mark of Bloomsbury Publishing Plc

First published 2014

British Library Cataloguing-in-Publication Data
A catalogue record for this book is available from the British Library.

ISBN: PB: 978-1-4725-1-8644
ePDF: 978-1-4725-1-8668
ePub: 978-1-4725-1-8651

Library of Congress Cataloging-in-Publication Data
A catalog record for this book is available from the Library of Congress.

Typeset by Deanta Global Publishing Services, Chennai, India
Printed and bound in India

CONTENTS

ACKNOWLEDGEMENTS

Many thanks to Stuart William Fleming for his friendship, and his excellent keyboard skills, and to David O'Leary for his help with recording. Thanks, too, to the wonderful vocal coach staff on *The Voice* auditions, especially Joshua Alamu, Mark De-Lisser, John Modi, Jai Ramage, Juliet Russell, and Fiona MacDougal who joined in the discussion and, of course, many thanks to Anna Brewer and staff at Bloomsbury for their help and guidance throughout.

This book is dedicated to Bijan Sharifi, whose love of music and unerring technical audio skills were inspiring throughout.

PREFACE TO THE SECOND EDITION

As Elvis Costello once famously said, writing about music is like dancing about architecture. I take his point, and when working on the first edition of this book, I was confronted regularly with the challenge of trying to describe sounds in words. But 9 years is a long time in popular music . . . and an even longer one in the world of technology. I began researching the first edition of this book early in 2004. iTunes was launched in the United Kingdom in June of that year, but like most people I knew then, I didn't start to use it right away. So you can probably imagine how things worked when I wanted to listen to artists like Big Bill Broonzy or Little Willie John . . . it was generally a fruitless trip into town to find old vinyl shops (from which I mostly came away empty-handed), or trawls on eBay for exotic record collections. YouTube launched in 2005 but wasn't really on my radar until after the book was finished. Pandora launched in 2005 and Spotify launched in 2008. These days, music is more available and easier to find than ever, so one of the great things about going back to rethink this book now is that there are so many more resources for listening. And that, in turn, gives me much more freedom in referring to singers and to specific examples of particular sounds, since I know that it will be relatively easy for the reader to track down and watch or hear a specific performance. This has inspired a massive rethink of the content and layout, and has resulted in a pretty extensive library of examples of all the vocal qualities and complementary elements of style considered here. I'm hoping that this alone will make this second edition a valuable purchase.

Over the years I've heard from many people who have bought the first edition of the book, mostly from teachers who have found it really useful in their work. But I've heard from rugged individualists too, who have used the book to help them chart a course for themselves as they listen and learn. Nearly all of the people I've spoken to have found that the material on earlier 'classic' popular singers seems to have proved the most interesting. That is because for many people, singers like Son House or Mahalia Jackson are a completely new discovery and that has provided much inspiration and pleasure. For these reasons, I've decided only to update the contemporary singers where I think it makes sense to do so, and I've referenced a lot more recordings and performances because they're so easy to find now.

You'll note that I've deliberately avoided too many references to pop music; there's little point in referring anyone to Bruno Mars or Rihanna as we spend most of our lives hearing these tracks in an ambient sort of way. Of course I address pop style, but I've tried to make sure that many of the references will be ones that you might not encounter on a daily basis.

I've also been asked by many people to include more here about one of the central themes of this book: learning to make the most of your voice, 'flaws' and all. To that end I've included a new section that addresses the questions and issues that vocalists I work with seem to worry about most.

Finally, I've tried to standardize some of the nomenclature used here. When I was first writing, there were copyright worries over using some terminology, but these days the use of 'sob' or 'cry' quality is so common that I feel comfortable substituting my old terminology (elongated) with the more commonly used 'cry'.

Nine years is a long time in all areas, and in the years since this book was published I've spent more time working in television than in training institutions or private teaching. It's been a fascinating journey; I've worked as a casting director and performance coach for shows as varied as ITV's 'Superstar' and 'Popstar to Opera Star', and BBC's 'The Voice'. Over that time I've done eight national audition tours and watched the increasing popularity of the television singing contests, all of which has convinced me that we're more fascinated than ever by the question of what it is that makes a great voice. The experience of seeing so many people in audition rooms across the country is a strangely humbling one.

Of course, there are some people whose auditions are more inspired by the 'quick-and-disposable' fame culture these shows promote, but many others come to sing because they love music, and they believe that singing gives them a powerful way to express themselves. Even when these voices are judged not to be right for a particular show, they are always an inspiration to me. In so many ways, this book is written for them.

Whatever your background, I hope that this book inspires you to forget the ideas of 'good'/'bad' or 'wrong'/'right' and just have the courage to listen, experiment, think deeply about what it is you want to communicate and sing with joy!

A note about references and examples

I've largely used Spotify throughout when looking for examples, but I've always included dates so you can check if your version is the same whether it's on iTunes, CD, Pandora or any other source. Occasionally I will refer to live performances on YouTube, and have included the YouTube link. These URLs are fiddly and long, however, for ease of reference I will also make sure that every YouTube link referenced is also on the website (www.donnasoto-m.co.uk) so that once on the site you can just 'click through' to the performance you want to see.

However you find them, try to listen to every example. I advise you to read this book with your laptop open and nearby, and I guarantee that if you read and then listen to every example, you'll never hear or think about popular singing in quite the same way again.

Introduction

Sometimes, I love beautiful voices. I respond to the purity of k.d.lang's great, rich autumnal tones. I appreciate the purity and elegance of the young Joni Mitchell's voice, or the earthy, almost funereal depths of Paul Robeson's. But my real passion lies elsewhere, because as much as I love beautiful voices, I am more fervently in awe of the whole of the spectrum of sound that the human voice can make – and I love that great spectrum of sound even more when employed honestly, in the service of heartfelt musical communication. Flaws, scratches, creaks, rumbles, screams, whispers, shouts, wails, sighs, grit, gravel and even dodgy intonation can move my heart when the artist has something deep and immediate to communicate.

Maybe my love of these artless sounds has to do with my general love of breaking the rules in the pursuit of frankly passionate expression. Perhaps it is to do with valuing the sense of abandon that so few of us ever manage to achieve in our day-to-day lives. Perhaps it's just simple admiration of artists who go their own way in spite of the good advice of others. No doubt it has something to do with the desire to hear things I've not heard before or to glimpse, ever so briefly, into the heart of someone else through their singing. But it must also be that the voice gets right to the heart of who we are; when singers are defiant, and different, and bold, and passionate, they are not only refusing to conform to imposed standards of 'beauty', but they are living proof that it is only in the great variety of individual human life and sound that we can discover what really matters.

This book is the result of my explorations into the way that these two vocal realms – the wild and defiant versus the pure and beautiful – seem to clash so often in vocal performance and in the approach to teaching vocalists.

This is a book about style. It is a book for vocalists, voice teachers and people who are interested in the varieties and the evolution of contemporary popular vocal styles. It is not a history book, nor is it, strictly speaking, a comprehensive book about vocal style, which would include much more about history and context. It is a practical book that aims to concentrate on the performance and practice of popular singing.

My method is to isolate and describe, where possible, the elements of popular singing, and to consider how one might learn these elements. As far as I know, there is no other book that attempts to do this. This is a very different approach to that of traditional vocal tuition or through books on how to train your voice. From the start, I will attempt to be clear about an area (popular singing/music) that doesn't seem to invite much clarity in written analysis.

Most definitions of popular music – and they aren't easy to find – are couched in some pretty careful language. This is because (as with most art forms) boundaries don't remain fixed for long. Most art forms grow and change through the blending and blurring of categories, and singing styles have certainly followed this pattern.

To add to the confusion, many singers, over the span of their careers, choose to explore songs in multiple styles or genres, and this can increase the confusion about something as seemingly simple as what kind of music one is listening to.

One thing that needs clarity from the start is the difference between style and genre. I am probably on safest ground if I begin by claiming this distinction as my own, and by explaining how I use this distinction throughout the book. The elements of vocal style that we will be covering here can be considered a series of vocal 'choices' that the artist makes. Some of them are choices that aren't available to all of us – few singers can successfully prolong the effort level or 'constricted' onset sound of Tina Turner, or match the extended improvisational ability of Christina Aguilera. Some singers, however, don't make such bold choices, and some prefer to remain within a rather narrow band of stylistic choices. And of course, that is their style (think of Norah Jones or Sade, for instance). Others make few but strong choices that leave their imprint unmistakably (Billie Holiday and Adele come to mind). Some have an extraordinary range of choices that seem adaptable to any number of song styles (Paul McCartney and Billy Joel are great examples of this).

These choices are what I will be analysing and describing as 'the elements of style'.

Genre is a more difficult thing, since you can't find two jazz musicians who will give you the same definition of jazz. Nor will you find two musicians who can agree on the difference between rhythm and blues and soul or even, simply, the blues.

In popular music, at the very beginning of the recording industry, the first strong detectable popular genres were the blues and jazz. As jazz branched out into many distinct subcategories, from the big swing bands to bebop, and through to more progressive forms, the blues remained more or less a 'shading' that infected nearly every style of popular music. While folk music has a long and wonderful history, country music (which might have been seen in its early days as a marketable brand of folk music, but which owes as much to the blues) quickly found its own distinctions and began to influence other forms once recordings were widely available. With the beginnings of rock or rockabilly music in the early 1950s, elements of jazz, blues and country were all detectable. Throughout this book, my interest in these histories will centre only on how such things influenced the stylistic choices made by singers working and recording at the time.

These days there are still large categorical distinctions but of course, these distinctions are only marginally helpful. We may have a general notion of what country singers sound like (which grows a bit more confused when we listen to the pop sound of a country artist like Taylor Swift), or of what jazz singers sound like (although jazz fusion styles have quite successfully blurred this category), or of what folk singers sound like (although I've seen the label applied to artists as distinct as Ed Sheeran, Mumford & Sons and Damien Rice, which is rather confusing), but it is often just as easy to let *Billboard*, iTunes or the recording companies sort it out for us.

Consequently, in any of the following chapters, we can only talk about genre in the most general way, always looking to specifics to help us thread our way carefully through the sophisticated and complex reality that underlies the blunt instrument of musical categorization.

Simply, then, the categories we will be looking at will include the elements of style that are common to blues, jazz, gospel, country and rock. But to make the distinctions between these genres clear, we must look backwards because pop music has been fusing and blurring these categories for decades. No element is exclusive to any of these genres, and indeed, that is the problem for voice teachers in the early twenty-first century. Pop has come to stand for a different listening experience altogether; where the five earlier categories can all be traced back to a kind of original 'pure' strain, pop is a massive fusion of all these early genres and it tends to mix them up and then re-present them in a 'lite calorie' version. It is the difference, for example, between Justin Bieber and Steven Tyler.

The backward look here is important in another way. Many of the examples I've included in this book are of artists whose works have been 'lost' to contemporary singers. I hope that the inclusion of artists you may never have listened to will provide a powerful demonstration of the kinds of brave, unique and exciting recorded sounds that we don't come across much these days. Given the somewhat homogenized sound of current pop playlists, the sheer bravado of some of these early recording artists should be a refreshing reminder of the full scope of vocal style and might inspire singers who are trying to find courage in their own style explorations.

Singing style is a highly personal 'signature' that artists develop over time, and it invariably involves experimentation and imitation. It demands listening and exploration, but often singers begin by just trying to sound 'good', 'correct', 'beautiful' or like someone else.

The history of popular singing has often been all about disrupting what we think of as 'good' or 'beautiful'; when vocalists like Hank Williams or Bruce Springsteen sound wonderful to us they may simultaneously sound anything but beautiful. The consequence of this is that the break from the 'beautiful' or '*bel canto*'[1] tradition of voice teaching has been a difficult one for many voice teachers to negotiate when working with popular singing, since the majority of the tools they work with are geared rather specifically to guiding voices towards that perceived aesthetic of good singing. To expect traditional voice teachers to train popular voices is rather like expecting an oil painter to sculpt – it requires different tools and an open mind towards a different kind of experience.

When I first began teaching pop singers and pop styles, I was surprised at how little was written for singers in this area. To provide a logical teaching pattern that would extend students' ability to approach a number of different styles and sounds, I began to compile notes on the kinds of vocal choices that singers in particular genres were making and of the various stylistic approaches they used. I spent much time sharing my 'style' notes and presiding over some critical listening sessions with my vocalists. This book initially grew out of that process.

Many years ago I read an article by Thomas F. Cleveland, the Director of Vocology at the Vanderbilt Voice Center in Nashville. I found it fascinating because he was making a plea for voice teachers to recognize that the growth of popular music meant that they needed to learn how to teach popular styles. His brief article made the point that for too long there

---

[1]*Bel canto* translates as 'beautiful singing'. The term is used to describe techniques that originated with Italian singing masters and performers many centuries ago, and these days generally means approaching voice training within the parameters of classical teaching methods and aesthetics.

has been the belief that singing in the classical style is the only 'healthy' way to sing. I hadn't run across any published work that was making such a plea before, although in my professional life I had encountered many who were convinced that singers can either sing 'properly' or risk ruining their voices completely. Professor Cleveland finished his article with an admonition that voice teachers would have to keep an open mind, and that they would have to learn the science of what makes commercial styles what they are.

I'm not sure there could ever be a science capable of accommodating just what it is about Bessie Smith's style that has such a sexual charge, or why Roy Orbison elicits such deep emotion when he sings, but I do believe that there are a number of elements that can be taught, which will allow artists to explore the possibility of creating such effects in their own way, should they so choose.

My own musical journey has led me, in what I freely admit to be a patchwork, uneven way, to some discoveries about teaching students the elements of style, and it is those elements that form the basis of this work. As a foundation, I still rely very much on things I've learnt over the years from great teachers like Jo Estill. But I know that when I was starting out as a teacher there were many times when I could have used some kind of reference or vocabulary for approaching popular style.

This is one good reason, I hope, for the existence of this book.

In short, then, this book is not about training the voice – there are many resources for this, from classes to videos to one-to-one tuition. It is meant instead to be a helpful resource for both singers and voice teachers who want to explore the ways in which they can add more style to their work, but are not sure where such an exploration might start. I hope that the following will inspire greater vocal experiment in the quest to find unique and exciting sounds that can add to the singer's own expressive ability – indeed this has been my mission throughout the writing of the book.

To begin with, we'll look at the weightiest elements – the various kinds of qualities that the singing voice makes. We'll follow that by looking at all the complementary elements that go into shaping those various qualities in a vocal performance. And finally, we'll go backwards, just slightly. Rather than looking at the long lists of category and sub-category that make up Amazon or iTunes catalogues now, we're going to follow categories back to their more 'pure', original strains and consider what it is that makes up those original categories of blues, gospel, rock, jazz, country and pop. It's important to note here, however, that I always recognize that there are no real categories, and that musical evolutions and fusions will always defy any attempt to put things into rigid 'boxes'.

Have the courage to experiment with things and spend as much time listening as you can. Remember that while vocal teachers can help you with technical things, nurturing your own personal style is something only you can do. And you'll only do it with some dedicated listening and experimenting in the first stage. Hopefully, you'll be lucky enough to go on from there to playing gigs. Do a lot: do good ones, bad ones, hopelessly depressing ones (we've all done them . . .) and that will be a massive part of shaping your sense of artistry and style. From Frank Sinatra standing in front of Tommy Dorsey's orchestra for years, to The Beatles playing to drunken sailors in Hamburg, style grows out of many years of experience and a lot of listening.

A note about the practice exercises in this book

Throughout the book I've included practical exercises that I use in workshops, but of course no one learns vocal style in this way. The exercises are not designed to make you a blues singer or a jazz singer – they are included along with listening sections to give you a practical framework for exploring your own voice and extending the range of your possibilities.

It's important to remember that we often sing in a pretty habitual way. In doing that we sometimes get trapped, either by our muscular memory or by the memory of what either we ourselves or others have decided sounds 'good' or 'right'. Try to think of these exercises in the way that a dancer exercises at a barre, the way a pianist learns through playing scales, or the way a tennis player lifts weights. These exercises aren't designed to be carried into performance in the isolated way in which they are done, but they will wake up muscles, they will get you used to using parts of your voice or sounds that you might not have tried before, and the more you practise them, the more they will become part of your expressive 'arsenal'. The more you 'exercise' these sounds, the more they will come to you naturally when you're singing. No singer ever plans a creak onset but they make them all the time because the sound is expressive and moving in the right context.

To expand our expressive capabilities we need to let go of our habits sometimes and remember the power of the unusual, the bold, the awkward and even the downright wrong/bad sounds that our voices are capable of. I once knew a right-handed painter who got so frustrated with his need to paint everything 'correctly' that he started painting with his left hand. He didn't expect to paint a masterpiece, he was just trying to avoid painting pleasant and forgettable work. I think it helps to think of these exercises as the vocal equivalent of the right-handed painter, painting with his left hand. Like him, you're bound to find yourself exploring something strange – you may produce a performance that makes you laugh or you may produce something that feels liberating. Hopefully you will find some unexpected sounds that can build a more direct pathway between the hearts of you and your listeners. Whatever you find, the exercises should help to disrupt some of your habitual singing patterns, and that's always a good thing if we want to keep growing as artists.

Before you do the exercises please remember the following:

1 **These are not vocal training exercises**. They're not designed to be done on a daily basis. They are purely to help you explore and to encourage you to work in different, maybe bolder ways. That said, you should certainly aim to add new sounds to your habitual ways of working, so the exercises that seem most foreign to you might be the ones you really want to keep working at for a while, until they feel like a natural part of your vocal 'palette'.

2 **You should monitor your vocal stamina and be responsible in what you do**. Don't persist in things that feel uncomfortable. If your voice is hoarse or husky after any of these exercises, you know you'll have pushed things too much. All voices are different and some are more delicate than others. But these exercises are relatively short and if you're careful about effort level they should be perfectly safe to do.

3 **As with any vocal exercises, remember to warm up before trying**. Don't try anything if you're ill (or still recovering from an illness); make sure you have a bottle of water and that you stay well hydrated when working.

4 **Working in different ways can sometimes mean that muscles get tired**. Try to learn to distinguish between muscle fatigue and vocal strain. If the muscles around your larynx feel tired but your voice sounds fine, you're perhaps extending the exercises longer than you should or your muscles might be tired from producing voice qualities or sounds that you're not used to. If in doubt about anything, reduce your effort levels.

5 **Don't panic and don't let others panic you**. Permanent vocal damage takes time to achieve. Allow yourself to explore some of the sounds you're hearing but make sure that you're only doing a little at a time with those sounds that feel really foreign to you.

CHAPTER ONE

Cultivating style

To train or not to train?

I've never had a guitar lesson, I've never had a singing lesson, I've never had a bass lesson. . . . Some people sound good when they've had lessons. But I have to say – all the people I've really admired have not had a lesson in their lives to my knowledge. That may just be something to do with my taste but I think that you will find generally that people who are really moving music on – say the early jazz musicians in New Orleans – these guys generally weren't taught.

–PAUL McCARTNEY[1]

In the years since I first started to teach voice, and certainly since this book was written 9 years ago, the rise of the popular singing teacher and popular singing courses has been notable. There has also been a huge growth in the number of websites focusing on singing which have done much to encourage

---

[1]This quotation is from an exclusive interview done for the first edition of this book, and is included here as an Appendix.

debate and discussion around the question of training voices for singing popular styles. There are also strong adherents of particular 'schools' of training, such as Speech Level Singing or the Estill Method. But it's no secret that a great many successful popular recording artists have not had training. The question of whether you should pay someone to help you with your voice or not is one that I am confronted with regularly and as strange as it may seem, I am never sure how I should respond to this question.

I would get a very knowing, approving nod of the head from most of my colleagues in the voice world if I simply answered the question about whether to train or not like this: it's a personal choice, but a few lessons won't hurt and might help you feel more confident about your vocal production. They might also help you with any vexed questions you might have about specific technical issues such as how to increase your range or how to produce more volume safely, or how to bridge the sounds between what you probably think of as your 'head' voice and your 'chest' voice. And of course, if you ever think you're experiencing some vocal damage or danger, you should consult a professional without delay. So I'm going to start this section with that answer.

But I don't think I can leave it there, because the question isn't only one that affects a single singer – it becomes something much bigger if we look at the question in the larger context of how popular singing has evolved – and perhaps, more critically, where we hope to see it evolve from here. From its roots (in folk ballads, blues, jazz, country and gospel) popular singing was never the province of the powerful; it wasn't commissioned by kings or bishops, by aristocrats or captains of industry, and it didn't require the great technical skill that the arts of the upper classes (ballet, opera, classical composition) did. It was the province of common folk: made and shared by non-professionals in non-professional circumstances. Consequently the raw, untrained and unique sounds we hear in the earliest recorded singers were never meant to be refined, but were instead meant to be reflections of the agonies or ecstasies of ordinary working folk. Of course, the rise of the recording industry changed all of that.

The question is whether that change will ultimately flatten, narrow and homogenize our tastes. Or perhaps it already has?

Could it be that between the interests of the big music industry companies, the mass market demands that are served by radio and television, and the increasingly tailored and targeted responses we get through our 'cyber-adventures' these days, our chances of discovering really new and exciting sounds – either in ourselves or others – are getting slimmer?

Manufacturing taste

I would hazard a guess that most of us have heard or been part of a conversation that centres around the question of how television shows like 'American Idol', or 'X Factor' or 'The Voice' have somehow 'warped' our tastes, and spoiled our pleasure in pop music. Many people I know feel that the 'manufactured' feel of these shows is in itself an off-putting thing. Of course, most people also recognize that the record industry has been 'manufacturing' things for years, so perhaps once you get past agreeing that 'manufacturing' things comes naturally to the popular recording industry (from the changed names and sounds of early singers, to the white cover versions of 'wild' songs in the 'race records' charts, or the studied market-analysis type approach of Motown and The Monkees) then what, precisely, is it that makes so many people suspicious of the domination of the television talent contest these days?

As I was writing this I came across a diatribe by Dave Grohl in Delta's *Sky* magazine that's gone viral:

> When I think about kids watching a TV show like *American Idol* or *The Voice*, then they think, "Oh, OK, that's how you become a musician, you stand in line for eight f****** hours with 800 people at a convention center and . . . then you sing your heart out for someone and then they tell you it's not f****** good enough." Can you imagine?. . . . It's destroying the next generation of musicians! Musicians

> should go to a yard sale and buy an old f****** drum set and get in their garage and just suck. And get their friends to come in and they'll suck, too. And then they'll f****** start playing and they'll have the best time they've ever had in their lives and then all of a sudden they'll become Nirvana. Because that's exactly what happened with Nirvana. Just a bunch of guys that had some s**tty old instruments and they got together and started playing some noisy-ass s**t, and they became the biggest band in the world. That can happen again! You don't need a f****** computer or the internet or *The Voice* or *American Idol*.[2]

I've quoted this at length because I think Grohl's concerns are timely. There is much truth in his idea that musicians have often found their own way best by experimenting and making some bad sounds in their early stages, without the pressure of being judged. And I also think that the fear of being judged (which is what these shows are all about) can stop great work from emerging out of risky exploration. Grohl is not, of course, alone in feeling passionate about the way that these kinds of shows work, and his distaste seems rooted in a sense that real rock music must come from a kind of raw, authentic passion.

Of course, 'authenticity' – particularly in rock sounds – has come to be seen as the touchstone of rock aesthetics. A. F. Moore, in a book called *Rock: The Primary Text*, is clear about the way that training compromises things for some people: 'the "untrained" ("natural") voice . . . is important in the ideology of rock as signifying "authenticity", since the trained voice is clearly held to have been tampered with'.[3] This is probably indisputable when it comes to rock, and probably also true when it comes to the blues. But is it the case for all popular sounds?

---

[2]This is available online: http://www.deltaskymag.delta.com/Sky-Extras/Favorites/Rock--n--Roll-Jedi.aspx

[3]Allen F. Moore, *Rock: The Primary Text* (Buckingham: Open University Press, 1993), p. 42.

Given the strong feelings about these things, the question of whether or not to train becomes a tricky one. I suppose I'm in an interesting position here, given that I serve as a casting director and a performance coach on some of the shows that Grohl rails against, and that my own musical journey began by making some 'noisy s**t' in a garage with friends. So I would be the first to confess to feeling a bit conflicted by these shows. Like most people, I worry that television shows seem to reward singing of a very specific type: the patently bankable type. Whether that bankable voice comes from Scotty McCreery, whose throw-back country and western sound was the surprise winner of 2011 'American Idol', or 2006 'X Factor' winner Leona Lewis, whose bland pop R&B floats lightly enough over any song to ease the listener, the search for bankable artists rarely takes us too far from well-worn territory. At times it feels as if the big riffing voice dominates most of these contests, and 'The Voice' even features a 'battle' round, which makes it very hard for contestants not to feel that big sounds and incredible vocal acrobatics will determine the victor. But the clash of commerce and art is an old one, and it only matters here – if it matters at all – when we start to think about the idea of training and vocal style, because we can't train for something without identifying what we value. And of course, we all learn our values from somewhere.

And do these shows influence our values when it comes to deciding what good singing is all about? Well, of course, the shows reflect mainstream public tastes. But in that reflection, are they convincing us that what they value is what we should all value in singing? If so, then singing training should (on average) be composed entirely of exercises aimed at:

1. increasing range and power, especially at the top end
2. increasing improvisational ability, especially in terms of ability to execute lengthy, acrobatic riffs at any point in a phrase.

Of course, if we look at some of the most notable recording artists in the very early days of recording history, what we hear is something very far removed from the slick (if often admirable) finesse of the TV talent show singer. We do, in fact, hear nearly the opposite: the rough-and-ready shout of Ma Rainey, the hard-edged, gritted quality of Lightnin' Hopkins, the plaintive rather nasal yodel of Jimmie Rodgers, or the ecstatic passion of Howlin' Wolf. Indeed, in the first 50 years of the recorded voice, the sounds are quite impressively individual, and in a way that we probably don't encounter much anymore.

But apart from the fact that the record industry has a heavy hand in determining our values and our tastes for us, a quick listen to the charts leaves us in a difficult position in terms of judging voices. Because these days recording techniques are so heavily layered and Auto-Tuned that it's difficult to know what we're actually hearing. In the middle of a great article on the Auto-Tune phenomenon, Lessley Anderson poses a chilling question:

> For every T-Pain – the R&B artist who uses Auto-Tune as an over-the-top aesthetic choice – there are 100 artists who are Auto-Tuned in subtler ways. Fix a little backing harmony here, bump a flat note up to diva-worthy heights there: smooth everything over so that it's perfect. You can even use Auto-Tune live, so an artist can sing totally out of tune in concert and be corrected before their flaws ever reach the ears of an audience. (On season 7 of the UK *X Factor*, it was used so excessively on contestants' auditions that viewers got wise, and protested.)
>
> Indeed, finding out that all the singers we listen to have been Auto-Tuned does feel like someone's messing with us. As humans, we crave connection, not perfection. But we're not the ones pulling the levers. What happens when an entire industry decides it's safer to bet on the robot? *Will we start to hate the sound of our own voices*?[4]

[4]Lessley Anderson, 'Seduced by "Perfect" Pitch: How Auto Tune Conquered Pop Music', The Verge: you can find it at: http://www.theverge.com/2013/2/27/3964406/seduced-by-perfect-pitch-how-auto-tune-conquered-pop-music (Italics are mine).

Will we? The indisputable truth is that what we hear in the popular sphere absolutely influences what we value. Anderson rightly wonders whether a generation of singers raised on Auto-Tuned pitch will have not only some unrealistic expectations of vocal performance, but might also fail to appreciate the sound of 'natural' voices, which often sail just the wrong side of pitch perfection. Are we in danger of no longer valuing the ways in which a certain generosity of pitch or slightly wayward time can add life, uniqueness and excitement to a vocal performance?

And if we can't hear Auto-Tuned perfection in ourselves, what will happen to the way we value our own voices?

All of this brings us back to my earlier point: before you ask 'should I train my voice?', make sure you know what you value. Unless I'm working with someone who wants to make a career in musical theatre (where the rules are 'fixed') or with someone on a reality television singing show (where the rules are becoming fairly 'fixed'), I'm always a bit anxious about working with any singer until I know exactly what they want to work on, or until I am convinced that there is something to work on. Because if we come from the school of thought that says the greatest voices in the history of popular music have always been somehow both unique and authentic (and despite the many worries I have over the whole concept of 'authentic', I confess to thinking this way), would we think that 'training' pop voices was a good idea? The list of singers that I find incredibly moving, but whose voices might have been 'corrected', is long, but I wouldn't have fancied anyone 'fixing' the voices of Otis Redding, Big Mama Thornton or Amy Winehouse, nor would the world have been a better place if any of them had simply concentrated on producing more power or adding more improv. But of course, I never underestimate the sheer pleasure of singing like someone you admire. And for many of us, that just might require some technical help.

So in the end, of course, to train or not to train is an individual choice, and if you do seek training, there are some helpful things to consider. The first, I think, is Richard Miller's assertion that 'one of the main goals of [singing] teaching in this or any age should be to do no harm'.[5] It may sound obvious, but it is important, especially in the area of popular singing. It is reasonable to assume that (as he is paraphrasing Hippocrates), Miller is referring to physical harm, because he follows this with a reference to 'healthy vocal function'. I would extend his worry about doing harm to the singer's psyche, since so much of my teaching seems to centre around trying either to undo the strict aesthetic 'rules' of singing which teachers have introduced into young voices (which although well-intentioned, often result in dull or uninspired sounds and a fear of experimentation), or else trying to encourage singers to consider what uses may be made of their vocal idiosyncrasies (which are usually seen and described as faults or flaws by traditional voice teachers).

It is no doubt this concern with sustainability that has inspired so many voice teachers to write books on how to train your voice. Vocal technique (of whatever kind) must be sustainable. In the absence of anything absolute in aesthetic terms, perhaps sustainability is the most important thing for popular singers to consider. And even though this sounds straightforward and relatively uncontentious, there will still be many who would insist that Tina Turner or Tom Waits sing in 'unsustainable' styles. For many other voices, these sounds *are* unsustainable, yet Tina Turner and Tom Waits are still going strong after many decades of performing. This means that sustainability must be measured against the individual voice and its capabilities.

The uniquely sort of 'constricted' or rather 'damaged' sound that these singers produce may be the result either of something unusual in the vocal anatomy itself, which results in a scratchy or rough phonation, or else the result of some vocal damage. But the real question is: would their many devoted listeners want these vocal flaws 'fixed'? I would hope not, but neither would voice teachers be working responsibly if they encouraged vocal damage. And herein lies much of the difficulty in teaching

---

[5]Richard Miller, *On the Art of Singing* (Oxford: OUP, 1996), p. 221.

popular style. It is undeniable that many artists work 'without a net' in popular singing – when the aim is gritty vocal realism, then 'pleasing tone' and 'flawless technique' are not important. That may be heresy to voice teachers but it is undeniably the case for many popular singers.

This means that if you decide to work with a voice teacher you should bear in mind that you need to find someone with whom you can communicate really well, who will be sympathetic to your desires to explore the styles you're interested in, who can keep an open mind about the kinds of noises you might want to make, and who can help you determine how best to guarantee vocal health and sustainability. And while it may be fine to work at all those things, traditional voice teachers concentrate on – beauty of tone, breathing, bridging the 'break' in the voice artfully, etc., – you must remember as you work on them that these things belong to a certain set of beliefs (that tone should be beautiful; that breaks need to be bridged or smoothed out). You also need to remember that this set of beliefs doesn't apply to Björk or Johnny Cash.

If you decide not to work with a voice teacher you should bear in mind that you alone will have to serve as the monitor of your own vocal health, and take seriously the responsibility for its well-being. Whatever your current musical passions, remember that life is long, and you want to be able to be adaptable enough to suit your voice to the styles you may be passionate about 20 years from now. Rod Stewart began with *Maggie May* but these days he's singing Cole Porter. Longevity and sustainability should be your aims and if you reach any point where you feel uncertain about anything you're doing vocally, you should seek advice.

From vocal training to vocal style

As noted in the introduction, defining style is a difficult thing. It could be considered, when talking about a singer's style, as a personal 'signature' in the execution of a work or perhaps as a collection of definitive traits detectable throughout a range of works. Whichever way you look at it, style is almost certainly a derivation from and a reaction to both the music and the world to which the artist is exposed. We often use the term style when we're talking about musical genre, such as rock-style or jazz-style singing. For singers who want to think seriously about their own style and who wish to find the ways to broaden or to adapt their own style successfully to different kinds of music, it is necessary to look at both uses of the word style.

Many young singers I've worked with (particularly those with an interest or background in rock music) seem to feel a kind of resentment towards the idea of thinking too consciously about their singing style. They point to the more extreme examples of vocal style (Layne Staley from Alice in Chains or Joe Cocker come to mind) and insist that style is something that should grow 'instinctively' and may wilt under the light of too much scrutiny. Like most young artists, rock vocalists can often feel that their own style – insofar as they may be able to describe or understand it – has evolved as a sort of 'happy accident' and they're reluctant to tinker with it too much. There's much to be said for such a theory, and I'm not at all against the happy accident mode of vocal exploration. But as most singers' careers go on, it isn't uncommon to find that some stylistic vocal choices can begin to feel limiting. All artists need to keep changing and growing, and since the voice and its own 'natural' properties (such as range and tone throughout varying qualities) can often feel like a rather stubborn thing to change, style is often an amenable place to start the evolutionary process, and that evolution almost invariably requires dedicated listening and practice.

The listening part needs to be as broad as possible, particularly because our own preferences can sometimes result in keeping us stuck in our 'style' patterns rather than leading us to new and exciting discoveries. But of course, listening widely these days means being proactive about the process. Not only are we being Auto-Tuned into some rather 'zombie-like' aesthetics, our very preferences seem to make us easy targets for more-of-the-same. The 'customisation' of things by companies like Amazon or Spotify, etc., means that we're continually being offered up a menu of 'if-you-liked-X,-you're-gonna-love-Y' choices. This is what Eli Pariser calls the 'you loop',[6] so prevalent on the internet these days, where information about you is gathered by companies who are keen to offer you more of what they're sure you like. For these reasons, I've spent quite some time while preparing this book looking for choices that I'm hoping will be surprising and a bit off the radar for some people. The examples included in the book are designed to help you look well beyond the usual experiences of 'chart hit' pop singers and are also largely targeted at recorded voices that haven't been tampered with. This means including older tracks that still allow us to hear some imperfections even while we marvel at the warmth or delicacy or power of an artist's performance.

What style is it?

And does it matter? There will have been a time, perhaps 20 or more years ago, when all this was simpler: most music stores I frequented as a teenager had five major sections – classical, rock, country, easy listening and jazz. These five categories were fairly blunt instruments of organization and it was easy to get confused when searching for an artist like Frank Sinatra, for example, who was sometimes found in jazz and sometimes in easy listening. At the time, easy listening for me seemed translatable as 'music your parents would like'. That didn't mean that adolescents like me never heard such music – most of us were growing up at a time when broadcasting meant *broad*casting; we watched television variety shows, knowing that there would be something for everyone – easy listening

---

[6]Eli Pariser, *The Filter Bubble* (London: Peguin, 2011).

and rock. Musical exposure was a little more mixed in those days, but nevertheless the categories seemed clearer to me and, of course, there wasn't so much recorded music available. The categories seem to be growing every time I look at iTunes or Amazon.com, and I get dizzy with the proliferation of new categories and sub-categories. Just under 'pop' on the Amazon site I have to make a choice between 13 sub-categories, including Korean pop and adult contemporary. I can think of six of the categories to put Daft Punk in, and six for Adele. Even the 'Large Category' section has expanded on the 'big five' of my youth to cover blues, gospel and Christian, classical, country, dance, folk, international, jazz, miscellaneous, opera and vocal, pop, rock, rap and hip-hop, and rhythm and blues/soul. The proliferation of categories has made the work of trying to define artists harder than ever, and clearly, companies like Amazon or iTunes are struggling with these questions.

But for the practising singer perhaps categories are of little use. For the purposes of this book, it's helpful to use some of the old categories, particularly those that can be traced back to where they began. But these days, style is such a mixed bag that there's little point in worrying about categories, since it is the singer's disregard for 'rules' that breeds style in the first place.

Sound, mystery, panic

Some of the sounds described over the next chapters aren't particularly pleasant in and of themselves. Some of them border on what many voice teachers consider bad or even dangerous. Most voice teachers will tell you that any constriction of any kind is bad/unhealthy/dangerous for a singer, and by and large, I wouldn't argue with that. But I also know that singers do it all the time, especially blues and rock singers, and I've come to believe that when we talk about bad/unhealthy/dangerous, we need also to realize that generalizations about the voice are always that – generalizations.

Particular voices can have particular qualities and capacities and this is an area of vocal work that desperately needs more research. It's very difficult to understand why some voices can sustain so much more hard usage than others. It's also difficult to know why, where the voice is being produced in a clear, unconstricted way, some vocalists seem to have unfailing endurance, while others must keep a careful watch over the length of time or the strength/volume of sound when they are singing.

One of the first rock bands I worked in had three front singers – an expensive but interesting option. One of my fellow lead singers was a young man named Roland who was passionate about Rod Stewart's raspy vocal quality. Roland was convinced that Rod had damaged his voice through hard drinking and hard living and that this damage was responsible for the wonderfully husky tone quality in *Maggie May* (a track he believed to be the greatest rock recording of all time). In the summer of 1970, Roland set out on his one-man journey towards vocal disaster. Every night after our gigs (which didn't generally finish until 2.00 a.m.), Roland took himself off to the shores of Huntington Beach and there, with a bottle of Southern Comfort (the preferred tipple of the raspy Janis Joplin), he would drink and sing at the top of his lungs for hours in a quest for vocal calluses. It was a fine plan – sandy, but promising. He usually sang until he fell asleep. Occasionally one of us would accompany him but it wasn't, to be honest, all that fascinating to watch.

Roland stayed with it for most of July and August, but despite his best efforts, results were disappointing. Worse than that, he found that his voice was stronger than ever and his one-time tendency to go hoarse on long nights or when he pushed notes particularly hard seemed to vanish completely. His voice remained disappointingly clear and certainly stronger, and I can still remember the suppressed laugh and the assumed solemnity all around the rehearsal room when Roland bitterly announced the failure of his nightly howling to the ocean.

What can we learn from this? To be honest, I'm not sure. Roland was young, his voice was obviously strong – perhaps the warmth and moisture of the Pacific Ocean air in a Southern California high summer was a tonic of some sort? Perhaps Southern Comfort has some little-dreamt-of qualities? Perhaps there was just something peculiar in his vocal constitution that thrived on this kind of 'abuse'? I couldn't begin to answer. But I know that general rules about voices have their limits and I feel convinced that if Roland had gone to any voice teacher to describe his plan, the teacher's reaction would no doubt have been panic. I am also convinced that if Roland had described the plan as one in which he intended to strengthen his vocal endurance (which is what, in the end, he achieved), a voice teacher would have laughed and probably then panicked.

In my own case, I knew that the amount of singing I was doing for most of my professional career was staggering. Apart from doing five sets, six nights a week for around forty-eight weeks a year, we often put in four to five hours' practice sessions up to four times a week. I was singing extremely demanding rock repertoire – some original, some cover versions – and I used to worry at times whether I would do some long-term damage to my voice. I worried about the long term, because I could rarely ever see a problem in the short term. The times when I did lose my voice were nearly always the result of one of two things: viral illnesses or time off. The first seemed understandable to me, the second mysterious. Most years, after the New Year, we would take a week or two off. When you're working as a musician there's no such thing as paid holiday, so time off is a rare thing. And as much as I looked forward to it, I always dreaded the inevitable vocal problems it would entail once we started up again. Always, the first month after a two-week lay-off would be filled with difficulties, rearranging sets and material to cover the hoarseness and the temporarily limited range.

Now, I know that I wouldn't generally advise a student to keep singing between 40 and 50 hours a week, that many weeks out of the year in order to maintain their vocal health, but for me, that was the recipe. I can't explain that any more than I can explain Roland's 'ocean therapy'.

Human voices make noises that are surprising all the time. I've heard noises made by indigenous folk singers that sound very unhealthy, yet the singers making them have been going strong for years. I've heard rock singers who can twang and belt for hours, even when I've thought they couldn't possibly go on without getting hoarse. I often try to imagine what most voice teachers would say to these singers, or to the gurgling, rasping 'overtone' folk singers of Eastern Europe. But then again, I often try to imagine what they would have said to Kurt Cobain or Big Maybelle. My point is that there comes a time when teachers have to realize that vocalists probably know the capacity of their own voices better than anyone else.

In this book, I encourage people to make some strange noises. As a voice teacher I've always tried to entice people away from the sounds they feel safest with, and to open their minds to the possible beauty in the 'unbeautiful' sound. I realize that in doing this I am courting some criticism from traditional circles. I also realize that there are many times when a voice teacher is working with a student who has no control over how many hours they must sing: for many singers that's often the greatest hazard to vocal health – not trying to imitate Rod Stewart or Tom Jones, but trying to keep the voice going for eight shows a week. In these situations voice teachers must remind the student of the safest and healthiest vocal choices available. But when a singer is not in this difficult position, then I think there's little need to worry about experimenting with sounds of all kinds, and in allowing the singer to find out just what their voice can and can't cope with.

I've been singing and teaching singers for nearly 30 years and I still think there's much to be said for respecting the mystery of the voice. Not only the mystery that surrounds each individual voice in terms of sound, ability, endurance, etc., but also the mystery that inheres in our inability to understand everything about its workings. There's great mystery to why we react so strongly to the sound of the human voice in the first place, and much to baffle us in the varieties of reception to the varieties of sung sounds. I've learnt that the voice is somehow so deeply entwined in the way we perceive and project our identity that changes in the sounds we make can elicit some extraordinarily surprising emotional releases that can't be explained. I've lost count of the times that I've coached young women who have been making quiet, breathy sounds into finding their own strong natural sound, and who have cried almost uncontrollably upon first hearing it.

Like most people, I've found myself unable to suppress my own unexpected emotional reaction to sung music, whether that came as a sudden outburst of tears while listening to a gospel choir in South Africa or a sense of overpowering spirituality that literally stopped me in my tracks while hearing a Russian Orthodox quartet at the Alexander Nevsky Monastery in St Petersburg. In its older sense, the word mystery was often used to connote both an individual craft (as in the Medieval Mystery guilds), and also a contemplation of the spiritual. I would like to think that the mystery I refer to here could be applied successfully in either sense.

CHAPTER TWO

Anatomy and sound

The basics

Before we begin, we need to consider what is fundamental to singing in any style. One of the great distinctions between teaching 'classical' singing and popular singing is that popular song has evolved out of years of free experimentation with sound and style. This means that the range of choices for popular song production is greater than the range for those you might hear in the Cardiff Singer of the World competition. For classical artists, the training is incredibly demanding, and the vocal skill necessary is daunting for most of us. For popular singing, as we know, neither of these is necessary. It takes a generous heart to think of Johnny Cash as a skilled singer, and no one imagines for a moment that Bob Dylan had much training. But popular music is an enormous category and most people know that a voice like Whitney Houston's is both very skilled and has probably had the benefit of some training.

Despite the relatively forgiving nature of popular music when it comes to technical skill, there are still two bottom-line skills that are truly helpful in enhancing a singer's ability. While these skills are important, the bad news is that relatively little is known about how they work, and even less is known about how to help the singer who doesn't possess them.

Intonation or pitch

It's become common these days to watch an 'X Factor' judge talk about a singer being 'pitchy', meaning that the singer's pitch wasn't entirely accurate. These days Auto-Tune does much in recorded situations to correct the flat, the sharp, the slightly wayward, so that worries about pitching in these situations aren't quite as critical as they once were. But in live performance (and I guess I'm 'old school' because I would say that in all performance) singers need to cultivate good pitch. The tone can be rough as a gravel-mixer or as piercing as a screaming cat; improvisational ability may be negligible and delivery rather artless; and even the overall audibility/comprehensibility can be obscured, but whatever the technical transgressions, a singer needs a reliable ear. Although a reliable ear is an important quality, sadly there isn't an easy remedy to help poor pitch, and I've never found any quick cures.

A large part of the problem lies in the way that a singer's pitching works, which is a combination of the variable mass and tension of the vocal folds, which are operated by both voluntary and involuntary musculature. We generally pitch a melody in terms of what we hear, but as we know from hearing recordings of our own voices, we're not best placed to be the judge of our own sound. The whole pitching process is mysterious, as Frank Havrøy points out:

> The complexity of the muscular process, and the chance of being deceived by the ears, together make sound production and pitch control an unpredictable affair. More than just depending on their ears, good singers try to think about singing as an automatic process by attending to their inner projection of their voice, rather than focusing on every muscular impulse needed for producing the desired sound and pitch. This inner projection is largely automatic and indescribable, like the skill involved with riding a bike.[1]

---

[1]Frank Havrøy, *Music and Practice*, Vol. 1, No. 1, 2013, which can be found at: http://www.musicandpractice.org/musicandpractice/article/view/18/6

Many people have proposed possible solutions to pitch problems, and many singing teachers will insist that there is no 'tone deafness', just a lack of confidence and familiarity, or problems of one sort or another in vocal production. While some or all of this may be true, there is still very little of a practical nature that I think can truly help someone build reliability into their pitching, if it's a problem. While there are some good theories, there is still little evidence to suggest that anyone understands exactly how we improve pitch in all cases; certainly, the more I read, the more contradictory is the advice I find.

Many people warn of the difficulty of learning pitch from hearing notes on a piano, yet I know of one singer who, after years of being told that he had a lovely tone but flawed pitch, decided to take some action. He spent more than a year practising daily with a piano and a tape recorder, matching the sound on the keyboard with his own and listening to the playback. He was convinced that hearing the note wasn't the issue – he had realized this when he listened back to the sounds he'd made when trying to accurately reproduce a note he had played on the piano. While he could hear the difference in pitch in this playback, he could not hear the difference when he tried to match the note 'live'. He found that for the first time he could hear the pitch problem (but only when playing sounds back on the tape recorder) which was an important first step towards correcting it. He kept at it with amazing perseverance, and found that by the end of the year he was being asked to do much more lead vocal in his band. He didn't stop there, but carried on recording and listening for another year. He was 21 when he sat down with the piano and the cassette recorder; he has now been singing solo professionally for more than a decade.

His story may be exceptional (there is need for much more research in this area), or it may be that anyone with his dedication could achieve what he did. I'm certain that what he was actually doing was not 'improving his ear' so much as learning to *feel* the pitch instead of relying solely on *hearing* the pitch. However, I do tell my students that I have seen someone 'fix' their pitch problem and that it may be possible for anyone to do so. But I never leave out the hard truth about how long it may take.

I have also learnt that pitching is closely connected to confidence and overall health. I have seen many singers 'lose' their ability for a time, only to rediscover it as they persevere. As with so many things about the voice, focusing too exclusively on any one area, like inaccurate pitching (even though this can be a fundamental problem), will often exacerbate the difficulty by causing tension or creating a loss of confidence in the singer. I've worked with a number of singers who were troubled by pitch problems, and I've learnt that it almost never helps to talk about it directly. Sometimes I just ask the singer to draw the melody as a continuous line; sometimes I just ask them to describe the melody as a pattern. For reasons I can't explain, these 'indirect' methods often resolve the pitching problem. I include this story here not because it clears up the mystery of pitching – in fact, if anything, it may confuse it further – but it is perhaps an illustration of how the language and the imagery we use in teaching and learning can be important. By making the challenge one of describing a pattern or drawing a beautiful melody (instead of one about pitch accuracy), singers can sometimes manage to conquer the problem.

Vibrato

The second skill is neither as difficult for most, nor is it as crucial as the first. It is the ability to produce or control vibrato. But I want to be clear: vibrato is not necessary for creating a good performance. Vibrato can be an asset (when it's reasonably even and controllable) and a hindrance (when it's too fast or uncontrollable). Vibrato is also one of the greatest mysteries of the singing voice. I have never encountered a singing teacher (or method) able to explain adequately what it is or how (or even if) you can teach a singer to access or control it, although many singers can naturally do these things without any difficulty. I have seen laryngoscopic films of voices while they were producing vibrato, and the only visible evidence of it is that there is a detectable movement or 'shake' of the whole of the laryngeal structure. If you have vibrato, you should be able to feel this movement simply by wrapping your hand very lightly around the front of your throat and observing the mild 'shaking' of the larynx during its production.

Some singers say that they sense their vibrato coming from the area of their throats; some say they feel it in their chest; and others swear that the sensation comes from their stomach. Some can control the speed and/or the width of their vibrato, and this control allows a far greater stylistic flexibility. Many singers notice their vibrato growing more pronounced as they grow older, and some, particularly singers aged over 60, can feel a tendency in the vibrato to 'wobble' very widely, producing an unpleasant sound that nearly falls out of the range of pitch.

Some people have no control whatsoever over their vibrato. If the vibrato is relatively even in terms of speed and width, this isn't a great problem. If it's very fast, it can lead to some great frustration for the singer but doesn't rule out the possibility of producing some interesting pop sounds (think of Michael Jackson, Antony Hegarty, or Randy Crawford). Most vocal experts suggest that control of vibrato is directly related to keeping tension out of vocal production and to ensuring an even supply of breath support, but I have worked fairly successfully with singers to reduce the speed of the vibrato. Often that work has included focusing on anchoring the head and neck muscles to restrain the 'shake' of the vibrato a little, although I've also seen that same anchoring work make the vibrato more pronounced. Consequently, the idea of keeping tension out of production can be tricky (assuming that anchoring introduces some tension) and probably needs to be approached on a case-by-case basis. Like pitch, problems with vibrato often grow stronger when under scrutiny and sometimes it's best simply to keep working towards relaxation to enable the vocalist to get in touch with whatever muscles are involved in the production of the vibrato. For many singers, vibrato is a strong muscular memory of their vocal production being teamed with a particular speed or width of vibrato.

Some voice teachers believe that a lack of vibrato is common in young voices and that with enough practice the singer can slowly learn to add vibrato to the sound. I have worked with students who have said they had no vibrato or could not imagine how to access it, and who then surprised both themselves and me by suddenly hearing a bit of vibrato while they were singing. This may be because for many singers, vibrato only occurs when they are fairly relaxed or confident in production. It takes a while to feel this way when you're singing in front of someone, so perhaps when a singer manages that, the vibrato occurs naturally. Often, when we're concerned about accuracy of pitching or about making a beautiful tone, we create so much tension that we simply stiffen all our vocal 'works' to the extent that the gentle laryngeal shake I described earlier can't take place. Certainly if you can sometimes suppress vibrato by adding a bit of muscle anchoring, the reverse should be true. In any case, I would say that it's best to 'discover' vibrato by not concentrating on it too much – you may just bring on enough tension through that concentration to suppress it! What the singer must remember is that while a lack of vibrato may be frustrating in some styles, in popular music there are a great many very successful singers who rarely ever use it (Paul McCartney, for example, never uses it, even in ballads, and in fact he actively dislikes the whole idea of vibrato).

All of the above leads me to the conclusion that there is still much research to be done on vibrato. I have seen teachers mistakenly explain to their students that it is a function of pitch oscillation, so that to create vibrato they should try moving rapidly between pitch variations. Any singer with vibrato knows that it is the other way around: pitch oscillation is a function of vibrato. In most vibratos, there is a variation of the pulse that determines how we hear the 'pitching' element. In other words, vibrato that sounds 'right' to our ears tends to be within the range of five to eight pulsations per second. Pulsations slower than five per second are those which we tend to hear as straying away from the pitch. Those faster than eight per second are generally described as a tremolo and can sound strange but do not tend to threaten the pitch. The best a singer can do in practising quick-pitch oscillations is to learn to produce a good vocal 'trill', but the sensation of moving quickly between two semi-tones simply isn't the same as the sensation most feel when producing a 'natural' vibrato sound, and doesn't have the same pulsation. But some voice teachers feel that learning to create this 'artificial' vibrato will encourage the creation, ultimately, of a 'natural' one.

In the end, it seems to me that pitch and vibrato have much to do with each other, since pitching in itself is not an exact science when it comes to the human voice; indeed, the more you know about it, the more confusing it can seem. In her analysis of the acoustic variables involved in pitching, Maribeth Bunch examines the work of F. Winckel, who asks 'is a certain inaccuracy in intonation actually necessary for satisfying auditory impression?',[2] and while the many variations that arise in perception studies on pitch and vibrato suggest that this may be so, she still concludes that these variations 'do not relieve the singer of the responsibility of producing correct pitches and of being "in tune"'. Perhaps. But we need to remember that some styles can tolerate more variety in the category of 'in tune' than others, and we also need to remember that confidence plays a major part in these areas. All this means that if you're serious about improving your sound, you need to sing as often as you can, you need to enjoy the sound you make – yes, even with all of its 'flaws' – and you must also be patient about your progress. Sometimes voices change slowly, but they do change and they do grow, all the more so as you work on and enjoy them.

---

[2]Meribeth Bunch, *Dynamics of the Singing Voice,* second edition (Wein, New York: Springer-Verlag, 1993), p. 75.

How the voice works

I'm going to keep this as brief as I can, since this is not a vocal training book, but I think a little knowledge is helpful. Most voice-training systems concentrate on three basic areas: the source of power (what actually 'drives' the sound – breath and lungs); the source of sound (anatomically, the point at which sound is created – contained within the larynx); and sound manipulation (anatomically, the controllable 'follow-on' areas which we use for modifying the sound – the pharynx, or vocal tract, resonators in nose and mouth, muscles all around the neck, the jaw and the face, lips, etc.). We're going to look at the first two briefly.

The source of power

In my teaching, I don't expend much energy on discussing breath as the power source of the voice, or worrying overmuch about breathing. In my experience, worrying too much about 'correct' breathing can sometimes create tension. Most singers know that inadequate breath capacity can be a problem: sometimes this is the result of something medical – asthma, bronchitis and other ailments of the respiratory system can all affect breath capacity in either the short or the long term. These are not areas in which to be 'guessing', so they always require professional medical advice. Some singers clearly have more capacity than others, and while there are exercises that can, perhaps over time, allow some expansion, change is usually very slow.

When I talk to singers about breathing, it's usually a way of getting them to contact muscles that can help support a large sound. In other words, instructions of the kind I used to hear endlessly (breathe into your diaphragm or, more interestingly, into your stomach or pelvis) are both good imagery and bad anatomy. There's only one place in the body into which we can draw air but we can use different muscles when we breathe.

Whether you move the muscles around your lower torso or the muscles around your shoulders when you breathe, you're still inhaling air into the same place – into little sacs in the lungs, where the bronchial tubes widen to complete the exchange of oxygen and carbon dioxide. Breathing deeply can require you to use muscles which must then move to make way for greater expansion of the lungs; it doesn't literally mean that you're 'breathing into your stomach'. In the following exercise, working with breath is a way of getting you to contact and move the muscles you will need for producing big sounds.

Practice

You can quickly get in touch with many of the muscles you need for singing, and particularly for making big, powerful sounds, by using the breath. Lie down on the floor and make sure you're comfortable (you might want to keep your knees bent). As you breathe, allow the air intake to move various parts of your body:

1. Breathe 'into' your collarbones and your shoulders. This is often the most common part of our bodies that we 'breathe into'. You'll notice that it's a fairly shallow breath and won't support you long under any stress or strain.
2. Now place your hands over your ribcage. When you breathe in, use that breath to make your hands rise or move gently outwards. Be aware of the muscles that move underneath your hands.
3. Next, place your hands on your stomach and use an intake of breath to make your hands move upwards. Again, be aware of the muscles that move underneath your hands.
4. Finally, try to use the image of 'breathing into' your back. You should feel some different muscles expanding and pushing down into the floor.

Using the image of 'breathing into' various parts of your body is a good way to identify the larger muscles that can help support you in the work of singing. When we're working really hard (and make no mistake – many varieties of singing require very hard muscle work!), right at the upper end of our range, or using a lot of volume, we need to be aware of anchoring that sound by engaging all the muscles we've just felt working. It wasn't only heavy-metal theatricality that used to inspire hard rock singers to swing their microphone stands up over their heads. The old mic stands used to have quite heavily weighted bases, and swinging the stand upside down while singing the big notes helped more than one hard-rocker to engage all the muscles needed to produce sounds of size and passion!

Perhaps the greatest reason why I don't like discussing breathing when teaching singers is that I have all too often experienced (either in myself or in others) the tension that this can sometimes create. When we worry about breath, we can sometimes panic about it, and I've seen many singers raise their tension levels trying to make sure they breathe in the 'right' place. There isn't a great mystery to breathing. We do it all the time, even if we are often doing it in rather shallow ways. We generally know instinctively how much breath we need to take to get to the end of a very long sentence, and, when speaking, we are rarely caught out needing more breath unless we have developed a habitual laziness about our 'tidal' intake. But because we aren't planning the lyrical pattern in a song in quite the same way as we plan our own day-to-day conversation, getting through a lyrical line can sometimes require that we breathe differently. Many singers have come to me with sheet music marked by some vocal tutor with little Xs telling the student where to breathe. It's hard to approach a song this technically and still make it live within your imagination. For the most part, I believe it to be a big mistake to divorce technique from imagination. At some point, you'll have to put the two together in performance, and you will inevitably find that process difficult if you've not been doing it from the beginning.

Of course, many songs from classical or 'legit' repertoire specifically challenge the singer's ability to get through it all with brilliant breath control (some Gilbert and Sullivan 'patter' songs come to mind, as do some Sondheim numbers), but the great majority of popular song can work if you breathe 'with your thoughts'. In other words, find out first what the thought patter of the song is – where your thoughts or actions are beginning and ending, or where you go on to a new thought – and then speak the lyrics. You'll know exactly where to breathe. For the most part, that's where you should breathe when singing the song, too, unless the phrases are incredibly long or tricky.

Because breath is often a source of anxiety or closely associated with a state of anxiety, concentration on breathing can too often lead to mild hyperventilation and tension. Concentration on breathing can also lead to 'over-breathing'. In other words, the singer takes in far more breath than needed, and then either blasts the air out at the beginning of the phrase or creates tension somewhere as he or she strives to release air as evenly as possible. Forget it. Unless you are training in classical repertoire, or have a very specific problem with capacity, or find yourself cast in one of those Gilbert and Sullivan roles, try to breathe with your thoughts. Try also to remember the lower torso area muscles we contacted in the breathing exercise – stay in touch with those stomach, back and ribcage muscles and try not to raise your shoulders when breathing. If you can manage that you should be fine!

The source of the sound

We'll be working a lot on this throughout our practical exploration of the elements of style, but let's start with a little anatomical understanding. The larynx itself is often the biggest mystery to the singer, as its workings are totally hidden. There are parts you can feel, you can easily feel the thyroid cartilage which houses the vocal mechanisms, and with practice you can find a way to sense when you're manipulating true and false vocal folds. There are a number of things it may help you to know about laryngeal anatomy, but I'm going to cover only the things I feel you'll need to know to make sense of the rest of this book.

The larynx that you're feeling when you touch the sides of your throat looks like this:

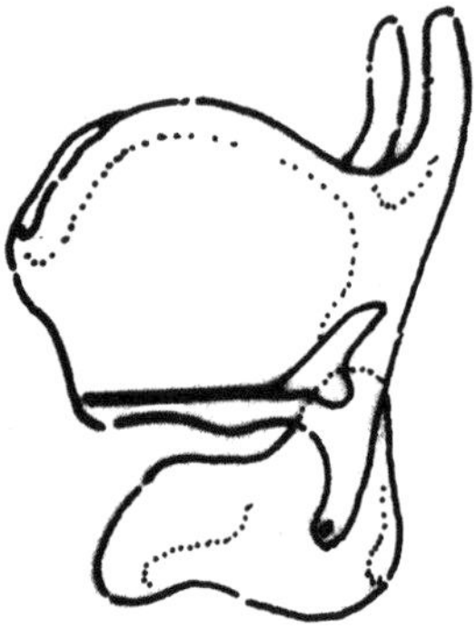

FIGURE 1 *Side view of the larynx.*

This is a diagram of the vocal folds, as if you were looking down on the vocal mechanism:

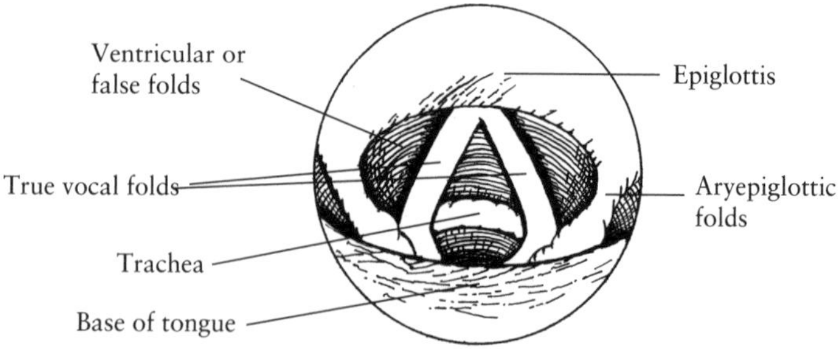

FIGURE 2 *View of larynx, inhaling, showing the vocal folds.*

The true vocal folds are connected in front to the thyroid cartilage, and attached at the back to two small pieces of cartilage, called the arytenoids. The movements of these small arytenoids determine the length and the width of the folds when the vocal process is operating. Just above the true folds are the false folds – something I never knew I had before studying Jo Estill's system. No other voice teacher I had come across explained the importance of learning to manipulate the false folds, and particularly the importance of learning to keep them 'retracted' if you want to produce a clear, unconstricted sound. The false folds are protection: they protect the delicate vocal mechanism, and they work in an emergency to protect the whole respiratory system.

Practice

To feel the sensation of these false folds closing quickly, grunt as hard as you can. That 'strangulated' sensation is the feeling of the false folds closing quickly. If they close while you're trying to produce tone, you can usually hear that your sound becomes 'constricted'; it has the same sort of strangulated property as the sound you made when you were grunting. Make that grunting sound again, but this time see what happens when you sing a note while holding all that tension.

Something strange (it could be terrible or it could be wonderful, depending upon your point of view!) will probably emerge. This is because when the false folds constrict over the true folds, they interfere with the free and natural vibrations that produce tone. Think of what happens when you place a piece of paper over a tuning fork – you still hear tone, and you know that the tuning fork is still vibrating, but there's a buzzing sound that interferes with the free, natural sound of the vibration.

Because the true folds are a more delicate mechanism than a tuning fork, prolonged interference from the false folds can, over time, cause damage. The health of your vocal folds depends upon their ability to vibrate freely. As the false folds are the source of so much anxiety for singers, it's worth taking a moment here to try to get a feel for their working.

Practice

We've looked at how to make the false folds constrict by making a grunting sound. Do that again, and this time try to hold onto that feeling. If you've got it, try sustaining the sound of a grunt and then releasing it quickly. At this point the false folds will have opened back, but they will not be as widely retracted as they could be. For that to happen, try laughing as hard as you can – silently. Make it a real 'ho-ho-ho' kind of laugh and notice that you feel a very 'wide' sensation in the area of your larynx. Try to hold onto that feeling. Breathe in and out a few times, and you should notice that your breathing is absolutely silent. In fact, breathing as audibly as you can and then consciously silencing your breath over four or five really deep inhalations is another quick way to feel that retracted sensation.

The true folds are open when you're inhaling, and they seem 'closed' when you begin to make sound. In fact, they are vibrating at incredible speeds (approximately 250 times per second to pitch a middle C), so unless you have a slow-motion film, they look as if they are closed in a laryngoscopic picture. They relax and open again when you take another breath. When you're singing loudly, the mass of these folds is generally thicker and they close in the vibration for longer. When you sing softly, the mass of the folds is thinner, and the folds meet for a shorter fraction of time in the vibration. Once we progress to looking at the various voice qualities, you'll see that the length and density of the folds themselves have a great effect on the actual sounds you're making; learning to change these variables is a part of expanding your possibilities as a singer.

Learning to keep those false folds retracted is an important skill that can help you to keep that 'constricted' sound out of your vocal production, unless, of course, you want to use it. This is an idea that is anathema to most vocal teachers, but we can't look at the elements of popular singing without admitting that there are many singers – particularly in the blues and rock genres – who employ constricted sounds at various times in their singing. This is another area that needs some careful research. In 2007 there was a fascinating segment about Steven Tyler in National Geographic's documentary, *Incredible Human Machine*. The piece follows Dr Steven M. Zeitels, who performed laser surgery on Tyler's vocal folds after he had suffered a ruptured blood vessel. Zeitels 'scopes' and studies Tyler's vocal mechanism while he's singing on stage and although the piece is well worth watching if just for the explanation of how the vocal folds work,[3] it brings us no closer to figuring out why some singers have voices that, like Tyler's, can sustain a great deal of hard use and others do not.

I have worked with many singers who can produce a mildly constricted sound for a fairly prolonged time, apparently without damaging their vocal folds. Equally, I have worked with those for whom even a short spell of trying to sing in this mildly constricted way causes an immediate sensation of dryness and the feeling of the need to cough. There may be good physiological reasons why one voice can produce such a sound and another can't, but I have not been able to discover any research on the subject. Still, in my work

[3]This is a good introduction to how the vocal folds work and you can see Tyler's working as he sings – creepy but fascinating: http://www.youtube.com/watch?v=9MDn5GgyxyU.

I have learnt that the brief use of mild constriction can be mastered by many, and can be extremely useful in raising the perceived level of effort that is demanded by some styles, for example, there is use for controlled constriction in some rock and gospel singing onsets. We'll look at these ideas in the next chapter.

Getting into sound

We're about to start an exploration of the sounds that you make, so it would be wise to do a little warm-up. One of the best ways is also one of the most common among voice teachers – it's called 'sirening'.

Practice

Sing the word 'sing' on a very comfortable note. Hold the 'ing' part of the word and very gently move up and down through the comfortable parts of your range. This exercise is called the siren because you'll sound like a very quiet siren. Be careful not to release the 'closed' sensation you have when you're holding the 'ing' sound. If you want to test the security of that 'ing' sound, release the tone very quickly into a 'ga' sound, and then move quickly back into the 'ing'. You'll quickly feel what muscles you need to hold that 'ing' securely in place. Keeping the back of the tongue high (and the overall volume low) will help to keep your siren in place. You will notice that this warm-up exercise doesn't produce much volume. It does, however, warm you up gently and if done for a few minutes will get you ready for singing.

The larynx itself is a moveable mechanism and you will find that it naturally moves up and down as you work through your range. If you want to test that, place your fingers lightly against the sides of your larynx and sing from mid-range to your highest note and then down to your lowest. You'll feel this 'housing' mechanism moving up and then down. There are some vocal qualities in which the mechanism stays down a little longer, but it will inevitably rise as you reach the top of your range. The larynx is also capable of 'tilting', and it is this 'tilting' quality that gives your voice its musical sound. In other words, when you are speaking, your larynx generally remains in a neutral state; sometimes, when you are singing, it tilts slightly.

Practice

To feel this tilt, place your fingers lightly on the front of your throat. First speak a sentence: you will feel the mechanism staying more or less in place. Next, make the sound of a puppy gently whimpering. You should feel a slight pressure against your fingers as the larynx tilts forwards. Now try singing – it's best to choose something towards the top of your range, since some people use their 'speech' quality in mid-range, which means that the larynx stays pretty much in the neutral position. You should again feel a gentle pressure against your fingers as the thyroid cartilage tilts down and forwards.[4] There is another part of the larynx that tilts (the cricoid cartilage) when the voice is doing certain things, such as belting, but this isn't easy to feel.

---

[4]Although this exercise will usually allow most people to feel this 'tilting', don't worry if you can't. I've lost count of the number of people in my workshops who swear they can't feel a thing, although they can always feel the tilt by placing their hands against my throat when I demonstrate. It must be that the larynx tilt is a more subtle process for some than for others.

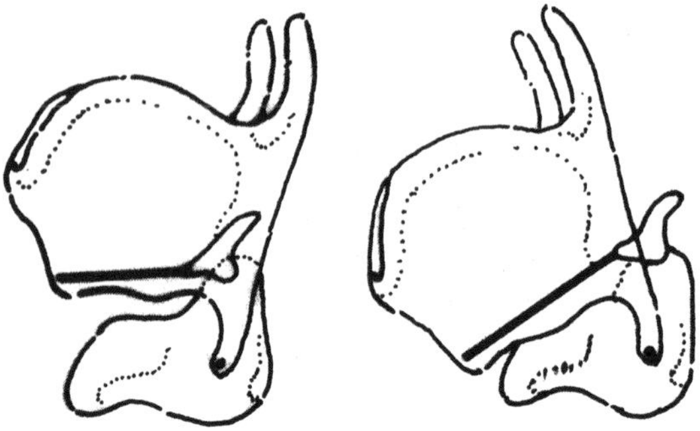

FIGURE 3 *Two side views of the larynx 'tilting'.*

The drawings above illustrate what's actually happening to the larynx when you do the 'tilting' exercise.

Exploring voice qualities

This is the part of the book where we start to make some serious noise! Take a bit of time with these exercises, and practise, perhaps where no one will hear you, as you'll no doubt be making some awkward noises at first, and you don't want to feel inhibited as you do so. I want to present the most useful and easily absorbed concepts in producing different vocal qualities, but I am aware that some people will require more detailed information or instruction. Not all people who pick up a book like this want to teach or even to do more than expand their listening skills, so I will attempt to provide as balanced an overview as possible, always knowing that since each person's needs are different, my overview may be too simple for some or too complex for others.

The idea of working through different voice qualities is a relatively new one, but it has grown greatly in practice among voice teachers who aren't teaching exclusively in the areas of opera or classical technique. I think that Jo Estill's research has been instrumental in this growth of interest, and many teachers have expanded and modified her work in this area. Simply, the idea of training through different voice qualities, rather than training just a single quality throughout the range was what made Estill's work rather revolutionary. Traditional voice training systems tend to see the voice through a single quality, which moves from a lower (sometimes called 'chest') register to an upper register (sometimes called 'head' voice), with a break or passaggio in between. By breaking down our analysis of vocal sound into various qualities, we can see the voice as capable of moving through that same range, but producing some distinctly different sounds throughout. This sometimes has the effect of helping to ease or solve the break or passaggio area (assuming that you want to – many popular singers never concern themselves with this), or even to alleviate the sense of a break in the voice altogether, depending upon the individual voice.

Various voice qualities have different vocal 'set-ups'. We'll learn these through simple access techniques as we go through each vocal quality. It is necessary, when both teaching and learning, to try to separate these qualities into their 'pure' forms (or as pure as possible), but the singer's art usually involves a skilful mixing of the qualities to achieve just the right sound for the right moment. In this section we will concentrate on producing the qualities in their raw state, so skill in 'mixing' and artistry will have to come later, when you've had a bit of practice!

As you go through the following exercises, which are designed to help you access the different qualities, don't be discouraged if you can't get it right away. Some people find it quite difficult to master more than a couple, especially at the start. If you find it easy to get all of them, you're one of those lucky people who possess a very flexible instrument. For the rest of us, repeated listening to artists who do use these qualities, together with lots of private experimentation (remember, you may not sound pleasant!), should slowly help you on your way. I've put examples on my website (www.donnasoto-m.co.uk) of each of the qualities but because every voice is different, the sounds will vary. Try to access the sound by following the steps and then check the following section that outlines what you should have noticed when trying the sound. Listening to the website example should be the last step; it's important to try it out for yourself first.

The common or neutral qualities

Quite a lot of popular music is sung in what I call the common or neutral thin-fold and thick-fold qualities. Some people think of these qualities in simpler terms – like the 'head' voice or 'chest' voice – but I find these terms less helpful when teaching. For me, explaining to singers about the variable density or thickness of the vocal mass helps to create an understanding of the ways in which we naturally mix qualities all the time, rather than always simply 'jumping' from chest to head. Let's start, then, by considering vocal-fold density. It sounds complex but it isn't.

In anatomical terms, vocal folds can produce sound in varying degrees of thickness. Look at this side view of the larynx:

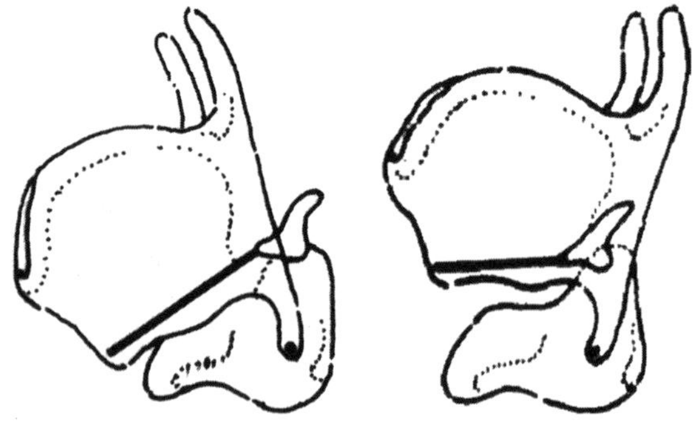

You'll see that when the thyroid cartilage of the larynx tilts forwards, the vocal folds (the heavy black line) are stretched thin. When the larynx is back in neutral position, the folds are thicker.

There is a third tilt, which occurs when the cricoid cartilage drops or tilts: this causes the back end of the cricoid to push up and in, thereby compressing the folds into an even thicker mass:

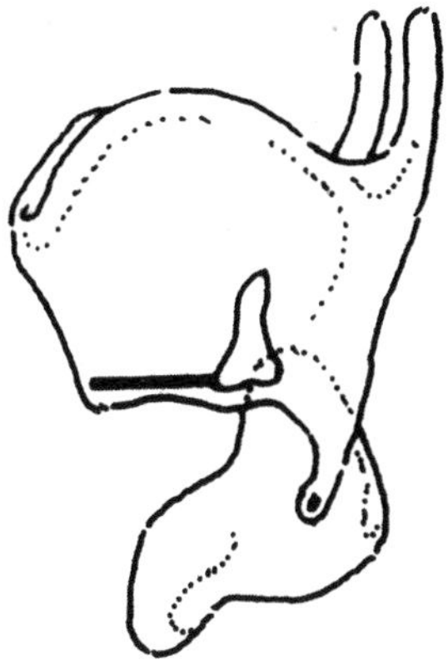

To understand why singing with a thicker-fold mass can be tiring, you could try thinking of the difference between beating two bricks together and beating two pillows together. Obviously because the pillows have less mass, they aren't likely to damage each other, even if you beat them together very fast. Whereas, if you had the strength, you could certainly damage the bricks if you beat them together even for a short period of time. That, in essence, is how you might think of the differences in vocal-fold mass – thicker mass naturally means more long-term wear and tear on the folds, whereas thinner mass is a safer bet. Still, you wouldn't want to build your house out of pillows. There's a time and place for all vocal quality uses; the smart singer simply knows how to pick them.

Neutral thin fold

The first common quality is probably the one with which we sing Christmas carols, or perhaps the one we use when we're singing lightly as we do the housework, or drive our cars (I haven't encountered many who use extreme voice qualities such as opera when driving their cars, although I'm sure they're out there). Many singers make a career out of using very little more than this kind of common quality. It's the quality that places, usually, very little strain on our voices; we're probably using most of our energy for vacuuming or driving when we use it. At times it is louder than at others, in fact, it can sometimes be remarkably bright and strong at the top end, which means the singer is usually mixing something else (like twang) into the quality. But even in its relatively higher-volume state, it is rarely hard to sustain. This quality is produced with thin vocal folds, and for most people it remains one used only for the comfortable upper range. When we get to the too-high end or the too-low end, we sometimes switch spontaneously to a different quality – possibly belt or twang (which we'll look at below).

Thin fold is of greatest use in the recording studio where, mixed with other elements of style, it brings us close to the artist through its intimate sound. Many singers work in their comfortable, thin-fold range when beginning a song, and for most this sound tends to come easily.

Practice

Just to make sure you're able to feel what I'm talking about when referring to neutral thin-fold quality, it is worth trying a practical exercise to access and identify this sound.

1 Start at the top of your comfortable range and once again make the noise of a puppy whimpering. You should be able to feel your larynx tilt gently forwards.

Practice (Continued)

2 Now slowly change the whimper into an 'ah' sound. Keep the sound light and try consciously not to engage muscles as you do this.

3 Get a real feel for exactly what's going on in terms of effort (which should remain low/relaxed throughout) and sound (which should be relatively quiet), and try to maintain it all the way through this exercise. Also be aware of keeping the larynx in its forward, tilted position.

4 Now very slowly move down through your range, holding on to the same effort and sound/volume levels. Once you get near the bottom of the range you might feel like increasing either muscle or volume, or else releasing the larynx tilt, but resist this and hold on to your set-up if you can.

5 Try a little phrase from a song and, again, hang on to your vocal set up and keep the effort and volume relatively low. You'll need breath for this, but don't overbreathe: just keep everything very light and relaxed. You should aim to have the same feeling when singing the notes in your upper register as you do when singing the notes in your lower register. The overall sound will be a quiet but pleasing one.

Overall, this quality should feel like what you may think of as your 'head' or 'falsetto' voice. The point in trying out this exercise is to demonstrate that we can hold onto this thin-fold set-up for quite a lot of our range. How far it can be carried into the middle or low range will vary with each individual voice. The larynx naturally rises as pitch rises, and this results in the vocal folds being stretched thinner. Often, as the pitch lowers into our mid to low range, we feel the larynx going into a 'neutral' or untilted state. This makes the vocal folds denser, so this exercise helps us to hold onto that thinner-fold mass for as long as it is comfortable.

Neutral thick fold

There is another quality common to popular singing that is rather like the neutral thin-fold sound, in that it is one which many singers use with ease. Often, if a singer has natural vibrato, it will appear easily in this quality. It is a sound that has greater power and potential for greater volume than thin-fold quality, yet, like thin fold, it is of most use in the singer's comfortable range. Again, once the singer goes into the very high or very low areas of their range, they will often spontaneously switch to another quality.

You may simply think of this as your 'chest' voice and, when singing in this thick-fold quality, you may or may not feel the larynx tilt. Because the sound is rich and strong, it seems certain that the mass of the vocal folds is thick. It doesn't require the same amount of effort as belting, and it doesn't feel as hard on the voice in production. It is often a very smooth quality and there are any number of singers who have made a career largely through the exploitation of this quality almost exclusively – Karen Carpenter and k.d. lang come to mind immediately. Again, because these neutral qualities are ones that many singers find easy (natural?) to access and use, they rarely feel the need to work on them technically, although some grow frustrated by the limits of their upper range in the neutral thick-fold quality, and wish they didn't have to sacrifice its power by switching over into their neutral thin-fold sound.

In the simplest terms, neutral or common thick fold is the singing sound you make when you are using a relatively moderate effort level and are singing in your low- to mid-range (where the folds will naturally be in thicker mass). Some people have great power in this quality, which can almost make the singer sound as if she/he is belting, but this common thick-fold quality doesn't require the same kind of muscle or effort level as belting does.

Practice

1 In what feels like the very middle of your range, try out the vowels A, E, I and O. Do your best to give the start of the sound an 'edge'. This is known as a glottal onset (which we'll work on again later).

2 While still in this mid-range area, sing A, E, I, O on one continuous breath but use the 'edge' of the start of the sound to really distinguish between the vowels, and:

- move up or down a pitch and hang onto that 'edge' to make the different vowels stand out from each other. Stay on one continuous breath, but you can hold onto each vowel longer now. Monitor what it feels like in terms of effort level and volume. This will be a louder sound than thin fold, but in mid-range it shouldn't really take too much more muscle than thin fold. Once you've really got a full memory of the feeling and the sound, hang on to both and sing a phrase from any song (staying in your mid-range). The sound probably feels more 'saturated' – full and pure and right 'on' the breath;
- move as comfortably as you can through the range, but don't push at the upper end. In other words do not 'drive' this quality by trying to engage more muscle or air to reach higher notes.

Doing these two practice exercises is a useful way of demonstrating that terms like 'head' and 'chest' voice aren't that helpful, even though it's true that people generally sing in thick fold in their 'chest' voice and in thin fold in their 'head' voice. It's important to note that most people can sing in either thin or thick fold throughout quite a substantial part of their range.

Every singer will mix these qualities in that middle area where they often experience a 'break' in the voice. These neutral qualities should just feel like a natural extension of the sounds you usually make in your life, but they are slightly sweeter, since they are sustained through your singing. In both of these qualities, you are often tilting your larynx forwards gently, so you will notice that this gives you – even in your easiest mid-range thick-fold sound – a slightly sweeter or perhaps warmer sound than your speaking voice.

Aspirate quality

In terms of voice quality, this is the only quality in which the vocal-fold mass actually stiffens slightly when you make the sound. The result can be a strange, airy tone, and many singers cannot, at first, imagine where or how they would use such a quality, but that is because we're using it here in its 'raw' form. Actually, once they begin the serious work of really listening to the elements of style used by any given singer, they are nearly always surprised by how much aspirate quality is used in popular singing, although generally in various blends and mixes of air and tone.

Practice

This is another relatively easy quality to access. First, imagine that you are doing that old trick of blowing over the top of an empty bottle to produce the weird, hollow sound that resonates from the cavity of the bottle. If that makes sense to you, you've probably just mastered the onset for aspirate quality. If it doesn't, try the following:

1 Set your mouth in the position to say 'ooh'.

2 Instead of actually voicing the 'ooh', keep your mouth in that position and exhale audibly (you'll sound like the wind).

Practice (Continued)

3 Next, voice the 'ooh'.

4 Now try to combine the two – in other words, voice the 'ooh' and sound like the wind.

5 With this sound in place, try moving gently through the mid- to upper-range.

6 Finally, hold onto the 'voice and wind' sensation and try singing 'Happy Birthday'.

If you got it right, you should have noticed the following:

1 ***When you made the sound, you could sense how much air was escaping freely as you did it.***

2 ***If you put your hand in front of your mouth as you simply voiced the 'ooh' (step 3), and kept it there when you added the wind sound, you could feel the difference in production. The simple voiced 'ooh' shouldn't have produced much more sensation on your hand than a slight warmth. The aspirate 'ooh' should have produced a strong sensation of air hitting your hand. If this difference wasn't apparent, try again!***

3 ***As you moved through the range, you may have found yourself losing the strong sensation of air on your hand – which may mean you switched into another quality.***

4 ***You may have noticed that you didn't produce much in the way of vibrato. If you did, you may have switched into another quality.***

5 ***When you sang 'Happy Birthday' you probably sounded as if you were doing an imitation of Marilyn Monroe (a famous example of aspirate singing!).***

Listen to Example 1 on the website and see if your sound quality is similar.

Most singers feel that if they produce this quality for very long, they become light-headed, thirsty or vocally rather 'tired'. They're probably not really tired, just unused to making this kind of sound, although they probably are light-headed and dry. The amount of air escaping can make you feel as if the throat is drying out quickly. This exercise is done with aspirate quality at its most extreme – most singers use it with far less air escaping. In fact, you might want to go back a practice, varying the amount of air you allow to escape while you sing. If you can keep the air present but somewhat minimal, you'll be able to employ this quality frequently without feeling dry or lightheaded. It's an extremely quiet quality and one best used in combination with other qualities.

Although aspirate quality is not naturally loud, some singers using it can produce more volume than others. It is not, however, the quality anyone would choose for power. While getting the hang of it isn't difficult, learning to use it artfully can take some time. Often students will claim that this is exactly the kind of sound they want to avoid making, but it all depends on where and how you use it. In the exercise you've just tried, you're using a lot of air to make the quality distinguishable to you; as you get used to finding and using it, you can decrease that amount of air and still gain the benefits that aspirate quality, or even a momentary stiffening of the vocal folds, can bring to song interpretation, particularly in terms of creating intimate or vulnerable vocal sounds. Few singers would use it too much, but singers like Norah Jones and Smokey Robinson have found terrific use for the aspirate quality.

Cry quality

There is no point in hiding it – we're getting into more unusual territory here. Cry quality took me much more time to appreciate, since I never 'naturally' used it in my years as a professional singer. However, having taken the time to understand it a little better, I now find it useful for all sorts of things – most particularly in getting a darker, more 'profound' resonance into the sound sometimes – and it seems to be a quality that I can use relatively easily over the passaggio or break area in my voice. I find it easy to access in the lower end of my voice (where many popular singers use this sound), but it can take a bit of practice to hold onto the sound as you move up in the register.

Practice

Some people find this sound easy to access if they think about trying to make the sound of an adult crying in a low, mournful way. It can be particularly helpful to think of 'swallowing back' the sound as you make it, since cry quality is a muted, soft and dark tone. If you can imagine and produce the sound of an adult very mournfully crying as they say 'Oh, no', you're probably well on the way to mastering this quality. If you're not too sure, try the following:

1 Assume the imaginary state of exaggerated sadness – think of tragic films you've seen.
2 Place your fingers lightly against your throat.
3 Imagine a lot of space at the back of your throat. Don't compress the tongue down at the back to achieve this, think more in terms of gently 'lifting' the top of the back of your throat. If you've got this part right you should feel your larynx tilting slightly forwards.
4 Now, holding on to that physical state and the emotional sense of tragic loss, 'sink' into the sound of saying 'Oh, no'.
5 Try this a few times and then hold onto the 'o' at the end of 'Oh, no'; sustain it, as if singing instead of speaking. Keep the sound soft.
6 Once you've got the sustain, try moving up and down through a very limited low- to mid-range – only three or four notes to start with.

You should have noticed the following:

1 ***Before you voiced the 'Oh' of 'Oh, no', you felt your larynx tilt forwards slightly.***
2 ***In those few notes, the larynx didn't move.***
3 ***If you tried to go up in the range, the larynx position began to feel a bit strained – this is because to make this sound, the larynx must stay in a low position. You can lower the larynx at any time, but because it has to rise when pitch rises, you need to reach the higher notes before you lower the larynx again. You can practise this by sirening up to a high note – not the very top of your range – and then (fingers lightly against your throat) trying to lengthen the vocal tract to drop the larynx again. This takes some practice, although most students can find this sound easily enough if they simply make the 'aahhh' sound that we sometimes make when we're yawning. This sound often starts high and comes down in pitch and it's usually in perfect cry quality. So if the access 'key' above doesn't work, try making that yawning sound – it's usually fail proof.***

Listen to Example 2 on the website and see if your sound quality is similar.

Again, in its 'raw' state, the cry quality can make students wonder where they would use this eerie sound, although from the beginning they usually recognize that it has an interesting resonance. And while it isn't a sound that a singer can use to create much volume or power, it is a quality that adds a richness and uniqueness to many voices. As with the other qualities, its use as a stylistic choice can be wonderful when employed by the artist. It is just this quality, coupled with a tremendous gift for improvisation that brings such pleasure in listening to singers like Donny Hathaway or Oleta Adams, who use a throaty, cry sound to great effect.

Twang quality

Because this quality is so useful to popular singing, it's probably the most important of all to master, so we'll spend some time on it. In my work, I've determined that twang has many subtle gradations. I often talk to singers about 'hard' twang, or 'baby' twang. In our consensual way, we usually experiment and try out sounds so that we understand what we're talking about in the sessions. That's more difficult when trying to write out a 'prescription' or guide to making a sound. First let's try to understand the sound.

Practice

Many people can access the 'hard' twang sound by thinking of the noise young children make in a playground when they are teasing each other: 'nyeh-nyeh-nyeh-nyeh-nyeh'. If you know what I'm talking about and you can do that little taunting chant with a really nasty reliance on the nasal sound encouraged by the 'ny' combination . . . well, you're probably a natural 'twanger'. It won't be a pleasant sound, so don't try to 'clean' it up or make it sound 'good'. Make sure you keep the vowel sound just as written above – 'eh'. If you can't find it this way, try the following:

1 Start with a good, fairly strong 'ee' sound in your comfortable mid-range. Imagine, as you are making the sound, that you are slowly 'compressing' it and pushing it out of your nose. It may help to 'squeeze' your face a bit as you do this. Now listen to Example 3 on the website and imitate.
2 Some people can access twang quality by doing an American accent, but you might want to be sure you don't carry the accent into the song (unless, of course, you want to).

(Continued)

Practice (Continued)

3 For a 'baby' twang, try to imitate the sound of an angry baby, crying 'wah' with a really nasal sensation. You may want to try to 'bend' the pitch upwards as you're doing it, just as the baby probably would. Listen to Example 4 on the website and imitate.

4 If you're having difficulty with these, try out the sounds of animals – either a sheep 'baa-ing' or a horse 'neighing' – these tend to be 'baby' twang sounds – or try the sound of a happy witch cackling.

For most people, one of these access keys works. Once you have it, you should notice the following:

1. ***The back of your tongue will be very high – the sides of the back will probably be just touching your back molars.***
2. ***The place where you really feel the sound is very high at the back of your mouth and in the nose.***
3. ***The sound is very sharp, probably loud (although not always), and very 'brassy'.***
4. ***The lower you are in the range, the 'harder' the twang sound, and the higher you go, the more like a baby you sound.***

Listen to Examples 3 and 4 on the website and see if your sound is similar.

Twang sound is created when the aryepiglottic folds just above the vocal folds 'tighten' into a circle. A good way of understanding this, without getting too technical, is to think of what happens to the air in a balloon if, as you release it, you suddenly pull the little ring of the opening very tight – it makes a higher-pitched sort of squealing sound. In a sense, that's how the aryepiglottic folds work in twang – they tighten and create a brighter sound.

One of the reasons that twang quality is so useful to popular singers is that it can enhance thin-fold quality. This is a surprise to most people, because they don't expect a thin-fold quality to have such power and volume. It is possible, however, for some people to have a very twangy belt, and they can often begin at the lower end of the range with thick folds. If they don't adjust as they move up in their range, they can find the quality very stressful. For those who access this sound through the 'nyeh-nyeh' method, they will often produce that thick-fold belt sound at first.

If you notice that you're finding it difficult to move up into your high range in twang, rethink your mental image – I tell singers either to remember the 'baby wail' described above, or to think of how they sound when they take a breath from a helium balloon. Make sure you don't force the sound at this point. Either of these images often sends them into thin-fold, 'baby' twang easily. If you feel you can't adjust as you move up in your range, try starting off the twang with the 'baby wail' sound or the animal sounds – they tend to start as thin fold. The thin-fold quality of twang is what makes it so useful for the pop/rock singer; you can produce enormous power and range in this quality which can be sustained for greater periods of time.

Belt quality

I think it's always good to look at belt quality after first having looked at twang, since having grown accustomed to the feel of twang production, you will find it easier to determine just what belt is, and for many, it is a confusing quality. Often we describe a twang sound as a belt, because the two can be very similar in terms of power. Also, many singers have a very twangy sound in their belt quality. On one level, it doesn't really matter, so long as you can produce the sound you want and if that sound is sustainable for you. But I think it's important for my students to know what belting is, and where they can use it, since I think it's a quality you must choose with some wisdom.

Practice

At its simplest, belting is much the same sensation as calling out to someone at a distance, but with pitch, sustain and (sometimes) vibrato added. When you're belting you feel the sound much more in your chest, but you will also be aware that much muscular energy is needed in the head and neck as well. When the volume is really high, or the pitch in the upper part of the register, it feels as if the whole of your upper body is involved in making the sound, so it's a very 'physical' quality.

1 Combine sound with a little movement. Imagine you see a friend across a wide boulevard but he/she is looking out of a first-floor window. With a vigorous wave, look up and shout 'Ay!' or 'Yay!' to your friend.
2 Hang on to the sensation, and now press your hands together in front of your chest. Keep your elbows close to the side of your body and press so that you feel the muscles in your chest and back working.
3 Call out again and this time call 'Ay, Ay, Ay!' (or 'Yay, Yay, Yay!') and hold each sound for about five seconds.
4 Before you go further, check to see that while you're definitely aware of feeling effort in your neck and chest, you don't feel strain.
5 Call 'Ay'/'Yay' again three times, holding onto the sound and letting the pitch rise to the highest comfortable note, but keeping all this sound well within your middle range.

You should have noticed that:

1. ***While you could feel muscle helping, you didn't really need too much air. If you were breathing too deeply, go back and try again. Belt doesn't need a lot of air.***
2. ***The sensation was really centred in your chest. You felt effort in and around the larynx, but not strain. And unlike in twang, there was little sensation in the nose or the facial mask area.***
3. ***The sound – especially as you kept your hands pressed hard against each other – was powerful.***
4. ***If you did this for long, you may have felt a bit tired.***

Listen to Example 5 on the website and see if your sound quality was similar.

For most singers, accessing or producing belt isn't much of a problem. Sustaining it can be, because although so much of what you do in this quality is similar to what you do in twang, the big difference is in the mass of the vocal folds: where twang is sometimes thin fold, belt is always thick fold. This is why in many cases it can sound very much like just a more musical version of calling out to a friend across the street.

Belt often becomes very difficult to sustain in the upper range, and this is where most singers either stop, switch into their neutral thin-fold voice (usually calling it their 'head' voice), or, if they've listened to much rock or gospel music, spontaneously carry on, having switched into twang quality.

For the listener, it can be hard to tell the difference between belt and twang but that's not so important, and these qualities are often 'mixed' anyway. What is important is being able to tell the difference as the singer. You should be able to feel the difference. If you're producing loud, high sounds with relative ease, and are able to sustain that for some time, the chances are you are twanging. If you can produce loud sounds through your lower- and mid-range but don't feel comfortable sustaining that for too long, you're probably belting. Twang is often experienced in and around the head, whereas belt is generally felt in the upper chest area. Belt often has a less nasal sound to it, but it can just as often have the same kind of brassy tone as twang. Each voice brings different harmonics to the quality and this is why the listener can get so confused when hearing belt/twang.

One of the easiest ways to tell the difference is to go back and access twang through one of the exercises described. In its 'raw' state, twang can sound very unpleasant. Belting, because it is closer in tone to thick fold or speaking, may be loud, but it doesn't usually ever sound unpleasant to the singer – it tends to sound simply like a very loud, more musical version of their speaking voice.

Think back to the pillow and the bricks, and you'll know that using belt can be harder, generally, on your voice than thin-fold qualities; because of its great volume, it can be much harder on your voice than neutral thick-fold quality. It is one of the more extreme sounds you can use as a singer but that doesn't mean you shouldn't use it. Popular music is full of belters – you simply have to know how to blend this quality with others in order not to overuse it.

Many voice teachers panic about belting, and consequently panic their students about it too. I believe that most singers instinctively know when they are producing a sound in a healthy way; when they aren't, their voices usually let them know. If you are attempting loud sounds and find that your voice goes hoarse soon afterwards, it's time to seek some guidance. But don't let that put you off experimenting – it's fine to try things out, in fact, it's part of the process of maturing as a singer. You simply have to be smart about it and make sure that you're not constricting as you produce the tone. If you are ever in doubt or feel that your voice 'goes' quickly, see a voice tutor, preferably one who is sympathetic to the kinds of music and vocal qualities you're interested in learning, who can listen and advise.

In your own practice, it's not particularly important that you monitor your vocal quality, but in terms of style it's helpful to increase your options, so you might find it worthwhile to practise these perfectly safe and distinct qualities. Of course when you practise them, you'll find that they often blend or mix and, as mentioned earlier, it is common to hear people with a twangy belt or somewhat aspirated thin fold.

The 'dangerous' qualities

There are a few qualities common to popular singing that I am listing as 'dangerous', frankly because to many voices they are. As noted earlier, much of what we respond to in popular music has little to do with 'proper' vocal production or pleasing sound. At the end of the twentieth century, the BBC conducted a listener's survey called 'Voices of the Century'. There are few surprises in terms of the popularity of the vocalists cited (with Sinatra, Presley, Nat King Cole and Ella Fitzgerald topping the list) but it is interesting to note how many singers on the list employ qualities that I would list here as dangerous. Freddie Mercury (10), Louis Armstrong (16), Stevie Wonder (26), Robert Plant (36), Bono (38), Otis Redding (48), Tina Turner (52), Sting (59), Rod Stewart (62), Meat Loaf (64), Little Richard (75), Howlin' Wolf (80), Bruce Springsteen (85), James Brown (86) and Tom Waits (92) all employ vocal techniques that involve some kind of constriction (to greater or lesser degrees).

Because so little is known about why constriction affects individual voices so differently, it is rare that the average voice teacher would want to try it with their pupils. While the resilience of each voice varies, prolonged constricted vocal sounds can result in lasting damage, and if used over a number of years, they almost certainly will. As we know, that damage is often what attracts us to particular kinds of vocal sounds, so this area is fraught with danger, but no book on popular singing style can avoid recognizing it.

In terms of voice qualities – which is to say, in terms of a sustained, 'sung' sound – there are probably three distinct dangerous qualities, most of which are used as a small percentage of the singer's overall vocal expression. I won't include website examples here, but I have provided recorded examples that will give you a strong sense of the sound. Listen to these and then try some of them on your own (if you're comfortable with them) in the Summary Practice at the end of this chapter.

Rumble

I call this quality the rumble, although some might call it a growl. Rumble sounds seem somewhat old-fashioned now, but they were once a mainstay of blues singing. The rumble is more or less the sound of Louis Armstrong's vocal quality. Apart from trying to imitate Louis Armstrong, or listening to the old recordings of Bessie Smith and trying to imitate her growling sounds, the only key to accessing the sound that I've found is to think of the physical sensation of gargling but keep the 'gargle' low in your throat (if you don't, you may just end up sounding like you're underwater!). If you set up the sensation of gargling low in your throat and then try to sing 'through' that feeling, you'll probably be able to produce a rumble sound. For most vocalists, this is a sound that can only be used sparingly. It will quickly dry out your throat and, if sustained for long, make your voice feel tired and rather 'croaky', although this is usually a short-term effect. Rumble is more often used as an onset because it takes such a toll on the voice, but whether used in sustaining an entire line of a song or only in the onset, it raises the perceived-effort level of the singer and gives a kind of high-energy immediacy to a performance.

EXAMPLE

k.d. lang: *Big Boned Gal* (1989). As noted, rumble is rarely sustained for long, but this track is full of exuberant style choices and features a lot of rumble. You can hear her switch quickly from thick- to thin-fold vocal qualities and as the track progresses she makes liberal use of the sustained rumble quality. She uses many interesting onsets and offsets (which we'll cover in the next chapter), a quick flip from belt or thick- to thin-fold quality as she goes. The whole thing is passionate and brave and perfectly captures the feel of the dance down at the Legion Hall that she's singing about.

Creak

The second 'dangerous' quality is a creak, the lighter form of which is sometimes called scratch. Creak has a dry sort of quality; it can be either pitched or not pitched. To access it, you can try making a noise, deep in the throat, which sounds like a creaking door. It will sound raspy and not necessarily 'pitched' in any sense. Some people can access this sound by talking until they reach the very end of their breath capacity and the raspy noise at the end of that very long phrase is usually a creak. It doesn't take much energy to sustain the creak sound, which is why it so often appears at the beginning or final stages of the breath. Like rumble, this sound is most common as an onset or offset (see next chapter), but some artists use it mid-phrase and can sustain the sound for a surprisingly long time. Creak is also called 'vocal fry' when it occurs right at the bottom of your range, and given the creaky sounds voices can make at the bottom of the range, this is understandable. But unlike vocal fry, creak can be used throughout much of the range. As noted, it's a dry sort of sound and can dry you out if you try to sustain it for long, although as noted above, some voices can sustain it just fine and still switch into a strong, clear tone at will. Creak can sometimes involve singing on after the breath supply is nearly exhausted, or a quick lowering of effort/breath in order to create the sound mid-phrase. The effect in performance is one of vulnerability and intimacy.

EXAMPLES

Rodney Atkins: *Cleaning This Gun* (2007). This is a wonderful and wicked track from Atkins. You'll hear that for the majority of the opening he uses a sustained creak sound liberally before opening out to a nice clean sound for the 'Come on in' chorus. He uses the creak in the more confessional and then the more threatening parts of the lyric ('I'll be up all night cleaning this gun') which gives both grit and intimacy to the performance.

Lyle Lovett: *That's Right, You're Not from Texas* (1996). This track features Lovett's amazing Western swing band to its best effect, and he uses a lighter kind of creak than Atkins – you can hear why many people refer to this as a 'scratch' vocal sound. He sustains it regularly on and off throughout the track and it gives a kind of 'street cred' sound that might be hard to achieve otherwise when singing with such a slick and sophisticated band.

Constricted

The last 'dangerous' quality is even more difficult to describe in terms of access, and that is a constricted quality which is, of course, singing while engaging the false folds to a greater or lesser degree. Many rock and blues singers do this quite consciously to raise the effort level of their performance and to take the voice to extremes when expressing emotion. You will recall that we tried this earlier in the practice exercise on page 39. You may have managed it or you may have found that not much sound came out at all. Pop singers clearly use various degrees of constriction in their performances. In some voices it can sound extremely hard (Janis Joplin) and in others it has more of a 'scratch' sound (Lyle Lovett). Some singers can temporarily constrict a tone to give a gurgling or raspy sound to the sustain and then follow on with a clear, full and unconstricted tone without doing any apparent damage to the voice. Many singers use this quality in short bursts to drive up the perceived-effort level of their singing, to match either the volume/energy of the band or the emotional intensity of a given song. The overall effect is one of raw, unmediated emotion.

EXAMPLES

Janis Joplin: *Piece of my Heart* (1968).This is one of Joplin's signature performances and you can really feel where she employs the constricted sound throughout this but especially on the 'You know you got it', the 'now' improv and the final scream before the last chorus. I love the kind of naked pain she displays in this track – it's old school recording, which really helps the overall effect – not a click track or an Auto-Tune in sight!

Nirvana: *Lithium* (1991). This track demonstrates the conscious switch from a clear to a constricted tone between the verses and the 'yeah' choruses (you can hear

(*Continued*)

it on the studio version but it's probably even clearer on the many live versions you can find on YouTube). The song is full of ambiguous images of a man who is caught between his own depression/paranoia and finding some salvation/survival in religion, so somehow the switch between a 'rational' clean sound and an 'irrational' constricted sound catches that dual mindset perfectly.

Nathan James: *Sweet Child o' Mine* (2012). This track is only available on YouTube (http://www.youtube.com/watch?v=XJWrOAJmn9o), but I've included it here because it's one of the clearest examples I can find of a singer who knows just how to use the power and excitement of constricted quality safely. Nathan is blessed with incredible range, and he pushes his voice quite hard, but you can hear very clearly here that he uses degrees of constriction – sometimes only using a kind of mild rasp to the sound (as in the first 'Sweet child o mine' chorus) and at other times allowing the full gutsy, no-holds-barred sound that full constriction can give (from about the 1:58 mark through to the amazing finish). It's a remarkable performance.

Only experienced singers should experiment with these kinds of sounds extensively, since you can only know what your voice will or won't sustain when you're extremely familiar with the way in which it responds to fatigue or any kind of new vocal production techniques. For this reason, it's probably best that you start simply by listening to the examples. If you decide to try any of these 'dangerous' qualities you should do so with a little caution, and only when you're sure you can assess for yourself whether a little experimentation is sustainable. While most singing teachers will shudder at this suggestion, the pop industry is now, and has been since its earliest days, filled with vocalists who can and do sustain some constriction in their style, and many have been able to do so for the whole of their careers. There are also a great many popular singers who are not interested in the 'rules', and who want to discover for themselves what kinds of sounds they can make. We know, of course, that most singing teachers wouldn't tolerate Little Richard. Then again, we can be pretty sure that Little Richard wouldn't tolerate most singing teachers . . .

Summary

Having spent a little time considering these sounds, you might agree with me that when it comes to popular music, most voices remain largely in the common neutral thin- or thick-fold range, but that many memorable voices use the other qualities – aspirate, belt, twang, cry, rumbled, constricted, etc. – for greater emotional impact as well as vocal shaping and shading. As such, they often aren't pleasant qualities, especially in their raw state, which is how you have been hearing and working with them while going through this chapter. For vocalists they are anything but 'neutral'; they are the wilder, more interesting parts of the vocal palette, which can create the vocal equivalent of an expressionist painting as opposed to a gentle watercolour landscape.

The difficulty in looking at these various qualities in isolation is that singers rarely ever use them this way. Most voices create their own spontaneous mix of sounds, which means it can be a challenge sometimes to identify all the qualities a singer like Tori Amos uses.

To help make some of the sounds we've just considered a little clearer in performance, and to discover what switching up vocal qualities can do for a performance, listen to the following examples below, which demonstrate style and courage. Listening closely to these tracks should also help you train your ear for listening. Take some time to explore these examples and I think you'll feel ready to have a go at the Summary Practice at the end of this section.

EXAMPLES

Rachelle Ferrell: *You Send Me* (1990). This is an extraordinary and confident cover of Sam Cooke's song. If you listen closely you'll hear a smooth cry sound in the opening lines, with a mid-phrase flip into thin fold and she follows that at various points with aspirate, thick fold and a bit of twang. It's playful and deeply musical and, for me, reinvents the whole song. Where Cooke's smooth and sophisticated version suggests a man trying to be rational in the face of his passion, Ferrell feels like she gives in to hers quite happily.

4 Non Blondes: *What's Up* (1992). This track makes me laugh – it was a massive hit for Linda Perry (the writer and singer), but it also made a couple of 'Worst Songs Ever' lists. It's easy to see why it was a hit though – Perry has such exuberance and the overall wackiness of her vocal choices really match the lyric here, which is all about a woman trying to come to terms with her unsteady mental state. We get aspirate, thin fold, thick fold, belt, twang and constriction as the track goes on, and also some nice mid-phrase flips from one quality to another. Whatever you think of it as a performance, you must admit that it's a bold piece of work!

Queen: *Bohemian Rhapsody* (1975). This is a kind of 'choral' work, but where Freddie Mercury sings solo you can hear some terrific vocal exploration. He starts with a twangy belt, and once we're into the verses ('Mama just killed a man') he drops back into a thick fold that melts into aspirate finishes and drifts from thin fold back into a scratchy belt. Sustains are raggedy, especially on the belted 'Mama' where the voice nearly fails. The piece is a classic, theatrical piece of rock kitsch and Mercury seems to have realized that half-measures would never serve his vision. Consequently the vocal sounds here go from 'legit' to absurd quickly.

Björk: *It's Oh So Quiet* (1995). Starting with a thin fold and aspirate sound before the big chorus kicks in and then we hear rumble, belt and some constriction. She runs through a lot of sound here which catches the excitement of the rush of infatuation. It's brave and funny and moving all at the same time.

Summary practice

The vocal qualities we've explored are best understood through both listening and practice, and that practice is best linked with the imagination. Once you've listened to the examples above, you'll be ready to try this practice, which is in two parts.

Practice

1 In a comfortable key (C usually works for both men and women) sing through the first lines of *Swing Low, Sweet Chariot* below. Sing the verse through once in either one or a combination of the neutral thin- or thick-fold voice qualities. Don't think about performing it, just sing it through in the most comfortable neutral quality. Try this twice:

Swing Low, Sweet Chariot,

comin' for to carry me home

(*Continued*)

Practice (Continued)

Swing Low, Sweet Chariot,

comin' for to carry me home

I looked over Jordan and what did I see

comin' for to carry me home?

A band of angels comin' after me,

comin' for to carry me home.

2 Now, before you sing through again, take a look at the lyrics and choose four phrases which you will sing with four different voice qualities. Because you'll be busy thinking about producing the voice qualities, it's best to choose your phrases and qualities before trying to sing. Your marked lyrics should look like this:

aspirate

(Swing low, sweet chariot)

Comin' for to carry me home

cry

(Swing low, sweet) chariot

Comin' for to carry me home

I looked over Jordan and what did I see?

belt

Comin' for to (carry me home)

Twang

A (band of angels) comin' after me

Comin' for to carry me home.

3 Don't think too much about what quality goes where – this is a totally random exercise at the moment. The exercise will probably sound a bit mechanical, precisely because it is so

Practice (Continued)

random. Don't worry about that right now; just mark at least four phrases with different voice qualities. Here is a blank lyric for you to mark in your own way:

Swing Low, Sweet Chariot,

comin' for to carry me home

Swing Low, Sweet Chariot,

comin' for to carry me home

I looked over Jordan and what did I see

comin' for to carry me home?

A band of angels comin' after me,

comin' for to carry me home.

Sing the piece through now, alternating between your neutral voice and the other qualities you've chosen. Do it this way a few times until you're comfortable switching vocal qualities quickly. Don't try to make the switches smooth – be as abrupt as you can.

4 After you've grown comfortable with trying this a few times, decide which parts of this verse or chorus carry the greatest emotional connection to your heart, or which you want us to have the greatest emotional response to and go through again. Reassign the vocal qualities to different phrases if you like, and try to use whatever feels to you like the more dramatic ones to bring greater life/colour to those parts. Make sure the quality switches are still very abrupt – don't worry about being 'correct' or careful.

You should notice that:

1 ***The more you get used to switching vocal qualities, the more interesting your performance sounds (even if interesting only means unusual).***
2 ***If you are already used to switching qualities quite a lot, you may have found this the easiest exercise in the book so far!***
3 ***When connected to your sense of performance or emotional truth, the qualities take on a much deeper and satisfying sound than when we worked through them earlier.***
4 ***Your performance didn't sound 'schooled' or trained; it may have sounded a bit wild.***
5 ***If you used the predominantly high-effort-level qualities (twang, belt, rumble, constricted or thick fold) you may have felt you were singing a rock or blues version of your song.***
6 ***If you used the predominantly low-effort-level qualities (aspirate, neutral, thin fold, cry, creak) you may have felt you were singing a jazz or pop version of your song.***
7 ***If you switched wildly from high- to low-effort-level sounds you may have felt that you were singing an R&B or gospel version of your song.***
8 ***However you worked it, your 'quick switch' version of the song should have proved more interesting to create (and to listen to!) than your initial neutral-quality version.***

CHAPTER THREE

The complementary elements of style

Sound and shape

Although this part of the book is all about sound, it might help to think about this section as focusing on how we shape sound. Sometimes, when I'm trying to describe this in workshops, I use the metaphor of shapes and it seems to make sense to a lot of people. They understand (once we've done a fair amount of listening to and talking about what makes up vocal style) what it means when we refer to a 'short thin' shape to a phrase, or a 'baggy' shape to a phrase. While we always start our work by exploring the sounds we can make in various vocal qualities, we then go on to look at how we shape that sound, and for me, the more interesting the shape, often, the more interesting the sound. The voice qualities we've been looking at are, of course, a primary part of the singer's sound; for most singers who are working with a teacher to train their voices, this is where a great majority of the work takes place. The difficulty for those vocalists or singing teachers who want to be able to explore popular style is that, while voice qualities can be more or less suited to a given popular style, they are certainly not the whole picture: there are many 'complementary elements' that frame and modify those voice qualities.

These complementary elements are what give shape, colour and distinction to a singing performance, and they will be the focus of this section.

In workshops, we often begin by considering the kinds of things we've been told about vocal 'shape' at classes we've attended – either in choral or solo singing. Most of us think immediately of descriptions like 'line' or 'arc' of the melody, and generally think that the way to create a 'good' line or arc in a melody is to make a sort of gentle 'hill' out of our sound. In other words, we allow the sound and the effort to rise gradually up towards the crest of this little 'hill' and then allow it to descend gently as we ease off the phrase. I usually find that when I ask singers to try to sing a line or two from a song as beautifully as they can (and I let them determine what beautiful means to them in this context), they tend to make these little 'hills' of vocal shape. Of course we can make these little hill shapes in any vocal quality, but most singers decide that 'beautiful' means either the neutral or the cry vocal qualities that we practised in the last chapter. Popular singing requires not only that you have the courage to move away from these 'beautiful' voice qualities occasionally, but also that you abandon any ideas you may have about creating the 'right' shape in a line or phrase. In fact, as we go through our exercises here, you'll discover many different ways to create interesting shapes in your sound; with enough practice you'll find that often, your most engaging and unique vocal work will come when you've learnt to create anything but 'gentle hills' of sound.

Effort level

This is the term often used by singing teachers who want their students to be aware of how much (or how little) they're working while singing. However, effort level is not commonly taught as an element of style and it should be because it is a major factor in how we are affected when listening to a singer's performance. Sometimes we want to be aware that the singer is working hard; indeed, that perceivable 'hard work' is frequently what convinces us that a singer is sincere. Effort levels influence our judgement about what kind of singer we're listening to, and usually the singer is working through a number of the complementary elements described below to create the impression of that effort level.

Analysing the effort level we hear is an important first step in considering a singer's style, and we have to analyse it in two ways: the perceived-effort level and the true-effort level.

The perceived-effort level isn't too difficult to ascertain, although whenever I'm doing this exercise in workshops (we work on a scale of 1 to 10, with 10 being the highest), we invariably have some debates over where to place artists. To illustrate the lower end of perceived-effort level – for the 2 or 3 we usually listen to 'smooth' voices or those artists who sometimes sound as if they could be relaxing in a beach chair. But often that low effort level has much to do with the way we respond emotionally to a song:

EXAMPLES

Norah Jones: *Good Morning* (2012). Jones's trademark aspirate and thin-fold vocal sounds are sustained through most of this track, which gives the impression of very little muscle or energy used in producing the vocal sound. Combined with the unusual sound of her backing, it all adds up to a kind of ethereal, haunting performance about a woman who is thinking about leaving but can't quite do it with conviction. The overall tentative sound of pain, sleeplessness and indecision are brilliantly conveyed in the singing.

(*Continued*)

Michael Jackson: *She's Out of My Life* (1979). This is an unusually low-energy, very intimate track from Jackson, which relies mostly on a twangy thin fold, and combines aspirate sounds with some interesting offsets. If you listen really closely in the final verse, after he does his only 'power' sound ('deep inside'), you can hear a lot of audible breath and as the voice just fails on the final 'life' it seems almost certain that Jackson was overcome by emotion in the studio at the end of this song.

For the 9 or 10 we might listen to artists whose whole style seems to be defined by sheer effort and energy:

EXAMPLES

James Brown: *It's a Man's Man's Man's World* (1966). This is one of James Brown's classics, if not *the* classic, and he absolutely drives the sound here with so much energy it's infectious. Brown was often referred to as the hardest working man in show business, and it was said that he lost up to five pounds in every concert. If you go back to watch some of his performances you can believe it.[1] This song relies heavily on Brown's explosive, gritty sound to convince you of its 'caveman' lyric. Brown uses a lot of constriction on the highest 'nothing' sounds, and because

[1]If you've never seen Brown, you're in for a treat. This extract from the T.A.M.I. concert in 1964 is probably as good an introduction as any: http://www.youtube.com/watch?v=b2nybY647F0

the effort level of the sound is so high he doesn't bother to exploit sustain much. You might enjoy comparing his track to Christina Aguilera's 2007 James Brown tribute at the Grammy Awards (http://www.youtube.com/watch?v=eg3wyv5iflk), where for all the rumbling, growling, heavy, slow note bends and massive sustains, I don't think she brings Brown's emotional impact. But it's certainly another 9 or 10 effort-level performance. Brown's intense growl and emotion in the final 'he's lost' screams combine to make you feel absolutely certain of Brown's commitment to the saving grace of the lyric line: that man is alone without a woman. Of course, few voices could sustain what Brown's did, but right up until his death in 2006 he continued to perform.

Tina Turner: *Proud Mary* (http://www.youtube.com/watch?v=EmH4YINdWAg). Of course you can listen to the studio version, but this YouTube clip is Tina Turner at age 69, holding her own with women about a third of her age. She doesn't really get going here until around the four-minute mark, but when she does it's absolutely extraordinary. She's been singing and dancing hard all her life and although you can hear that she doesn't have as much range as she did 30 or 40 years ago, she's still a force of nature. When she started singing in the late 1950s, there would only have been classical voice teachers around, none of whom would have encouraged her to sing in the way that she did, but she clearly knew her own voice well: she knew just what it could take and what it couldn't – what else could explain her incredible stamina and the ability to deliver like this at the age of 69? She's an inspiration and living proof that rock and roll keeps you young.

Figuring out the true-effort level, though, can be much more difficult. Most singers mix up the effort levels as they go through a performance, and some are actually working much harder than you think:

EXAMPLES

Karen Carpenter: *We've Only Just Begun/Rainy Days and Mondays* (1970). While you don't hear a great deal of effort in songs like Carpenter's *We have Only Just Begun* or *Rainy Days and Mondays*, both songs are dominated by a deep, rich thick-fold quality; long, even and muscular sustains, often capped with beautiful vibrato releases. If you try Carpenter's style out for yourself, you quickly find that the true-effort level is significantly higher than what you're hearing.

Hall & Oates: *One on One* (1983). Although there are no 'power' sounds here, if you try singing along you'll quickly find out just what a challenge Hall's sinuous phrasing and extended melodic additions are. Just finding places to breathe while maintaining his even, fluid delivery is a real challenge – sing along and you'll see. It's a beautiful track that achieves its effect through what sounds like Hall's 'effortless' ease, created through sheer hard work!

Learning the difference between a true and a perceived-effort level is important for any singer thinking about the choices they make in creating a given style or working in a particular genre. In rock, gospel, and rhythm and blues, so much of what distinguishes these genres is that the singers use great effort and energy to perform. But vocal longevity and health can often depend on being able to learn how you can create the effect of a high perceived level of effort without always having to produce a high true-effort level. Much of our work on the complementary elements of style below will make this clearer.

We're going to look at and practise a number of elements:

Onsets
Offsets or release
Sustain and vibrato
Phrase weight and placement
Note attack
Breath
Diction
Improvisation

As we look at these, keep in mind that the purpose of all of these elements is to help you communicate your thoughts/feelings effectively. I always worry about presenting these elements without making that point – perhaps repeatedly – because I believe that singers should never separate what they learn technically from what they do imaginatively.

These elements are part of the creation of a more imaginative vocal expression. Having said that, I would suggest that as you read through, you should start giving each of these a try, even though you may be doing it out of context. Some may come easily; some may not. Again, I've included many examples for you to listen to so that you can hear the sounds in practice (on Spotify, YouTube, iTunes, etc.). Ideally you should go through this section with your laptop or tablet close by. The examples are deliberately wide-ranging – some contemporary and some old. All the examples have been chosen to help make the sounds I'm describing clear, but also because I think the artist is using that sound as part of a great performance.

The examples also demonstrate the way that each voice is unique, and that means one singer's creak onset can sound very different from another's. I've tried to choose examples that are clear but there are always some very fine distinctions (glottal flip, for example) that can be difficult to describe, and may also be produced very differently by different singers. Some people respond initially in terms of muscle or the way a sound 'feels' when it is made. Some simply respond in terms of the way things sound. But listening first and then experimenting in whatever way works for you is really critical.

Onset

Onset is the way in which you begin the sound. Most singing teachers work with three standard onsets: simultaneous, aspirate and glottal. They are onsets that anyone can master.

Simultaneous onset

In this onset, the tone and the breath seem to occur simultaneously. This quality has a kind of 'neutral' sound since it doesn't require as much effort as the glottal onset, nor is it as distinctive an onset as the aspirate. For this reason the simultaneous onset has no particular emotional effect on the listener in itself – it must be coupled with other elements.

EXAMPLE

Joan Baez: *Diamonds and Rust* (1975). This gentle, evocative track (written by her of her early romance with Bob Dylan) is typical of Baez's style, which is based in simple storytelling. You can hear that all of her onsets are very 'even' sounding – you don't get the sense of any particular energy in coming into the note. Her vibrato is fast and she uses it in the fade of every phrase. Emotional reaction to the song relies heavily on the story, the romantic associations it evokes, and the quality of Baez's voice.

Aspirate onset

This is the onset you will have used in creating aspirate quality. The air actually precedes the breath, and it gives a singer's performance a softer, more tentative quality. It can be sexy or vulnerable and it always creates a genuine sense of intimacy between singer and listener. Sometimes a singer switches into another voice quality quickly, and sometimes a singer may hang onto the aspirate voice quality through the line.

EXAMPLE

Kenny Loggins: *This Is It* (1979). Loggins typically uses a wide dynamic range in his singing and often moves from a gentle aspirate sound to twangy belt and even rumble very quickly. He's a master of mixing air into his sound to create the emotional effect he wants, and this track demonstrates that so well. Inspired by seeing his critically ill father in the hospital, you can really sense both the intimacy and the urgency that Loggins must have felt when recording this anthem, which is about choosing life. The use of the breath in those opening phrases immediately matches up with his lyric, which is all about a man who isn't sure how things are going to turn out. This recording is full of bold style choices and quick changes which, despite Loggins's reliance on aspirate sounds (usually a low-effort quality), really boosts the overall effort level here.

Glottal onset

This is the most 'abrupt' onset, and we've worked with it already in creating our thick-fold sound. The easiest way to feel this onset is by saying 'uh-oh'. Try that out before listening to the example below. You'll be able to feel that the sound at the beginning of the tone is a little edgy and well defined. As a little experiment, try making the 'edge' of the 'uh' in 'uh-oh' as hard as you can. If you manage to make it very hard, you will almost certainly have done that by adding a little muscle and creating what is called sub-glottal pressure, which is the building up of air just below the glottis as it is closed, and then releasing it quickly into the phonation of the 'u' sound in 'uh-oh'. It almost feels as if the tone comes before the breath in this onset, and it will feel like an onset that requires a little more effort than the first two. Because the sound gives vowels a definite edge as you come into it, this onset, when combined with 'poppingly' hard consonants, is most useful for dynamic styles, particularly styles where you want to create a high perceived level of effort. It can sound emphatic and definite, and give the listener a sense that the artist is certain about what she/he is saying (singing). Of course, a glottal sound isn't only used in onset – Amy Winehouse and Adele (among many others – listen to the Patsy Cline example on page 86) both use the glottal sound mid-glide, either as they move from note to note or simply mid-sustain to give their sound a bit of muscle.

EXAMPLE

Christina Aguilera: *Ain't No Other Man* (2007). Aguilera works with a lot of glottal pressure here (which basically means that she lets the breath build up before releasing) and this pressure gives her onset its sense of urgency and edge. You'll hear this really specifically on the word 'ain't' in the chorus – the 'a' vowel just pops when she releases it and has real power. That sound mirrors the synthy-horn sound in the opening and ties the whole track together. The combination of those high-pressure glottals and all the big twang/belt/rumble sounds result in a very high overall effort level.

Along with these onsets, I think there are four other identifiable onsets used regularly in popular music. Not everyone can master these, although some can master all. As they can give you some interesting vocal variety, it's worth trying to get a feel for them.

Flip onset

You may make associations between this onset and country music, and you may be familiar with the sound of it from hearing someone yodel. According to some singing teachers, the yodel or flip sound is created when the plane of the vocal folds jumps rapidly between a thin or thick fold and an aspirate position, quickly changing qualities from thin/thick to aspirate, or the other way around. Strictly speaking, this isn't always an onset phenomenon: you can't flip into a consonant; you can only flip into the first vowel. So on a word like 'swing', you would have to voice the 'sw' consonants and flip quickly into the 'i' vowel. But it would still strike us as part of the onset in this example because it happens so quickly near the front of the phrase. Nor is it only used in onset – many popular singers use this flip sound mid-phrase – Jennifer Warnes, Sarah McLachlan and Alanis Morissette come to mind immediately – and others use it frequently to move from note to note or to 'switch gears' very quickly into another voice quality.

While many vocalists can't find the way to use this sound mid-phrase (any more than they can yodel, which is essentially what is required), the majority of vocalists I've worked with can learn to imitate the sound for use in onset. The emotional quality of the flip sound is variable. It can sometimes be a vulnerable one if used gently and with low-effort voice qualities. But hard rock singers use this onset to gain power and give a hard edge to the opening of a phrase. There are degrees of 'width' to the sound that can vary its effect: a slower, 'wide' flip is often associated with country, and has a naïve, 'untrained' sound, whereas a quick, 'narrow' flip is more often associated with pop music and can lend a kind of sophistication or nuance to a song. Remember when you experiment with this onset that you have to flip on a vowel, which means that you come into the consonant sound first and then flip quickly into the vowel sound.

Most people can master the flip in time, but it often takes a variety of vocal 'cues' to try and familiarize a voice with this sound. If all else fails, try a Tarzan yell! This usually helps people find the sound.

EXAMPLES

Patsy Cline: *Crazy* (1962). A flip sound is used at various times throughout this track and you can hear it quite clearly on the choruses and on the middle-eight ('Worry, why do I let myself worry'). The flip gives her song a plaintive, yearning sound and given the heartbreak story she's singing to us it suits this piece beautifully. This track is worth listening to closely, as you'll also hear a liberal use of mid-phrase glottal technique (listen especially to the first 'lonely' and 'long', where she uses a glottal stop mid-word).

Sarah McLachlan: *Angel* (1997). As well as the occasional onset use, McLachlan frequently uses a flip sound mid-phrase in the changeover from thick- to thin-fold quality. It gives her work that rather wistful or heart-rending effect, and it always makes McLachlan's work memorable. There's something both delicate and ethereal about the flip sound in this track that matches the lyric – about the desperate search for inner peace – beautifully (listen especially to the word 'hard' in the first verse, but of course, she uses this mid-phrase flip liberally throughout the track).

Glottal flip

This is a rather strange combination of both glottal and flip sounds and it has a compelling and edgy sound. It's both powerful and strangely vulnerable as it has a kind of 'cry' feel to it. It's difficult to describe, but it needs the same kind of sub-glottal pressure that the glottal onset uses, but in the release there's a slight flip or yodel sound as well. This one really takes some listening to and some practice. Not everyone can master this one (I can't), but everyone can hear it. From there it's just a question of experimenting to see if you can match the sound of it. Listen carefully to this example and then give it a try.

EXAMPLE

Adele: *Rolling in the Deep* (2011). She uses a glottal flip for so much of this track and you can hear it in its most extreme form on words like 'how', 'underestimate', 'go ahead', 'heard' (in the phrase 'I've heard one on you'), 'all' (in the phrase 'could've had it all'). It takes muscle and air, and it gives a very unique power to the onset sound, that drives the perceived-effort level up and feels like a combination of vulnerability and defiance. That works extremely well with the overall lyric of the song, which is entirely about heartbreak and revenge.

Creak onset

As in its sustained application mentioned in the chapter on voice qualities, this is another onset best understood through listening. Once you're specifically listening out for it, you'll be surprised by how often it is used and in how many different styles and genres. As mentioned earlier, the sensation of creating the creak onset is very like the feeling you have when you speak until you come to the end of your breath capacity and your tone breaks up into a kind of creaking sound. You can also try to imitate the sound of a creaking door on an 'ah'. When you use this onset, it feels as though you're dwelling in that low, throaty, creaking area of your voice very briefly just before you come into your tone. Some vocalists can extend this creak sound, and some seem to hit it only briefly on onset, but it is a very common sound that has the effect of softening the onset. It can have the emotional effect of suggesting great pain or vulnerability if coupled with low-effort-level voice qualities. Used with thick-fold qualities, creak can give a more spoken or conversational feel to a song. It always creates some intimacy between singer and listener.

Creak can give an almost unsung sound to a lyric if combined with little or brief sustain. It is also useful for singers who want a slightly grittier sound in their interpretation – it isn't a clean onset.

EXAMPLES

The Fray: *You Found Me* (2009). Isaac Slade is terrific at creating a kind of intimate sound that gives way to real power as he progresses, and the start of this track is typical. He creaks into the most intimate phrases and then floods the sound with air. His use of the creak is subtle, and you might want to listen to the opening verse a couple of times. The combination of creak and aspirate quality gives fragility and anger to the opening of this song about a difficult conversation with God.

Beyoncé: *If I Were a Boy* (2008). Beyoncé uses a lot of creak onset in the quiet verses, especially in the opening two phrases, which makes sense as creak is an intimate sound. She is singing with minimal accompaniment in some sections here, which gives her the freedom to use such a delicate onset. As the track progresses into the big sounds, you'll hear a lot of switch up in the onsets – glottal, rumble, flip and glottal flip, so it's a great track for hearing a lot of different onsets.

Des'ree: *You Gotta Be* (1994). This is a nice study in creak because she uses it as an onset and an offset. Listen closely and you'll hear that whenever the track gets intimate she uses the sound. The overall vulnerability of her style here, combined with lyrics about having to be tough, give you the sense that she's speaking from painful experience.

Rumble onset

This is the onset version of the 'dangerous' quality we described as sounding like Louis Armstrong, or feeling as if you're gargling and singing at the same time. It is a very old stylistic technique (in its sustained form it can be traced right back to the very earliest blues recordings of the twentieth century), probably because for singers working without microphones it was a way of driving up the power and volume as they came into a phrase. You can hear it in a slightly gentler form in the work of singers like Stevie Wonder and Whitney Houston, where I think it's used to great effect. Most singers can't (mercifully) hold onto this sound for very long – it feels hard on the throat and sometimes makes singers cough if they carry it on too long. It can have the same effect on the ear as it has on the throat: hard. It sounds very consciously unnatural and can be very effective in making the singers seem to be trying to convince themselves or their audience of something (listen to Stevie Wonder singing 'I'm a big boy now' in *Land of La La* or Whitney Houston singing 'Tonight is the night!' in *Saving All My Love*), but it can also sound very playful. Many blues and R&B singers have used this sound to heighten a sexually suggestive lyric. It appeals emotionally through humour and sensuality, and it convinces the listener of a singer's inner strength and resilience.

EXAMPLE

LaVern Baker: *Saved* (1961). One of my all-time favourite tracks, this is LaVern Baker letting rip on Leiber and Stoller's *faux*-gospel hit. She has energy and passion, and gives an earthy authenticity to a piece by a couple of Jewish writers from New York who knew how to write great songs for pop artists of all genres. The rumble onset throughout sets up every phrase with an attack that reads as 'found' religious ecstasy that's convincing enough to make you want to grab a tambourine.

Constricted onset

This is the riskiest onset, but it can be very effective in raising the perceived level of effort. It is produced by constricting the false folds quickly (think grunt) and then letting the pressure of air build up behind the closed folds. Sing through the grunt and then quickly release the folds and the air into the (unconstricted) sound. This takes a great deal of practice because, with the exceptions noted above, you might not want to carry the constriction into your sound. It's a very popular gospel, blues and rock onset as it creates the sense of power and extreme emotion, which conveys extreme conviction to the listener. The singer is leaving us in no doubt about how high are the emotional stakes and the level of commitment for them, and it suggests that the situation is almost too important/immediate/demanding to sing about.

EXAMPLE

Etta James: *I Just Wanna Make Love To You* (1961). Etta's performance here is the perfect illustration of how the constricted onset works. Her constricted sounds mirror the raunchy sound of the sax solo in the middle. You can hear that she doesn't carry the constriction into the verse, she just uses it to come into each phrase with passion and it brings a very sexy and powerful sound to a song that's all about desire. It's little wonder that this song is as popular today as it was 50 years ago when it was recorded. As you listen you're never in any doubt about what Etta wants, and this is a superb match of style/sound to lyric!

Offset or tone release

There are many kinds of release or offset, but all affect the way a singer finishes the sound.

Vibrato fade

This is a common offset used by a great majority of singers, regardless of style. As we discussed earlier, because vibrato speeds and width can vary enormously, the sounds of vibrato fade offsets can also vary. It's generally a sweet way to finish your sound; it has an artful, 'sung' quality about it, although combined with other kinds of release it can have more punch. On the whole, unless the final note is held for an unnaturally long time at a high effort level, this release usually has the same kind of neutral emotional impact as the simultaneous onset.

EXAMPLE

Rumer: *Aretha* (2010). This is a really catchy tune, with a beautiful, very straightforward approach from Rumer. There are a few compressions and some 'falling off' finishes, but the majority of her phrases finish with a subtle vibrato fade. Even though it's contemporary, the overall feel of the song is very 1970s, set off by a 'Bacharach-style' trumpet opening. Rumer's simple style is a critical part of the whole retro-feel of this blues song about teenage angst, which is simultaneously homage to the great Aretha Franklin.

Aspirate offset

Depending on the kind of effect the singer wants to produce in the offset, this may include a full stiffening of the vocal folds (which means there is no vibrato to it), or it may just be a very 'airy' sounding thin-fold tone, which can include vibrato. Most people can master this finish but it takes some practice to use it artfully. The emotional effect can be varied – aspirate can lend a kind of gentle or contemplative mood to a performance, and it often makes the singer sound as if he or she is turning the sound (and perhaps the thought) in on himself or herself.

EXAMPLE

Damien Rice: *Eskimo* (2003). This is quite an extreme version of the aspirate offset, and Rice uses breath to great effect in all of his work. This is an enigmatic song that responds well to his strange, whispered intensity. The uniquely quiet sound of this opening leads ultimately to the surprise of a huge operatic build-up at the end. As a recording, it's a real piece of modernist art – it defies your attempts to make sense of it on all fronts, but has an undeniably haunting power.

Falling off the note

This release works just as it sounds: the vocalist bends the note downwards, as if 'falling off' the phrase. There may or may not be vibrato. Some singers use this 'fall' with vibrato when gliding from note to note (think of Judy Garland), so that it has a very definite place to 'fall' to. When used as an offset, singers generally just bend a note downwards to nowhere in particular. There's almost always a fade to it, but sometimes subtle. In harder rock sounds the fall neither fades nor has vibrato. It is a deliberately artless sound in singing, and its effect is always strong. It might suggest that the singer's feeling is too strong to be 'sung' about, or that the singer is more concerned with the overall musical feel of the piece than with the lead vocal. Emotionally it appeals to our sense of defiance.

EXAMPLES

The Pretenders: *Don't Get Me Wrong* (1986). This is an example of a middling effort level use of the offset. Chrissie Hynde uses the 'fall' to give this song a kind of light rock sophistication. She doesn't labour the sustain, which would somehow have transformed this into a kind of 'jump' ballad. The fall offset gives Hynde some emotional distance from the song; it suggests a bit of irony and allows the track to breathe.

U2: *Pride (In the Name of Love)* (1984). This is an example of the high-effort-level use of the offset, and the big choruses really use the falling off finish to good effect. This is a classic rock anthem, which demands that the singer keep all 'sweetness' out of the sound. The lyric was inspired by the assassination of Martin Luther King Jr, and the emotional drive of the piece is evident. The massive belt that Bono uses in the choruses contrasts well with the sometimes aspirate/creaky sounds he uses in the verses. The whole effect is one of terrific heartfelt power.

Pushed or flip release

This is sort of the opposite of falling off the note. It's quite distinctive in sound, and has become rather fashionable in pop music. There are two kinds of pushed releases: the first is when the singer actually pushes the note upwards, just before releasing. The sound can sometimes have an almost flip quality to it. It's a high-effort-level release and takes real energy to produce. The second is related to the flip onset and has the same sound and effect. When used gently it can create a kind of wistful sound. When used with high effort it has real urgency. It's a release that has usually only been used by vocalists who are brave and secure in both their power and in the uniqueness of their style.

EXAMPLES

Kings of Leon: *Sex on Fire* (2008). This is a song of primal passion wed to a kind of paranoia, and Caleb Followill's masterful performance captures that strange combination magnificently. Everything here – creak and powerfully built-up glottal flip onsets, belt and constricted qualities but most especially the urgency of the releases – speaks of pure, naked desire. Listen closely to the way he uses his releases: it's a real signature of his style and he uses it to up the overall effort level and to convince you of his commitment to the lyric – a man with so much desire it can never be satisfied.

Avril Lavigne: *Smile* (2011). You can hear a quick flip finish to a lot of the phrases in this song, but they have most effect on the 'I, I, I' phrase in the chorus. The song is about losing control and the quick flip finishes give a kind of uncontrolled freedom to her vocal sound, which works perfectly with the bluntness of the lyrics.

Ruth Brown: *Mama He Treats Your Daughter Mean* (1953). The flip finish can have a very different sound with different artists. Here Ruth Brown uses this sound with such exuberance that it dominates the whole track. She sounds like a real survivor here – despite singing of her mean man – and it gives the performance strength and a super sassy sound.

Compressed release

In this release the singer simply stops the note, with no attempt to soften or ease the finish. This offset is also often combined with a fast improv fill, or a short, quickened vibrato, but it still finishes sharply; in other words, it doesn't fade, it doesn't fall, and it is always abrupt. Again, this offset seems to want to defy any sweetness or comfort in the sung sound. It can make a singer sound angry or defiant, or it can sound sophisticated and cool. Its emotional effect is varied but usually makes the singer sound strong and in control of their emotion and their sound.

EXAMPLES

Peggy Lee: *Fever* (1958). This is Peggy Lee's cover of Little Willie John's song, and it's said that she did this 'bare bones' arrangement herself and rewrote quite a few of the lyrics. It's really interesting to listen to the two versions – both of which are great – but Lee's just has such a fabulously timeless feel to it. She deliberately compresses all the phrases right the way through. Her 'cool' delivery of the hot lyrics creates a sexy irony that – more than 60 years later – still delivers the goods.

Suzanne Vega: *Luka* (1987). This is Vega's biggest hit and she wrote it after watching a young boy in a playground who seemed very different and somehow a bit damaged. She uses compressed finishes right the way through this track, which gives the whole thing a very conversational feel. The song is written from the abused young boy's point of view, and seems to suggest that he is wary and knows that he must keep his emotional distance. Compressed finishes always allow a singer some distance and here we just sense that if the song had been given a really 'sung' treatment we would not have been able to believe this unusual hit song about an abused child.

Gospel release

There are strong and mild forms of the gospel release. The strong form has a burst of air on the finish. The burst can be subtle (Michael Jackson, Sarah Vaughan) or quite strong (Jennifer Holliday, Stevie Wonder). In the case of singers with a very strong gospel influence, like Holliday, you may even hear an added syllable on an 'ah' or 'hey' sound. This is often the sound of extreme ecstasy or pain, as if the song is not enough fully to convey the singer's feeling, which must overflow into an extra syllable or sound. The milder form may have a much more subtle finish, but is definitely a singer punctuating the end of a phrase with air. Like the pushed release, gospel offset quickly raises both the true and the perceived-effort levels and it takes great energy to produce. Not surprisingly, its emotional effect is inspiring – we feel absolutely inspired, either by the singer's conviction or by their passion. It creates a sense of excitement and energy.

EXAMPLES

Jennifer Holliday: *His Eye is On the Sparrow* (2011). I'm including this as a nice example of gospel release but in truth this is a little master class in nearly everything we've run through so far – she's very brave in terms of the sounds she's willing to use. In the opening verses you'll hear nice examples of 'baby' twang, cry quality on the low notes, aspirate onsets and offsets, belt and the neutral qualities, and as the track goes on she kicks it all up a gear. She begins to use much greater effort, and that means more glottal and glottal flip onsets, a lot of glottal mid-phrase on an 'um' sound, and she combines all this with big energy expended in the gospel offsets. Holliday is passionate in her faith and you can hear that every step of the way in this committed performance.

(*Continued*)

Stevie Wonder: *Livin' for the City* (1973). Stevie uses audible breath throughout this track to give a very high perceived level of effort and no doubt about it, he's working this vocal hard. There's a liberal use of the gospel release throughout the second, third and fourth verses in the first part of the song, some of his releases literally just sound like hard breathing but many have an audible burst of air on the finish. The song includes a small dramatic section and when Wonder comes back into the verse (along around the 5:15 mark) you can hear an extended use of sustained rumble as the anger that has been building up through the whole tale of lost innocence and racist abuse. Wonder's performance here captures the weight of social injustice. It's hard, gritty, exasperated and brilliant.

Creak offset

This sounds exactly like the creak onset. Some people find it much harder to produce creak at the end of a phrase than they do in producing it at the beginning, and many have difficulty using it as a 'stand-alone' release of sound. More often it's used to fade the sustain of one note as the singer 'glides' into the next note. It is very effective because it can have a defiant, artless quality about it that suggests a kind of pain which can't be alleviated through singing – as if the sound must melt back into a kind of never-ending agony or deep thought. It's a highly vulnerable sound that creates immediate intimacy between singer and audience.

EXAMPLE

Kenny Rogers: *The Gambler* (1978). Rogers makes great use of the creak onset, sustained creak and offset throughout this almost cinematic classic track about two men on a 'train to nowhere'. The creak sound brings us right into the story of a lost and jaded man who trades the last of his whisky for advice from a dying gambler. Creak is never a power option and Rogers uses it here brilliantly to evoke the exhaustion felt by both men. Rogers's masterful use of the sound creates a wholly believable sense of an intimate moment with a stranger on a train and allows us to feel close to the action.

Sustain and vibrato

In popular music, the vocalist has many options when it comes to sustain, and this is especially true in R&B, rock and gospel styles. For many, sustain is where we (either as singers or as listeners) feel that the biggest expression of the emotion occurs, and this is why singers who use a minimum sustain time (Peggy Lee, later Dionne Warwick, for example) often strike the listener as having more emotional distance from their material than those who exploit sustain (Shirley Bassey or Liza Minnelli, perhaps). In classical music, the singer's sustain is by and large dictated by the composer; where there are long, held notes, there is little choice for the singer in how that is done. Classical style generally requires that the singer builds to the fullest, richest sound and then eases out of that sound with a vibrato fade, creating an arc within the line. Popular singers have much control over how long they hold a note and how they choose to do it. In highly improvised styles, the singer rarely builds sustain in an even manner, and may even do a 'multiple build' of sustain within a single phrase. Lengthy sustains using thick fold, belt or twang qualities or sung in a high part of the register will, of course, raise the perceived-effort level. Long sustains at low- to mid-range in less demanding voice qualities can strike the listener as relatively low effort. Because the slow-build-to-vibrato-offset is so common, having the courage to really play with sustain is a difficult thing for many singers. No one starts out sounding like Al Jarreau or Bobby McFerrin but with time, most people can add much more interest to their sound by simply experimenting with all the possibilities in their sustained notes.

The speed, width and use of vibrato can sometimes indicate style. For example, a very fast vibrato can be acceptable in many jazz and rock styles, whereas a very slow or wide vibrato is almost never heard in rock styles. The wide but evenly paced vibrato is usually most artfully employed by the big show-tune voices (Barbra Streisand). As discussed earlier, there are no quick fixes for singers who want to create vibrato if it isn't present in their voice, but it's important to remember that even singers who swear that they are unable to produce vibrato may discover some in time if they carry on singing and begin to relax and gain confidence. Suppressing or adding vibrato to the sound has a strong effect on the listener and learning this control can be helpful in creating the sound you want. It's hard muscle work to suppress vibrato, especially on high notes, but that suppression can bring a kind of purity of emotion to a sound and give a terrific 'relief' to the listener (and the singer!) once the vibrato is slowly added in for a fade.

Phrase weight and placement

For many artists these choices can change from song to song, or even within a song. Phrase 'weight' is basically where you hear most of the emphasis in a phrase – and here is where it really helps to think of the 'shape' of a phrase. A good example might be the first two lines of Aretha Franklin's *Respect*: '**What** you want / **baby** I got it'. Because she makes such a powerful sound, I think of the phrase as sort of pear-shaped, with the heavy end coming first. Think how differently you might hear the song if she'd shifted the weight of the phrase towards the back. Of course, highly skilled improvisational artists like Aretha, Christina Aguilera or Bobby McFerrin can sometimes throw the weight of a phrase all over the place – rising and falling in equal measure at times – this can give it a kind of 'baggy' shape. Some artists build a phrase towards the middle with very clean onsets and vibrato fades, and this can give a kind of oval shape to the phrase. Creak or aspirate onsets, or offset coupled with a build mid-way, never feel 'rounded' in the same way; both ends of the phrase feel too thin or wispy for that.

Phrase placement is about where the vocalist starts the phrase against the actual ground beat of the song. Some vocalists are very even about this and sing right on the beat most of the time. Others are 'back phrasers', letting the track go on a bit before coming in. This generally compresses a phrase, but can be very effective in shaping both phrase and performance. There are times at which a vocalist will push the phrase forwards, although this is not quite as common as back phrasing: Bette Midler does this with regularity and it gives a kind of breathless urgency to her performances. Many artists use a combination of forward/backward phrase placement to achieve a kind of ease or looseness about their interpretation.

Listen to **Example 6 on the website** and with this one, tap along with our beginning count 1 – 2 – 3 and note that the phrases are deliberately being started behind the beat:

I sing because I'm happy
I sing because I'm free
His eye is on the sparrow
And I know he watches me

Now listen to **Example 7 on the website** and again, tap along with our beginning count 1 – 2 – 3 and note that the phrases are deliberately being started ahead of the beat:

I sing because I'm happy
I sing because I'm free
His eye is on the sparrow
And I know he watches me

Now that you've heard the examples of back/forward phrase placement, play **Example 8 on the website**. This has the same accompaniment you heard on the examples above. Play it through once and practise back phrasing everywhere you can. It may feel like too much – never mind, this is just for practice! Now play it through again and push phrases forward wherever you can. You may get a little lost on this one but don't worry, just let the accompaniment hold it all together for you – you'll find your way if you go through this exercise a few times.

Note attack, breath and diction

Note attack is different from onset in that it is not about the way in which the singer comes into sound, but about the way in which the singer actually comes into the pitch. In other words, some singers come straight onto the pitch with no variation in attack. For most classical, choral and musical theatre styles, this accuracy of note attack is important: it's clean, and it sounds 'legit'. For most popular music, though, vocalists often employ a slight upward bend in the note, which, when combined with ease and substantial sustain, is often called 'crooning' or 'sliding' and was always ground for chastisement in my choir days.

The amount of bend used varies greatly from singer to singer.

Listen to **Example 9 on the website** and notice that the first line is sung with 'straight' note attack:
Why should I feel discouraged
The second line has subtle 'bends' in the note attack:
Why should the shadows come?
and the third line has very exaggerated 'bends' in the sound of the attack:
Why should my heart feel lonely and long for heaven and home.

Now play **Example 10 on the website** and just experiment with your note attack. Move between subtle/radical/no bends in the sound and just do it in a playful way. It will help you get a feel for how your voice sounds on various note attacks and help you have a sense of what your own natural note attack tends to be.

The sound of breath as an element of style is an area that doesn't come under much consideration in classical music styles, since for the most part, the singer is trying not to make the breath audible. In popular music, however, audible breathing can be an important and relatively easy way to raise the perceived-effort level without creating any vocal stress whatsoever. We've already explored the ways in which audible breath sounds in aspirate onsets/offsets or gospel releases can give a powerful shape to a phrase, but many singers are creative with the use of audible breath mid-phrase. Remember that audible breath can 'up' the perceived-effort level without putting any strain at all on your voice, so be bold about using this technique if you can!

EXAMPLES

Michael Jackson: *Bad* (1987). The use of percussive breath makes this whole track pop. If you listen just for the use of breath alone you'll be amazed at how much it occurs right the way through and really pushes up the effort level of a song that is for the most part delivered in aspirate and neutral thin- and thick-fold qualities. Jackson really knew how to work in between sung phrases to create an extraordinary excitement, yet most of the things he's doing here are easy on the voice.

Bobby McFerrin: *Thinkin' About Your Body* (1986). McFerrin is a genuine one-of-a-kind artist. Here he uses his whole body and the range of his voice to make a sort of one-man band out of himself. His accuracy in some massive jumps is just so impressive, but he also uses the audible breath sound as part of the aural landscape that he's creating here. You'll have a master class in breath and improv if you listen to Bobby McFerrin doing almost anything, but this performance really demonstrates his bravery about making noise.

Diction can tell you a lot about the way in which an artist sees his or her material, and what he or she's trying to achieve with it. 'Storytellers' (musical theatre, country and folk singers) always value the lyric and work hard to make the listener understand it all. Some people's accurate diction can still operate within a relatively relaxed, low perceived-effort level – Sinatra is a case in point. Others, however, can so hammer a consonant that you are deeply aware of the energy it takes to get it out, or else hang on to the consonant in what can almost feel like Herculean effort.

EXAMPLES

Carrie Underwood: *Jesus Take the Wheel* (2005). Underwood has quite a tale to tell here, and although she doesn't really hammer the diction you get every word with just one listen – she makes sure that she doesn't sacrifice the lyric to her style choices. There are just enough interesting choices to keep us engaged, but you can just sense how much the overall story is the dominant factor in this recording.

Nancy LaMott: *Skylark* (1995). LaMott's beautiful reading of the Hoagy Carmichael/Johnny Mercer delicate jazz standard is a great example of clean diction. LaMott was a celebrated cabaret singer and she relished every word of this lyric and clearly wanted her audience to do so as well. Crisp, careful consonants along with a fluid, sophisticated delivery adds up to a quietly stunning recording.

'Atmosphere' vocalists go for an overall sonic ambience and don't worry too much about how many times you have to listen to get the lyric. They generally aim to paint a mood or picture with their songs and the mood can be enhanced by a kind of mumbling delivery. With these singers the perceived-effort level can sometimes seem low because of their soft consonants and rather 'blurry' sound, but with a singer like Tom Waits who has such a constricted vocal quality, the perceived-effort level seems high whatever he does with his diction.

EXAMPLES

Amy Winehouse: *Me and Mr Jones* (2006). The loose diction here really adds to the overall retro sound of this track – you can hear that Winehouse loves to play with the vowel sounds within a phrase, and she enjoys pulling a phrase around with some really interesting, twangy and edgy sounds, sometimes she doesn't even bother to finish a word. The whole thing adds up to really louche, sexy sound.

Rickie Lee Jones: *Weasel and the White Boys Cool* (1984). Like Winehouse, Jones sort of immerses herself in the dream of some kind of retro-world that relies heavily on the overall sonic ambience that they can create in a track. It isn't that the song doesn't have a story, and it isn't that you don't catch some of it; it's simply that the story isn't quite as important as the sound of the cool and driving acoustic guitar and the way it counterpoints against Jones's loose and sometimes rather wispy, 'little girl' vocal sound.

Improvisation

This can be one of the most intimidating areas for a singer, particularly those who are used to reading music as it is written. Improvisation applies not just to patterns of notes or alternative melody lines, but also to some of the other elements we're exploring – sustain, phrase weight and placement, and note attack.

I've often thought that my own tendency to improvise was born out of the sheer boredom of singing the same songs in clubs six nights a week when I was younger. To improvise well, a singer must be very comfortable with the harmonic structure of the song and feel as if they know it inside out – and singing the same songs six nights a week will certainly do that for you! It's possible, of course, to improvise over any structure, but more complex chord patterns require a terrific ability to anticipate the sound of the change before it comes. I think this only happens when you've heard a song enough (i.e., many, many) times. Most vocalists have some 'natural' improvisational tendencies and for the most part these tendencies include a descending melodic pattern. Improvising with an ascending melodic pattern is far less common and is a lot trickier.

Minimal, easy or very logical sequences that are evenly weighted are often associated with the old big band/jazz singers (Rosemary Clooney, June Christy) or a lighter R&B sound (Peabo Bryson, Denise Williams). Big octave swoops and glides, massively weighted or extended fills tend to belong to the R&B/pop or gospel singers (Aretha Franklin, Smokie Norful, Christina Aguilera). Highly complex intervals and detailed or complex percussive fills remain mostly in the R&B or jazz areas (Rachelle Ferrell, Ella Fitzgerald, etc.). Trademark riffs or repeated vocal improvisation patterns can often help you identify the singer (Mariah Carey, Sam Cooke).

To begin with, it's good to understand what your own natural patterns are. Feeling comfortable in what you're doing is always a good place to start, but you won't want to stay in that comfort zone for long if you really want to create some excitement in your sound. Many of the older jazz vocalists (Frank Sinatra, Billie Holiday) have said that listening to instruments, rather than voices, taught them much about how to improvise freely. That's a good place to begin, especially since instrumental improv is almost always more daring in terms of rhythm and far more 'percussive' in that sense.

Spend some time listening to instrumental improvisation. To begin with, most singers find it easier to think of improvising like an instrument, possibly because it allows them to forget about lyrics and melody while they experiment. Most also tend to feel more comfortable if they are specific about what instrument they want to imitate – trumpet, guitar, sax, etc. It's especially good to imagine your voice improvising as different instruments: the kind of notes and rhythms you'll find for improvising like a trumpet are very different from what you'll find if you're improvising like a guitar. Find a backing track (the rise of karaoke has made this easy) to a couple of songs you know well and improvise. Be patient – you'll make a lot of mistakes. Be prepared to make some strange sounds and try to make sure you're not overheard, you'll only feel free to experiment if you know that no one is listening. You'll only learn by trying (and laughing!) and trying again.

The most important thing to remember is to work through your boredom threshold. It is probably the hardest thing of all to do, but unless you keep at it – well beyond the usual practice time you might spend with a song – you simply won't identify all the possibilities in the song. Also bear in mind that becoming bored with a song is the starting place of a lot of good improv! Remember that you have a number of elements to explore in improvisation. I'm very reluctant to advise people to imitate another singer's improvisation – it almost never works. You'll notice that I've not included examples for improv; this is because the joy of improv lies in its spontaneous nature. As a listener, I am always uncomfortable hearing a singer try to do another singer's improv – the sound of imitation takes all the spontaneity out of the performance. I do, however, think it's a perfectly good idea to imitate an instrumentalist's improv – in fact I think you should feel free to try Miles Davis anytime!

Practice

To explore melodic improvisation for a specific song, I usually ask singers to do an entire song without ever singing the melody. They invariably find this a difficult exercise and the first few times through they usually find a few 'home' notes that seem to work for long stretches of time. It takes time and courage to move away from these 'home' notes and really explore what else is possible. You can try this either with karaoke backing tracks (as long as you've chosen a song you know really well and have a passion for singing), or you can simply sing along with a recorded piece but never land on the same note as the singer. In other words, sing all around the recorded artist but find different notes and seek out the gaps in the singing that you can fill yourself.

You must always remember that improvisation, either with or without lyric, is about communicating and the purpose of this exercise is to make sure you have a reason for doing it. Sing the song a few times just as you know it, and then sing it through without using the actual melody. Be patient and do this until you've done it so many times that it seems simple. Once it feels (relatively!) easy to do, that's the point at which you'll find going back to melody is really interesting. You should find both relief and liberation in your performance because you'll feel much more confident about where you can go both within and without the melody. And that's when you'll really find out where – or if – improvisation can help you to communicate more effectively than you could by singing the melody line as written. Remember that improv for the sake of improv has limited communicative use.

However, not all improv is about changing or 'decorating' a melody – there are other things to consider in making a song your own:

Phrase Weight. See what happens when you change or add a weighting in your usual phrasing of a song. Try breaking up even passages of phrasing in this way and find out what it does to the sound and how it affects your breathing.

Breath. Use the breath in improv and not only in percussive sounds or onsets/offsets. Find out what happens when you force the sound through more than one phrase, right to the end of your capacity. You'll not only get some interesting tones, you'll almost certainly create an audible intake. Try this a couple of times until you find a comfortable way to use it in a song – it's a good way to raise the effort level without stress.

Phrase placement. Be bold about where you come into the song, let the music carry you for a bit before you enter. Don't sustain so much, it will give you time to think of more interesting places to start in again. See what happens if you come in before the count of one. You'll get lost sometimes as you're starting, but learning how to phrase in less even ways can make your delivery much more interesting.

Sustain. See what happens when you consciously try to change your sustain pattern. If you tend towards the 'classical' slow-build-to-vibrato fade, find out what happens when you mix those elements up. Try building and then releasing with a compressed offset. Try multiple builds in the sound. See what happens when you start the vibrato fade and then suppress the vibrato into a falling offset. There are many combinations you can try and no doubt some of them will sound strange to you at first, but stay with it. Interesting singers rarely do things the obvious or 'even' way.

Diction. If you're used to singing with very clean diction, see how the song sounds if you relax that as far as you're able to and concentrate much more on varied and interesting onsets and offsets/releases.

The amount of work you can do in this way is unlimited – all of it will pay off. Any singer with a relatively good ear will progress quickly with some dedicated practice. But be warned: it's not a linear process. In other words, you don't begin and end it like a lesson; it's something that you need to keep going back to in order to keep increasing your confidence. Good, imaginative improvisation is a key to many popular styles and it can make the difference between a good singer and an exciting one. This process is also a good one to go through in a student/teacher context – it allows for much more play and feedback, and will give both of you a starting point when trying out things like a pop or jazz piece.

A Summary Practice

Our final practice will involve trying out as many of the various vocal qualities and complementary elements as we can. You can use this part of the book as a 'workbook', as we review all the materials from Chapters 2 and 3.

Begin by putting a tick next to every voice quality you were able to do (go back and review if you've forgotten any of the 'access keys'!):

Neutral thin fold

Neutral thick fold

Aspirate

Sob/cry

Twang

Belt

Creak

(*Continued*)

A Summary Practice (Continued)

Rumble

Constricted (watch this one carefully and don't do much, even if you're relatively comfortable with it)

Now put a tick next to every onset you were able to imitate successfully:

Glottal

Aspirate

Flip

Glottal flip

Creak

Rumble

Constricted (again, careful with this – even if you have it comfortably, you may not have had enough practice to do it safely for long)

Tick every offset or tone release you were able to do with relative ease:

Aspirate

Falling off the note

Pushed/flip

Compressed

Gospel

Creak

You will notice that I didn't include some of the easier elements. This exercise is about really experimenting with sound, not about playing safe.

A Summary Practice (Continued)

On the blank lyric sheet below, do the following:

1 At the beginning of the phrases, mark in as many onsets as you can (at least 3)

2 At the end of the phrases, mark in as many tone releases or offsets as you can (at least 3)

3 Choose four phrases and underline them. Now mark in at least four voice qualities over the underlined phrases

4 Write BP (back phrase) or FP (forward phrase) at the beginning of at least two phrases.

Your marked-up lyric sheet should look something like this:

creak cry
Swing low, sweet chariot

BP **Comin' for to carry me home**

cry compressed release
Swing low, sweet chariot

flip
Comin' for to carry me home

FP **I looked over Jordan and what did I see?**

Belt gospel release
Comin' for to carry me home

Twang vibrato fade
A band of angels comin' after me

aspirate flip aspirate
Comin' for to carry me home.

Swing low, sweet chariot

Comin' for to carry me home

Swing low, sweet chariot

(Continued)

A Summary Practice (Continued)

Comin' for to carry me home

I looked over Jordan and what did I see?

Comin' for to carry me home

A band of angels comin' after me

Comin' for to carry me home.

Now, using **Example 11 on the website**, go through the verse and try to do every marked quality and element on the page. This is a purely random exercise and it's going to sound random. That's okay. We need to get used to making the noises before we can do anything else with them. There is only one rule here: make your voice quality changes abrupt – don't try to smooth them out or go into them elegantly. Let them be as quick and artless as you can. Go through this at least three times. Enjoy the sounds you're making – they will probably be a bit strange to you at the moment.

Once you're feeling more secure at just making the sounds in the right places, go back and look closely at the lyrics. The song is about things that all of us can relate strongly too – about freedom and redemption; about going home to some place safe and secure; being with people we love. Think about what you really want to communicate when you sing the song. Do you want us to feel comforted or inspired? Should we feel confident that you'll survive? Should we help you survive? Try to connect the meaning of these words to your heart and your head. Speak the lyrics through once and see if you can make your meaning clear. Now play the website accompaniment and go through the song one more time with all your voice qualities and elements intact. Keep all your voice quality switches abrupt.

A Summary Practice (Continued)

This time, after you've gone through, you may feel that you want to change where you've put some of the elements or qualities marked up on your lyric sheet. Take a bit of time and switch things around if you want, but don't lose the number of qualities or elements you're doing. Sing through again, really holding onto the things that give the song meaning for you. If you're feeling happy with what you've tried, go on to **Example 12 on the website** which is the same accompaniment but has a looser, slightly jazzier sound. That may inspire you to connect even more closely with both what's in your head/heart and with the kinds of sounds you're making.

I do this exercise in workshops and I'm almost always amazed at the results. While we rarely ever achieve great artistry, there is almost always something extraordinary in what we hear. That is partly because it takes real bravery to sing like this, and also because the singers in the workshop are not concerned with pleasing anyone or sounding beautiful. That means that whatever we think of their final performance, we usually find it moving and engaging. Even though the exercise begins in a completely random way, if the singer keeps holding on to what they feel in their own hearts about the song, they usually manage to get that across to us in a variety of ways, which does much to remove the randomness of the exercise. Wherever you land with this exercise, you're bound to have made some singing choices you wouldn't ordinarily have made, and you're bound to have explored outside your usual ideas of 'good' singing. That is a good beginning for exploring who and what you can be when you sing!

CHAPTER FOUR

Blues, gospel, jazz and what came after

Communication is the heart of style

While learning to practise and perform the elements of style is a great way to expand your expressive ability as a vocalist, listening to the ways in which other artists put these elements together is just as important. In this section I want to lead you through the works of a number of artists in different genres, which I hope will help to make the relationship between the elements of style and the art of combining and employing them artfully a little clearer. In the interests of brevity, most of the analyses of the songs covered in this section below are quick, they're meant to increase and deepen your knowledge of how singers have worked in various genres. Singers grow their own style best when remaining open to the widest possible range of influences, so try to keep an open mind as we go through even the kinds of music you think you don't like.

In reading these last two sections you've probably discovered that I have been suggesting two things all the way through. The first is that you have to know what you want to communicate with a song before you can think about style. The second is that although there are a great number of elements to learn and to enjoy experimenting with, perhaps what is of greatest importance to the listener lies in knowing that the singer has something to communicate.

As listeners we can sometimes be put off by singers who simply sound beautiful, or singers who are singing artfully but not (as we may perceive it) soulfully or truthfully from their hearts. For me, what makes a great performance is the sense that I am being let into the singer's personal realm. We may find it in a tearful delivery, or we may find it in great soaring notes; we may find it in sheer energy and bravado, or we may find it in quieter, 'creakier' sounds. But wherever we find it, we will probably also find a singer who is not as concerned with 'singing' as they are with communicating.

I recently watched an episode of 'The Voice', in which Jessie J was trying to make a decision between two singers. Her difficulty, she said, was that one singer had a beautiful voice, but that the other was an artist. The 'artist' won out – and in watching the performance it was very clear that he had something deeply personal to communicate in his performance. It was a nice reminder of the fact that a beautiful voice and a great performance can sometimes be two very different things.

The early style artists

It's difficult to talk about good or bad voices when listening to early recording singers like Ma Rainey, Woody Guthrie or Jimmie Rodgers, because in a sense, these artists worked against such notions in the attempt to strip away the 'art' or artifice in their singing, and to convince the listener that their work was neither contrived nor beautified, but simply honest. One may still argue, perhaps, that these artists were still deeply concerned with the 'art' of creating a soulfully convincing sound, but they nevertheless did so with absolutely no recourse whatever to classical or traditional ideas of good vocal production.

Vocal style since the early twentieth century (like other arts since the first stirrings of modernism) has been marked heavily by the attempt to bypass accepted ideas of 'good' or 'bad' and, in some cases, by completely subverting the listener's expectations. This subversion was done against extraordinary and specific social conditions and if anyone has doubts about the political importance and dimension of style, a quick look through the history of ragtime, blues and jazz in turn-of-the-century America will convince even the most sceptical.

This section looks at the various ways in which popular singers use the elements and qualities described in the last section to create an overall impression on the listener. That impression may be one that the listener 'categorises'; in other words, choices that the singer makes may relate to particular elements or qualities that are often associated by us historically with certain genres of music. For example, a strong nasal twang, coupled with a high frequency of flip onsets and slow bends in the note attack are vocal qualities and elements of style that are often associated with country music. These qualities are, of course, common to nearly every style of popular singing, but put together in this way they usually remind the listener of an identifiable country sound.

Although such crossover and hybrid approaches in contemporary recorded music of the last 50 or 60 years has made classification in this sense more and more difficult to maintain, I believe there are still some pretty fundamental popular genres; among these I would count blues, gospel, jazz, country, rock and vaudeville/music hall or Broadway styles. These all, of course, crossover themselves, and trying to follow the threads of each style back to where one might locate a 'pure' strain of style is a particularly difficult task.

Perhaps of all these styles early American blues, jazz and gospel would be the most likely forms to sustain and reward such a search. In a sense, too, perhaps the very early years of Broadway and music-hall styles (which were in essence a popularization of opera and light opera) could be said to form a fairly distinct if derivative style at some point. But while one might argue, for example, that there is a popular strain of 'legitimate' singing style that could be traced from Jeanette MacDonald or Deanna Durbin through to Julie Andrews, which remained for some time relatively untouched by the great jazz and blues influences of American popular music, it would still have to be acknowledged that now musical theatre styles are thoroughly immersed in pop techniques. There could also be said to be strong distinctions in the early years of this century between jazz and blues, but such distinctions do not hold for long.

In the following sections I'll be looking closely at a few specific artists and recordings. In the attempt to look at some descriptive qualities in these areas, I've largely had to avoid anything too current. In the contemporary world of fusion and crossover it can be difficult to separate the country world of Carrie Underwood from the pop world of Avril Lavigne. This means that any effort to take an overview of such categories is bound to be a fairly historical one, and my analyses below will in most instances be of older recordings, but I believe these early works established much about the styles under consideration and remain part of a common working vocabulary in popular music today.

You will also note that I am only providing detailed practice notes for the early genres: blues, jazz and gospel. This is because in their early forms, they are not so 'fused' with other sounds and you can reasonably talk about and practise the things that constitute the style. For country (which is a genre that mixed European and early American folk, blues, swing and jump) and rock (which similarly fused hillbilly, jump blues, jazz, western swing, etc.) and pop (which is a fusion of all these early styles), the sections are geared towards helping you to think about the most common things a singer might want to listen for and apply when exploring these areas.

I've come to believe that listening and imitating are still the greatest ways to expand your repertoire of the elements of style, so I hope you'll combine your reading in this section with close listening and practice. I'm often surprised when an artist mentions who they're listening to at a given time – I'm sure I wasn't the only one who found it curious to read in an interview that Randy Blythe (the gloriously unique lead singer of thrash metal band Lamb of God) cited Barry White and the Pet Shop Boys as influences. I was equally fascinated when interviewing Paul McCartney to hear of his passion for Nat King Cole. It shouldn't be surprising though – any artist who really wants to extend their stylistic ability should have eclectic tastes.

In compiling the examples in this section, my concentration remains on what the style and the artist are communicating and what elements the artists are employing in that communication. I also hope that in providing a relatively brief introduction to key artists in each style, those wanting both to teach and to learn will be inspired by listening to those who were indeed charting new territory and (in some cases) struggling to find their own distinctive voice and style. Great artists have always studied those who have come before them and I hope that in discovering (or rediscovering) some of these songs you'll find the courage to push yourself in new directions and to be brave enough to abandon whatever 'safe' vocal places you might customarily inhabit.

Blues

I didn't hate [Ma Rainey], she was all right, but I never cared too much for her. I seen her a lot, you know, she always sounded flat to me. When she sings, she sang flat. . . . I never did like that kind of singing.

LITTLE BROTHER MONTGOMERY[1]

---

[1]Giles Oakley, *The Devil's Music*, second edition (New York: Da Capo Press, 1997), p. 94.

Oh Lord, don't say anything about Ma. . . . Ain't nobody in the world ever yet been able to holler 'Hey Bo Weevil' like her. Not like Ma. Nobody. I've heard them try to, but they can't do it.

VICTORIA SPIVEY[2]

In a sense, considering vocal style almost always means considering what the word 'art' means, and not only in its aesthetic sense. Art is an interesting word, which grows more interesting still when you consider some of its cousins: arty, artful, artificial. In itself, the word simply means practical skill or the application of practical skill, and we both admire and distrust it as a description. If we were to consider the idea of 'singing as art' we would probably think of the principles of classical singing. We would probably also expect that 'art' means something mediated – something taught, learnt, considered and then applied. The blues is an 'artless' style – it is a kind of musical 'defiance'.

Blues singing is the result of a kind of historical melting pot – many influences can be traced. The first blues singers were male, members of black minstrel shows who worked itinerantly throughout the American south, in large tent shows, church halls, etc., always without a microphone. This last point is significant because the history of vocal style is, in many ways, the history of the microphone and of sound technology in general. When we listen to contemporary vocal recording, every tiny shade of sound is available to our ears because recording technology is now so sophisticated (and many would say too sophisticated) that singers can move from a whisper to a roar and a good engineer can balance it all out for us so that we don't miss anything, but at the beginning, microphones were either non-existent or very rough instruments and singers had much to do to compensate for this.

---

[2]Oakley, p. 94.

The idea of the 'blues singer' may have been a relatively new one in the early part of the twentieth century, but as the quotations at the beginning of this section show, that didn't mean early listeners weren't applying their own aesthetic judgements to the songs. Little Brother Montgomery's assessment of Ma Rainey may have been fair (although in her recordings there are no discernible pitch problems), or it may simply have been a response to the downward inflection and general lack of sustain in her delivery that gives it a 'flat' and somewhat 'artless' style.

In its 'purer' forms, blues singing has an extraordinarily consistent vocal heritage that can be traced with ease from, say, the earliest recordings in the 1920s of Bessie Smith right up to Keb' Mo's 2005 collection, *Suitcase*. Blues include a number of distinct shadings and styles (rural, Mississippi Delta, Chicago, etc.) which, while often influencing each other, have their own identifiable kinds of vocal sounds. But perhaps what unites the form is that for the most part, traditional ideals of musicality or beauty or tunefulness are not prioritized in this work; instead, blues singers have from the very first employed a wide variety of all the kinds of sounds that human voices make, from the piercing, to the raspy, to the raw in order to take their listeners on a highly personal journey of the heights and depths of the human soul. It's a form that actively embraces and rewards an enormous range of vocal sound.

Many early blues songs were accompanied by guitar and banjo, and this perhaps accounts for the musically less adventurous sounds of some of the singers as opposed to those of later blues artists who were singing with piano, bass, drums and horns. The variety and complexity of these added instruments no doubt inspired these later singers to experiment both tonally and improvisationally. Nevertheless, the overall emotional impression of these early recordings is strong. Although the lyrical content of the songs could vary greatly – some narrating stories of love or tragedy; some dealing with everyday problems of cleaning, cooking and washing, and some very obviously sexually suggestive – the sense one has when listening is that of hearing the sound of a survivor. Despite being called the blues, these songs use humour and innuendo to suggest a world conquered by those who can best appreciate the simple things in life. The 'unsung' quality described above creates a sometimes conversational, sometimes passionate, and sometimes intimate style that reflects this fundamental theme.

The fundamental 'authenticity' of adverse experience that marks the blues as a genre is an effect many singers employ to create a sense of intimacy with the listener and to imply a life experience that has been at once rich, painful and endured with great spirit. The voices may not be beautiful, instead they seem to carry the scars of old battles and the weariness of unrelenting toil, but the very fact that they still 'sing' out to us is what gives blues music such a life-affirming quality. Vocal 'flaws' in this context have meaning and power – it makes little sense to talk about improving or fixing the vocal sounds of Big Mama Thornton or Sonny Boy Williamson, since such unique voices convince us of their honesty.

Bessie smith: *Gimme a Pigfoot and a Bottle of Beer*, (1933)

Perhaps the best known of the early blues singers, Bessie Smith's style was no doubt influenced by the need to sing without amplification in large tent shows throughout her early years. In a song like *Gimme a Pigfoot and a Bottle of Beer*, her sound can probably best be described as a 'wailed shout'. This is one of Bessie's last recordings and she's a decade into her recording career. At this point she's working with some legendary musicians – Benny Goodman and Jack Teagarden played at these sessions – and she's come a long way from her first recorded hit, *Down Hearted Blues* (1923).

If you listen to the two recordings together the first thing you notice is how much sweeter and more lyrical the early song sounds, even though in many ways she's working with some very similar stylistic choices. *Gimme a Pigfoot and a Bottle of*

Beer seems like a vocal illustration of the hard-drinking life Bessie had been leading up to this point. Her predominant vocal qualities are always neutral thick fold and belt with a large share of rumble sounds thrown in to increase the overall effort level at the moments she wanted most to emphasize. Her onsets are hard, with an impressive number of rumble onsets (many voices simply couldn't cope with employing this high-effort effect so often), her diction in the onset is always clean and never 'eased' into. She doesn't improvise much, although she adds a 'Yeah!' on the piano player verse, which sounds like something beyond her usual rumble. When you hear her quality on this, you can understand why so many people have described her higher-effort-level sounds as a 'growl' – this is definitely growled, and combined with the fall off the note finish, she sounds both dangerous and sexy here. Melodically, this is a very simple tune. Structurally it is just a series of repeated verses, with only one variation, for which Bessie adjusts very quickly up into a thin-fold sound (just slightly flat at one point) and comes right back down onto her comfortable thick-fold/belt sound. The overall effect of these things is to keep the perceived-effort level of the song consistently very high.

Her note attack here is often a light upward bend, and sustains are mostly brief; indeed, this is one of the things that really distinguishes this track from the earlier *Down Hearted Blues*, where she used much more sustain and vibrato, and also linked her phrases together a bit more elegantly. *Gimme a Pigfoot and a Bottle of Beer* features very little sustain, which means that phrases are often broken at the midway point. Where she sustains she never fades – she either compresses her finish quickly without vibrato or employs a fairly brief vibrato that finishes with a compressed release or the occasional fall off the note. Phrase placement is very even and apart from a little spoken intro, her improvisation is generally confined to her growls. The spoken intro is interesting to listen to since you can hear how closely her singing voice matches her speaking voice.

Overall, the song adds up to much more than the sum of its relatively simple parts. You can sense that Bessie would have been a great singer to see live. This track doesn't feel like a 'sung' track, she is shouting at you to come and join her. Recording feels a kind of 'cold' medium for her since there's an immediate energy and raunchiness that you feel can't be entirely captured in the studio. In listening, though, you feel in no doubt that she knows what she wants to communicate – she wants to get this party started. She uses her growls and shouts to suggest that she's ready to have a good time and wants you to come along. She isn't drinking champagne and it's not a 'champagne' delivery – she's singing about beer, gin and reefers. The rough-and-ready sound of her voice is at once incredibly physical and perhaps this is the greatest impression you get upon hearing her – her voice never comes from her head, it comes from her whole body, once described as 'just this side of voluptuous, buxom and massive, but stately too, shapely as an hour-glass. . .'.[3] To modern ears, perhaps, this recording now sounds dated and maybe even a bit repetitive, but you can imagine that to a public only just discovering recorded music, this was probably a pleasurably scandalous work.

It was perhaps the overall emotional effect created by her stylistic choices that led to an extraordinary advertisement for one of Bessie's recordings in the 1924 *Chicago Defender*: 'Wow – but Bessie Smith spills fire and fury. . . . You can almost see hate drip from the piano keys. Fury flies off the violin strings. Every note is a half-note. No quarter for anyone.'[4] Witty as it is, it's unfair – I don't think I hear anything in her recordings that I would associate with 'hate'. But she makes strong choices when she's singing and it leaves you convinced of her own personal strength, and the overall rough-and-ready quality to her singing still nearly defines what it is in blues singing that appeals to so many.

---

[3]Ibid., p. 99.
[4]Ibid., p. 101.

Robert Johnson: *Terraplane Blues* (1936)

Perhaps the most influential blues artist of all time, Robert Johnson's singing is distinctly different from other blues singers of the time. Many people see Johnson as the link between early country blues and the more urbanized Chicago blues form. Descriptions like restless, haunting, anxious are commonly applied to his vocal sound and in this track I think you hear all that, but with a powerful measure of joyful defiance thrown in. Johnson was a guitarist of skill and this song works particularly well in the interchange between his singing and playing. In this track you can really hear him attempting to make his voice sound like his guitar playing, especially in his upper register. He was deeply influenced vocally by the way in which he played guitar. He was exceptional in his instrumental exploration and his playing was never heavy-handed or droning, as so many of the country blues guitarists were. You almost get the sense that he was impatient with his playing, constantly adding small improvisational pickings where others players would ordinarily just keep a rhythm line steady. He also had a love of the upper range of the instrument and you hear that clearly on this track, where he explores that range continually through quick, high riffs.

Unlike many sung blues recordings, this song isn't dominated by a single vocal quality; in fact the most arresting thing about it is the quick and interesting changes of vocal qualities. From the high neutral thin-fold sounds of the 'oohs', which flip mid-phrase into twang sound, to the low-effort neutral thick-fold quality that gives way to the song's only spoken line. He is running through quite a range both in terms of pitch and approach. There is little attempt to shape a phrase, apart from using the melodic arc to create a sense of a rising weight mid-phrase. He uses much note bend throughout.

Because of this variety, as well as a wide mix of compressed/falling releases and sustain vibrato fades in neutral thick fold, the song does very definitely have a 'sung' feel to it, even if that sung feel is rather thin and pinched at times. But it never sounds schooled, and he never sounds as if he comes fully onto the voice. Perhaps that's what gives his recordings such a jumpy, restless quality. He is bold with his quality changes, which are quick and have an unsophisticated feel to them. He doesn't exploit sustain at all – he uses it when it seems to lead naturally into the guitar break he's planned, and that seems to keep the emotional weight we often associate with sustain at bay.

His lyrics are sexy, couched in an extended metaphor about his 'terraplane', and he sings of raising his woman's 'hood' and tangling with her wires to get to her spark plug. Not great literature, but self-consciously not so. As he runs through his metaphor the range of vocal colour and boldness allows you to feel his joy at the exploration of both his music and his machine.

Sonny Boy Williamson: *Dealing with the Devil* (1940)

Before listening to this track I wouldn't have thought it possible that one recording could put me in mind so strongly of both Bob Dylan and Mick Jagger at the same time, as these artists' styles differ widely, but this piece by Sonny Boy Williamson does just that. A blues legend whose career spanned many years, Williamson displays what might be described as a classic male blues sound here. The diction is very loose but it isn't really hard to pick up the lyric. Williamson was known to have had a speech impediment, which perhaps influenced the loose diction. As with nearly all blues, his performance evokes a very 'spoken' sound and in the middle section of the song he abandons any pretence at singing and just speaks in time – you can hear how closely alike his spoken and sung sounds are. There is really only one vocal quality throughout the song (a neutral thick-fold sound) although you can hear a bit of creak or scratch overlaid onto that at times.

Williamson was considered one of the early virtuoso blues harmonica players and his real melodic flights take place in those instrumental solos. The singing has a 'straight' feel to it, as does the whole track, and he weights his phrases quite evenly. He pushes the placement just forwards of the beat in most places, which gives a little sense of forward weighting, but for the most part, the overall effect of evenness adds to the conversational quality of his performance.

His note attack is heavily bent in the 'devil' choruses, and instead of the compressed or quick falls off the note that he uses in the verse, he holds onto the end of 'devil' (which he almost pronounces as 'devim') and allows a little fluttery vibrato into a notable bend downwards as the pitch falls off. This particular release reminds you a bit of the sounds he makes later in his harmonica solo. And although the word 'devil' remains heavily weighted throughout the song, that little vibrato and backing off the full consonant in the end foreshadows his ambivalence about 'dealing' with the devil as the song goes on. In his spoken break he assures us that he's only been a little 'friendly, just friendly' with the devil, and goes on to admit that he 'got in trouble', and that he 'don't do that no more'.

It's a thoroughly playful song, which emphasizes joy in survival – the lyrics are a kind of mishmash of the usual blues preoccupations: mean, perfidious women, and the hapless men who are taken in by them. But he's not defeated at all – he's ready to find another woman because he refuses to travel this 'big road' by himself – and you know that he finds something life-affirming in the ongoing wars between men and women.

Big Mama Thornton: *Little Red Rooster* (1968)

An extraordinary song that has been recorded by artists like Sam Cooke, the Rolling Stones, Junior Wells and Howlin' Wolf; this is a truly unique effort, filled with an entire barnyard full of sounds. Big Mama Thornton doesn't so much sing as wail her way through this atmospheric performance. She relies almost entirely on neutral thick-fold and belt qualities and you can sense the size of her instrument – particularly in the final verse. I wouldn't want to guess exactly what voice qualities she's using for the animal effects! Rather than rumble, she uses glottal and (both mildly and heavily) constricted onsets most frequently, which really ups the perceived-effort level.

She does nothing to 'beautify' the sounds she makes – there is relatively little sense of the song being 'sung' – it's filled with the classic kind of defiance that Ma Rainey and Bessie Smith were exhibiting decades earlier. This was recorded in the 1960s and sound technology had moved on quite a bit. Where Bessie Smith's recording feels almost distant in the hearing, this track has a great sense of immediacy to it.

She doesn't build to her final verse, she comes straight in with a powerful constriction and maintains high-effort voice qualities throughout. She is completely in control of where she employs the constricted sound and also knows how satisfying it is to the listener to hear that constriction ease into a full and saturated neutral thick-fold or belt tone. Her note attack is consistently playful; she bends the sound both up and down. She uses little sustain and the quick compressed finishes keep a spoken quality throughout most of the song. Although in this track she includes improvisation, she saves most of her improv efforts for the animals and the occasional, more heavily constricted 'Whoa!'-type sounds. But you feel her strong gospel roots in the last short improv; strong, and with a downward inflection. She keeps the phrase placement even but always slightly behind the beat. That evenness can sometimes feel a bit imposed on blues songs since they are so often structured like 'call-and-response'. Here she exploits that form playfully with the lead guitarist. She heavily weights the first part of her phrases and although there is great energy to the animal sounds at the ends of phrases, the finish of the 'sung' phrase tends to feel light as she compresses the finish or else adds a light sustain and very quick vibrato fade.

It's a joyful and defiant sound, certainly not a sophisticated one. She refuses to be embarrassed or intimidated by the range of sounds she can make, pleasant and thoroughly unpleasant, and she really explores the lot. Like Smith, Thornton's music is always something of a triumph in the battle of the sexes. The song has always been seen as an extended sexual metaphor about a philandering man, but this is anything but the sound of a helpless or heartbroken woman; she wants you to know that women can and will survive their wandering men. She's changed the lyric around to fit a woman's perspective and you certainly get the sense that her 'little bitty' rooster will return.

Summary

Blues singers from Memphis Minnie to Muddy Waters have always given the listener an almost voyeuristically personal experience of sharing the singer's pain and their ultimate survival. It's a form that really champions equality of the sexes – both men and women survive here with strength and style. The 'basics' of early blues vocal sound, include:

1. A downward inflection in the vocal delivery that almost imitates the downward inflection of someone wailing or crying.
2. An 'unsung' sound that is achieved largely through the use of thick fold and sometimes belt qualities that give a close-to-spoken feel about the voice.
3. Dramatically varying effort levels. For the women the effort level is usually very high, largely owing to the predominant use of belt, twang and neutral thick-fold voice qualities. For the men, most of whom played instruments while singing, the effort levels were not always so high and in most cases remained closer to medium level since they most often employed neutral thick-fold qualities. There are, of course, many exceptions to this (Howlin' Wolf comes to mind).

4 A tendency to fall off the note – a part of the downward pattern of inflection noted above – with either little or no vibrato, or else to compress finishes to give a more 'spoken' sound.
5 Little build or improvisation in the sustain.
6 Even phrase placement, and often a tendency to weight the beginnings of phrases;
7 Frequent upward or downward bend in the note attack.
8 Little attempt to 'beautify' the sound of the tone – a kind of rough-and-ready feel to the delivery.
9 Inconsistent diction, sometimes mumbled delivery.

Practice

These general elements of blues style are not as evident in this 'pure' form today as they once were, but learning to work with them can help free you as a vocalist from some of the limitations we place on ourselves when we're singing for someone else's approval. You'll find this exercise a lot more effective if you can record your sound – it doesn't have to be great quality.

Find a song that fits comfortably into your neutral thick-fold range. Ideally, you might know a blues song that you could use for this exercise, although the traditional spiritual songs I've used in examples so far work really well so you could use one of them.

Sing your song through once, concentrating on what you want to communicate with it. Don't worry about anything technical, just concentrate on communicating something important with it (perhaps just in terms of where the song feels most emotionally connected to you?).

Practice (Continued)

Now that you've worked the song through once, try again and this time, particularly in those areas of the song you feel the strongest connection with, see what happens if you concentrate on using the highest-effort-level voice quality you can. You may find it easier to belt 'wail' or 'shout' if you move the song up a little way in your comfortable range. Resist the urge to sustain notes, and when you come to the ends of phrases, either compress your finishes or fall off the notes. These finishes can feel really unnatural if you've not used them before.

Listen back to your performance – it may not 'sound' like you but it's bound to have a different sound from your first attempt.

If there was anything you liked in that performance – even if only your own bravery! – hang onto it and try again. This time, maintain a thick-fold quality in the singing, but see whether you can add weight to the beginning of phrases, either with hard glottal onsets, slightly rumbled or slightly constricted onsets, and some bend in the note attack. Let the diction slide a bit, especially towards the ends of phrases. If you can, also try to keep in mind what it was that you made your strongest emotional connection with, it will help to keep these exercises from being too mechanical!

Finally, choose a blues artist whose style you really like. Spend some time analysing their work. Notice what they do with voice qualities, onsets, tone releases, phrase placement, diction, improv, effort levels, etc. Now find a song that your artist has not recorded and attempt to do the song 'in the style of' your artist. This isn't an imitation effort – you're not trying to sound like the artist – you're trying to put into practice the elements of style that you think really mark their performances.

If some of this comes easy to you, and you liked the roughness and the immediacy of your sound, you're probably a blues natural! If you couldn't stop laughing – well, don't give up. You may not see yourself as a blues singer or you may find this style too demanding/foreign. It will help to do more listening in this style because it gives you real freedom in terms of making sounds that aren't correct or beautiful, and that calls for a bit of bravado on your part! The more you listen, the more you'll learn to appreciate the humour, strength and generosity of blues singing.

FURTHER LISTENING – BLUES

Keb' Mo': *Perpetual Blues Machine* (2003). This is a great contemporary blues track. The scratch of his voice somehow comes across as both strong and vulnerable. He manages to bring the whole Delta blues sound right up to date and yet still be the 'real deal'.

Muddy Waters: *Hoochie Coochie Man* (1954). Waters was considered the father of Chicago blues, which was an amplified blues style that influenced so many other artists in the later twentieth century. This is typical of the Chicago blues sound; kind of defiant and more urban than the older acoustic Delta sound, but Waters's voice remains squarely within the older blues vocal aesthetic – a downward inflection, a very spoken and 'unsung' sound with compressed or falling finishes.

Son House: *Preachin' Blues* (1930). House is considered the father of Delta blues and the power of this piece demonstrates why he was so influential. There's a certain irony to hearing him sing about getting religion here, as House began as a preacher before turning to blues. This is a lively track from him and his gritty, warm sound is really inviting.

FURTHER LISTENING – BLUES (CONTINUED)

Victoria Spivey: *Dope Head Blues* (1927). I love Spivey's voice, which has a lighter and more fluid sound than Smith or Rainey, but you could never call it pretty – the sustain very nearly fails. This is a great track about the delusions of a dope head and her scatty sort of sound suits the crazy lyric well.

Memphis Minnie: *Me and My Chauffeur* (1941). This is a kind of jump blues track and it's said that she once beat Big Bill Broonzy in a 'blues contest' with this song. Minnie lived a tough life and most of her songs were autobiographical. Like most blues women, you can feel her strength and her survivor's spirit when she sings.

Gospel

Gospel is the great Mother, the church a repository of women's memory, nurture, liberation and catharsis. Its moral codes may be strict, but it is a place where women feel safe in a full expression of self. When [Aretha] Franklin's father, the Reverend C.L., who in the mid '50s could command up to $4,000 fees for an appearance on the Gospel circuit, let loose his million-dollar roar, working women would surrender themselves to ecstatic prayer, some having to be carried away by strong-armed nurses.

LUCY O'BRIEN[5]

Gospel is closely allied with blues in the sense of its strong roots in black American history and experience, and also in its overall sound and the vocal choices made by gospel singers. There are many styles that seem to operate under the category of gospel, and singers as diverse as Elvis Presley and Louis

[5]Lucy O'Brien, *She-Bop* (London: Penguin Books, 1995), p. 86.

Armstrong have recorded gospel songs or albums. Gospel is also, of course, a group style – from quartet to choir – and the range of sounds in these groups moves from highly syncopated and rhythmic almost barbershop-style close harmonies to the fuller more traditional sounds of liturgical choir music sung in response.

Gospel as a movement has mutated greatly from its earliest manifestations in the crossover between the field 'spiritual' and the Southern church 'witnesses'. Early gospel stars were highly celebrated by their audiences as they travelled the 'Gospel Highway' circuit, and they worked in various group/solo combinations. It is generally held that the first great crossover artist from gospel to popular, secular 'chart' music was Sam Cooke, and although his was certainly the success with greatest impact, there were many others whose crossover attempts preceded his. Cooke's impact inspired many other gospel singers to take the high-risk gamble of crossing over into secular music, and it was indeed high risk as the gospel community could be very unforgiving of such a choice. This crossover gospel sound is often referred to as soul music or rhythm and blues, and it is distinct from blues in many general ways, but of course, the links between these sounds are obvious as well. The vocal style of contemporary gospel artists, such as Smokie Norful or Karen Clark Sheard, is barely distinct from contemporary R&B artists.

The sound of a gospel soloist is one that also varies widely, but perhaps the most identifiable gospel solo quality is a big belting sound. Although some of these belts can be quite twangy at the top end, they often maintain a very 'chesty' belt sound. Gospel style is also associated with wide sweeps up to the note, and a kind of hollering style in the improvisation. There is less reliance on the downward inflection of blues, and much more upward bend in the note, as if trying to suggest through song the way to heaven.

Very early gospel singers were working acoustically and often singing over a large church choir. It is possible, perhaps, that the call-and-response sound of many gospel numbers originated from the early call-and-response of church liturgy. But it seems just as likely that the call-and-response was a way of allowing the solo voice some audibility against the large choir. Perhaps the tendency to wail and improvise on notes in the highest part of the singer's range was similarly an attempt to cut through the sound of the choir and be heard. Metaphorically, of course, the high wailing style of some gospel singers seems to reach right up to God.

There is physicality and muscularity to gospel singing that seems to attest to the depths of the singers' belief – strong and rich, that belief seems to need to permeate the singer's body as if overtaken by the 'holy spirit'. This, perhaps, leads to a kind of freedom for the vocalist, since all sounds made in this context must be holy, and perhaps that's why some of the improvisation is so free and exuberant. Indeed, gospel granted a kind of extraordinary license to both its artists and its audience – complete abandon and expression of passion was licensed in this spiritual sphere. This tradition of wails, shouts, moans and utter ecstasy occurring within the sanctified church realm was no doubt the reason that so many within the gospel audience turned their backs so completely upon those artists who stopped 'singing for God' and started singing 'for the world'. It must have felt like a betrayal not only of that sphere but also an act of sacrilege.

Gospel music has many vocal ensemble forms, some in more traditional choir mode, some of them quite at home next to contemporary R&B groups, and some of the older, smaller groups, like the Golden Gate Quartet or the Heavenly Gospel Singers are most distinguished through the close, syncopated style of the harmonies, which became a clear forerunner of so much of the early R&B, Motown and 1950s rock groups. A singer like Sam Cooke while pure gospel, was remarkable for the way in which his uniquely smooth, sandy tone almost belied the high effort he put into so many of his performances. But for most people, it's the female gospel solo, with its extended melismatic displays and sheer power, that has come to define the style. Lucy O'Brien's analysis, quoted above, perhaps explains why, for many, it is the women gospel soloists who have always captured something particularly extraordinary in this form and proved the most popular of the gospel artists.

The very early recordings of gospel singers suggest that they were very clearly influenced by the style of their blues and jazz-singing sisters. Listening to Sister Rosetta Tharpe now is an interesting experience because she was capable both of the raw blues 'shout' in her work, but also had a more artful sound in most of her singing – and some of the later recordings sound remarkably close to sophisticated jazz. She was capable of a wide range of stylistic elements and these, along with the dominance of belt quality in her performances, raises the perceived-effort level of the songs. Songs like *Rock Daniel* or *God Don't Like It* both draw on a number of blues techniques, including high-effort-level onsets like rumble and constriction, and a 'shouted' sound combined with a downward inflection at the ends of phrases. Overall the songs sit in a higher register than many blues songs and while there is more improvisation than in most blues recordings of the time, they remain relatively modest by contemporary standards.

Five Blind Boys of Mississippi, *His Eye is On the Sparrow* (1964)

This is a really fantastic track for illustrating so much about what really makes the gospel sound so unique. The lead vocal is combined with a kind of short sermon, and the whole recording demonstrates very clearly the connection between the preaching and the singing sounds of a gospel church service. The first full minute of the track is spoken and there is another spoken break midway through the song that continues the inspirational storyline, a story about the way in which we can seek comfort through the strength of our spiritual belief. The opening part of the sermon is delivered in a fairly relaxed if beautifully resonant spoken voice, and the rich sound of the voice seems to continue quite naturally into the very 'schooled' and beautiful sound of the singing voice in these first few lines. With just solo voice and piano, we can hear very clearly how the play of improvisation and extension between these two really are at the heart of this kind of solo gospel delivery.

Gospel really thrives on short, isolated phrasing. Rather than pursuing a sense of melodic 'line' through a song, gospel artists tend to chop phrases (sometimes even single words) into small parts and dwell upon them either through improvisation or lengthy sustain. Here is a part of the broken pattern of this version of *His Eye is on the Sparrow*:

> Why should my heart // feel lonely //
> and long // for my heaven // and home
> When Je // sus is // my portion //
> a con // stant / friend // is he //
> His eye // is on // the sparrow //
> And I know // He watches // me

These six lines take up over a minute and a half, which gives you some idea of just how disjointed the performance is. There are a lot of unexpected breaks in the words or phrases, certainly not adding up to a sense of a sung-through 'line' – something highly valued in classical singing style. In between all of these small broken phrases you can hear the play of the piano, which is mirroring the vocal with a series of arpeggios running up the scale. There's a wonderful moment in the spoken part in the middle of the track, where the really bold and passionate sounds of a proselytizing preacher leads to a bit of constriction and very high effort level in the speaking voice, and that is matched once the singing comes back in. There is most definitely a 'sung' feeling here and along with a lot of sustain in the short phrases, there is much variety in the vocal colour – we hear belt, neutral thick fold and even some delicate thin-fold sounds (especially on the final 'sparrow' lyric), combined with a beautiful fluttery vibrato sustain that fades gently.

But the great majority of the finishes are compressed in the way the piano player quickly stops between phrases, or else falls quickly off the note. There are many short improvisational extensions – rarely more than three or four notes at a time – and very definite heavy upward bend in the note attack. It's difficult to talk about phrase placement because this kind of gospel style always feels 'out of time'. The vocalist and piano player sort of follow each other in a kind of call-and-response. Where most tracks of this kind usually come into some kind of rhythmic groove, this one stays thoroughly out of time all the way through – a fairly common technique in gospel solo singing. It's an incredibly uplifting and fascinating recording that convinces you that it's being delivered with unshakeable conviction and great physical commitment.

Aretha Franklin, *Precious Lord (Take My Hand), Part One* (1956)

Perhaps nothing comes closer to defining what I think most contemporary singers have come to think of as gospel style than the recordings made of 14-year-old Aretha Franklin in 1956, as she sang live in her father's New Bethel Baptist Church in Detroit. The recording is far from perfect, but the passion is unmistakeable. It's difficult to attempt to render a musical notation of what the young Aretha does with a gospel standard like *Precious Lord (Take My Hand)*, and for our purposes, I think it might be more instructive to try yet another kind of graphic notation – one that simply looks at the way in which the lyric carries the weight of the vocal style. Here is the first verse of the hymn:

Precious Lord, take my hand
Lead me on, let me stand
When my way grows drear
Precious Lord linger near
When my light is almost gone
Hear my cry, hear my call

Hold my hand lest I fall
Take my hand precious Lord, lead me home

I want to attempt a kind of rough graphic depiction of the
way in which the highly complicated improvisational patterns
that Aretha uses in her performance actually lie within the
phrases, and you will see the familiar small, isolated chunks of
phrasing. Each repeated vowel represents an added note, and
each bold letter (roughly) indicates a heavy upward bend in
the note attack:

Leeead
leeead
lead me **o**ooon
To the l**i**ight (wh**ooo**ooa)
take my h**aa**and
Preci**oo**ous l**o**ooooooord
and l**e**ad
y**ou**r chi**iiii**ild **o**oon home
When m**ii**y
when my way gro**ooo**oows drear
Pree precious l**oo**oord
pl**e**eease linger near
And **oo**ooooo when m**y**yy when my light
ii**iiii**is al**mo**oooooooost al
mooooooost almost g**oo**one
Father, f**aaa**ath**e**eeeer
father hear my pr**a**yer looord
and**oo**h hear my caaaall
And h**oo**ooooold hold m**y**yy h**o**ld m**y** h**a**aaand
peace of jesus
l**e**st **I** f**a**all wh**oo**o
Take my haaand,
pr**e**eec**i**ous l**o**ooooord
and l**ee**ad
m**e**eeeee
l**e**ad me h**o**ooome.

This is a strange way to look at a singing performance, no doubt, but it serves to demonstrate something about the gospel style that is difficult to explain in any other way, and this is about the way in which these isolated gospel phrases are both extended and weighted. In this version, you can literally see the way in which this classic performance isolates and then weights those small phrases very heavily towards the front and the middle. As you look through you can see that although there are some 'weighty' phrase finishes in terms of improvisation, they don't tend to feel heavy in the listening because the massive upward swoop in the preceding note attack tends to throw the emphasis squarely onto the first part of the word. Stylistically, phrase weight and note attack are the most distinctive things about such big, belting gospel performances. The dominant vocal quality here is belt with twang on the really high notes. Most onsets are simultaneous or glottal, and tone release is gentle, sometimes with final consonants unvoiced. The perceived-effort level is extremely high throughout the song – even from the very start – and the true-effort level is likely to be as high as the perceived level.

The emotional quality of the performance is undeniable, although for many it may simply be all too much; there's no doubting the passionate spiritual quality of the performance. And perhaps this is one of gospel's enduring traits, as while it takes great technique and artistry to perform it well, it does, at its most basic level, seem to want to deny any sense of 'art' insofar as 'art' may be linked to anything artificial. This particular recording is 'flawed' at many points, there are moments of wayward pitching and at times her voice fails altogether. But, as is so often the case with emotionally charged raw performances of popular music, it is doubtful that any gospel aficionado would want to see these 'flaws' fixed.

Mahalia Jackson, *Amazing Grace* (1971)

Many consider Mahalia Jackson the sort of 'godmother' of all gospel singers and her sound is very different from Franklin's, although this is largely an effect of overall tonal quality. Her dominant vocal quality is belt, but she has a very 'dark' sound in the belt which feels as if she's mixing it with cry quality at the lower end. In mid-range she's producing a pure belt, which naturally has a very dark timbre; it gives a great resonance to the sound. It is a very powerful voice and the overall cry feel of the tone lends both significance and a real dignity to her performances.

Although the differences between the two singers feels strong in the listening, I've come to see how similar they are in terms of their basic style choices, and it is this which leads me to think that the difference felt is largely one of vocal quality.

Below I've taken a small fragment of a live recording of *Amazing Grace*[6] and I've done a similar graphic analysis to the one on *Precious Lord*.

Ammmmaziing Graaaace
Hoooow // Sweeeeet
theeeee // sooound
Thaaat // saaved
aaaaaa // wreeeetch
liiiike me
Iiii once
waas looooost
buuut noow // Thank God I'm fooound
Hallelujah I been bliind // buut noooooow
Iiiii caan seeee

I've found this rather unusual method helpful when listening closely to performances of such overwhelming power and improvisational flight and I think these graphic representations make clear how, despite the very different tone qualities between Aretha Franklin and Mahalia Jackson, the fundamental choices they make about phrase placement and phrase weight are very similar. It seems that Mahalia is less inclined to break

[6] You can find this on YouTube at http://www.youtube.com/watch?v=dB8g WUIE1D0

the phrases into the much smaller chunks that Aretha does, although this is extremely hard to judge when listening to her sing. What she does tend to do is to treat each word almost as a separate unit in itself. There is very little sense of 'flow' in the sung line. She places the weight mid-word with much bend coming into the vowel that she's about to improvise around, and in the section shown on the previous page, there are only two points ('wretch like **me**' and 'can **see**') at which she sustains an end of phrase. All other tone releases are compressed (with one pushed release), and many of the final consonants are either unvoiced or very softly voiced.

Summary

The overall impression is that each word has great weight within the overall performance, and the power and solemnity of Mahalia Jackson's tone give this performance a truly church-like quality. The improvisation here is neither as spontaneous nor as (occasionally) wayward as the young Aretha Franklin's, but for all their differences, both artists exemplify what I believe is still at the heart of the Gospel solo singing genre:

1. Vocal qualities dominated by belt and twang
2. A heavy reliance on upward bend in note attack and extended sustain
3. A tendency to break phrases into small chunks, and to weight the phrases very heavily towards the front or the middle; less tendency to sustain in phrase endings
4. Little sense of 'flow' in the performance
5. An extremely melismatic approach, often concentrating improvisation mid-word, rather than at phrase endings. Very high effort levels – both perceived and true.

It's probably sounding mechanical (and not a little weird!) but go through a few times (and feel free to drop or add a few notes when you want to). For reasons I can't wholly explain,

Practice

You'll want to be somewhere very soundproof or home alone so you can make mistakes without worrying who will hear you! Try the verse through first in a range that allows you to use a lot of belt and twang voice qualities, if you can access those easily.

Example 13 on the website is a gospel-style accompaniment that should help get you in the mood. First try the lines freestyle:

If you get to Heaven before I do

Comin' for to carry me home

Tell all my friends I'm comin' there too

Comin for to carry me home

Now try the lines like this, and make sure you find a different note for every vowel you see here:

Iiif you get to heeeaven

Before Iiii doo

Comin for to caaary me home

Teeel all myyy frieeends

I'm comin' there tooo

Comin for to caaarry meee hoome

Make sure you're not allowing a sense of 'flow' as you sing, break the phrases up into bits. Now try this through once more, adding a few very hefty bends in the note attacks – perhaps on the words 'you', 'home' and 'all'.

when we do this in workshop, singers have always found this approach to the exercise easier than when asked to just try doing long extended melodic improvisations spun out of their own imaginings. Maybe they are concentrating so hard on figuring out how many vowels/notes are written here, it releases some of their self-consciousness.

Even if this feels quite difficult for you, or you have a very hard time finding enough improvised notes, with a little practice you can really start to get the feel of this style, so it's worth sticking with.

Make sure you keep the weight of the phrases towards the front. Don't always hang onto your sustain at the end of each phrase – allow long improvs in the middle to take that work from you. There's a great deal of sustain in gospel, but much of it tends to happen mid-phrase. Remember that gospel style doesn't really flow – it's very 'chopped up' and the weight occurs within individual words usually. If any of this comes easily to you then you're probably a gospel natural! If it doesn't, spending some time really listening and then trying things out will pay off in terms of increasing your confidence with R&B/soul as well as gospel sounds, and the joy of being able to do this kind of music well is indescribable!

FURTHER LISTENING – GOSPEL

Maurette Brown Clark: *Just Want to Praise You* (2002). This is typical of contemporary gospel recording, where solo style is much closer to contemporary R&B. The choir provides the base of the work and allows Clark to work in and around that sound, and she uses her grainy power alto to get the congregation on side.

Kirk Franklin (with Stevie Wonder): *Why* (2011). This track gets me going every time. It's another good example of contemporary gospel's call-and-response play between choir and singer. Franklin isn't a singer so much as he's a gospel facilitator. He began directing choirs at the age of 11 and here he lets Wonder work his wonders. Franklin's choir is in incredible form here. They address a lot of contemporary issues in the lyric and the addition of Stevie Wonder's performance makes this an outstanding 'urban' gospel track.

FURTHER LISTENING – GOSPEL (CONTINUED)

Kurt Carr: *God Blocked It* (2005). As this track progresses you hear Nikita Clegg-Foxx and Nikki Potts soaring above the sound of Carr's powerful choir. This track is testament to the fact that gospel is alive and thriving in its own right, no matter how much its style has been appropriated by R&B.

Smokie Norful: *I Need You Now* (2002). Norful is a practising African Methodist Episcopal pastor, and one can only imagine how inspired his congregation must be when their preacher sits down at the piano and breaks into song. This gentle, evocative track features his unbelievably fluid, melismatic sound and like all contemporary gospel, his sound is closer to Peabo Bryson than it is to Mahalia Jackson, but his spirit and his absolute faith are well reflected in this gorgeous recording.

Marvin Sapp: *Never Would Have Made It* (2007). Sapp's fluttery, warm and visceral sound just lifts this piece into something between a raw confession and a life-affirming testament. He puts himself into this track body and soul, and it's hard to listen to this without being absolutely convinced of his belief. See y'all in church!

Jazz

Jazz exists (and came to exist) through tensions, which ultimately became syntheses, between black/white (the European musical traditions versus non-European, African-American sound); hot/cool (the sometimes wild and reckless solo sounds versus the cool, urbane musical sophistication); heart/head (free expressive instincts and untrained musicians versus a structured and profound musical knowledge); raw/refined (growling, rasping, passionate noises versus a purer aesthetic with regard to timbre). These tensions give jazz the strangely indefinable character that makes analysis so challenging. Because jazz began first as an instrumental form, jazz singing seemed to have to search to find its form. It wasn't, like blues, just a matter of allowing the heart to lead. Jazz musical form was fairly sophisticated even in its early years, following on from ragtime and march music, and involving instruments that required a higher degree of musical knowledge to play than the guitar/banjo/harmonica instrumentations so familiar in blues form.

The early influential jazz orchestra leaders (Fletcher Henderson, Duke Ellington) were well-educated artists, whose musical skills brought significant changes to the form. It was not a vocal form in its infancy and many of the vocal performances recorded with jazz bands in the 1920s and 1930s drew heavily on blues form, but this wasn't an entirely happy marriage. The blues form was in many ways dominated by the vocal performance. As an instrumental form, jazz singers often had to take the part of the 'straight man' – they were left to sing the melody while all around them erupted spontaneous instrumental flights around and away from the melody. Still, the singers couldn't be too straight with the melody, or they would inhibit the 'swing' sound of jazz. People often think that jazz singing has to include extended improvisational skills, which can make it seem as if the form is rather ornate, but in truth, the great jazz singers often did quite the opposite: they reduced and simplified as often – if not more often – as they embellished. Billie Holiday's great influence was in her ability to simplify a melody line, often allowing some tension or dissonance between the sung line and the harmonic changes beneath the singing. Those tensions had a 'blue' sound and along with this she employed a kind of 'wayward' style in the note attack. This is the smallest kind of improvisation – just a very fast rise and fall in pitch sound before settling on to the note. Like many other 'cool' jazz singers she brings a truly unique tonal quality and has a profoundly unusual ability to phrase against the expected ground beat. It is a subtle but very skilled playfulness.

Early distinctions between European tradition and blues could be heard in the voices of Armstrong and Holiday, particularly in the desire to deviate from the European standards of 'timbre'. Early jazz instrumentalists often went to extreme lengths to adjust the sounds of their instruments, modifying pianos so that they lost their 'concert' purity, or finding various ways to mute or change the sound of instruments like the trumpet. These same desires can be heard in some of the unusual sounds of some of the singers. In a way they also typify a split that might be characterized as the 'hot' or 'cool' sound of jazz vocalists – the 'hotter' sound working perceptively harder in effort level and generally using the voice as a band instrument. The 'cool' sound often brought beauty of tone, and lent a kind 'silken', floating feel to the melody, which was always creatively (rather than 'accurately') placed, allowing a 'swing' jazz feel to a track.

Absolutely no one is comfortable with trying to define jazz, although a number of people would insist that there are defining factors that unite all its disparate camps: syncopation and improvisation. As I must talk in general terms here, for the singer, I would suggest that there are perhaps some identifiable traits in jazz singing, although of course there are no 'rules'.

Overall, jazz stylists always tended to value (and want their listeners to value) musical skill, and the ability to extend harmonic territory. Quite opposed to the rough-and-ready similarity found in the tonal quality of many blues singers, nearly every great jazz singer has displayed an arguably distinctive sound to the voice. That distinction may lie in the very smooth and somewhat 'sandy' tones of 'cooler' artists like Mel Tormé, June Christy, Nat King Cole or Norah Jones, or in the utterly unique tonal qualities as well as the range of complementary elements employed by 'hotter' jazz singers like Dinah Washington, Sarah Vaughan or Nancy Wilson. All these singers share certain musical attributes, chief among which must be the accuracy and confidence of their pitching.

Jazz has always appealed to an urban ideal: it is the musical background of city living and to that end the kind of raw emotional connection with material that is common to blues or gospel is deliberately avoided. There is little to comprehend, emotionally, from Nina Simone's absolute certainty in *My Baby Just Cares For Me*, other than mere mortal appreciation of her supreme confidence. It is a life-affirming sound that proposes music as the joyful expression of reason and, in its more progressive forms, an almost mathematically precise reason, mastered and rendered unique in the solos of musical virtuosos.

So how does the jazz singer achieve this more reasoned, less emotional sound? Overall I think jazz singers tend to see less distinction between the voice and any other instrument in the band. To that end, then, there is often more attention given to diction and the sound of lyrics generally. This is less to do with 'telling the story of the song' than with actually employing consonants and vowels in the way that an instrumentalist concentrates on the various components which make up their sound. There is often much more sense of play between vocalist and instrumentalist. As jazz instrumentalists became increasingly concerned with the purity of the tone they could coax from their instruments, similarly, jazz vocalists seemed to reflect their concern with achieving a kind of purity of tone. Perhaps a close listen to something like Peggy Lee's *Why Don't You Do Right* (1942, with Benny Goodman) comes closest to exemplifying some of these ideas. The play between her cool vocal performance (which is never really 'sung' in any sense) and the massive, 'hot' orchestral swing and sound behind her is a good example of the way in which jazz, as a medium, seems to want to find better, more interesting ways to incorporate the human voice as an instrument with other instruments in an ensemble. Lee uses one vocal quality throughout, never exploits the sustain of the voice, and doesn't bother with much melodic improvisation, apart from a very interesting sort of 'wayward' finish on the phrase 'why don't you do right', a slight lifting of the melodic line at the end of the song. Her whole delivery speaks of a woman who doesn't care enough about this no-good man to even get angry.

Improvisation is part of jazz singing and it is here where I think the voice-as-instrument approach is important. Of course, one of the greatest differences between the voice and most other instruments is that you don't have valves or keys on a keyboard to help fix a pitch. Vocal pitching is a fairly mysterious process in which we simply 'know' where to place a sound. In jazz singing there is often much improvisation and much of it is more complex than standard blues or gospel vocal riffs. There are often difficult patterns to the improvisation, and sometimes those patterns can feel more 'instrumental' than vocal. In other words, where many vocalists feel safest improvising around a range of notes within a comfortable proximity of one another, jazz vocalists can sometimes dazzle with the unexpected, in perhaps the same way that a keyboard player can move as easily from one note to a minor third as they can from that same note to octave or more away. There is often more experimentation in phrase weight and placement, and again this may be related to a more 'instrumental' approach to vocal solos.

Louis Armstrong, *You Rascal You*[7] (1931)

I love this track – it gives us a great chance to hear the whole spectrum of sound that Armstrong could make, and it really makes clear why so many people see him as the first great jazz singer. He talks through the opening and in the end, and you can hear that in his speaking, as in his singing, he has real control over how much rumbled sound he makes. The whole piece has a spoken quality, he uses the same sounds in speech as in the singing voice. It's a song that really builds in terms of looseness and swing, and in keeping with that, his diction gets fuzzier as

[7]Armstrong recorded this track a couple of times but the version I refer to is on a collection called 'You Rascal You'.

the song goes on. As with his horn playing, he approaches song with great freedom and his improvisation pattern as a vocalist very clearly imitates his horn improvisation. He brings a nice easy bend to the note attack, but there is no real 'sung' sound here, which means that his vocal improvisation has a highly percussive sound, he clearly enjoys singing the way he plays his horn. He sings and plays in and around the beat, often lagging just behind or playfully pushing the phrase forward of the beat. Towards the end there is a great, syncopated play between his vocal and the rhythm section.

He draws a lot on the blues styles of the time in his rough-and-ready vocal delivery and his phrase weight relies on a kind of rising weight towards the middle, which falls away towards the end of lines. But you can really hear the influence of the jazz music of the time too – the melodic range here is just so impressive. He uses a lot of his trademark rumble sound and when he's not rumbling there's still a great deal of air/huskiness in the tone. He begins the piece by talking about how happy he'll be when the rascal he's singing about is dead, but it's a very funny song and uses some outrageous sounds to exaggerate the humour (presumably you can't get away with singing about how happy you'll be when someone dies unless you do introduce humour!). He has great confidence in the 'blue' notes, which can sometimes sound as if he veers on the flat side but he always gets to the pitch he's heading towards. Like so much of Armstrong's output this is an experience of absolute joy and proves that even when he's talking about death he can't help but affirm the great pleasure of life.

Trying to judge the effort level here is a challenge. The heaviness of the vocal quality and the exploration of range should lead it towards the high end of perceived effort in listening, but in a manner typical of jazz, the ease of his reading, the lack of sustain, the overall 'relaxed' approach to singing (he clearly doesn't care about sounding beautiful or correct), the laugher, and the way in which he seems to just bounce so easily over the ground beat makes it feel almost effortless.

Ella Fitzgerald, *The Midnight Sun* (1964) and *Lady Be Good* (1947)

Midnight Sun is a beautiful and rather gentle track from the great lady of jazz and I've included it here largely because some of her bigger flights of improvisation and musical imagination can be a bit intimidating! Legendary jazz vibes player Lionel Hampton and big band leader Sonny Burke originally wrote *Midnight Sun*, and like most jazz instrumental melodies it has a beautifully catchy but very complex structure. This makes it fairly difficult even for a virtuoso scat/improvisation artist like Ella Fitzgerald to take the piece too far afield and for that reason it's really interesting to look closely at what she does with the piece.

She never pushes the effort level at all – she stays very comfortably within her neutral thin- and thick-fold tones with only some slight shadings of aspirate sounds on the upper end of the first lines in every verse, and a hint of cry quality as she gets towards the lower end of the register in the last lines of the verse. Her onsets and releases are not highly varied – she consistently uses simultaneous or very soft glottal onsets. Releases are predominantly vibrato fades, and these things combined give a very smooth and very 'sung' sound. Her tone is beautiful, if not passionate, and her pitching is, of course, remarkably accurate. What is interesting in her interpretation here is the way in which she manipulates the phrases very gently to allow herself some breathing room within them. This is a particularly 'wordy' piece with an extraordinary lyric. It is said that lyricist Johnny Mercer heard the original instrumental version on the radio while driving along the coast in California and that he composed it all in his head then. Whatever the truth of this legend, you certainly feel that Mercer was pushing poetic lyric form quite hard with some spectacular results (just the 'chalice'/'palace'/'borealis' rhyme of the first verse is so impressive) and along with a very evenly placed and constantly moving descending melody line, the singer needs to stay close to the melody as written. Ella gets around this very neatly, nearly every phrase is placed just forward of the beat. This gives her time to linger now and then on the lyrics mid-phrase, either stretching them just gently beyond their natural 'fall' within the line (thus allowing her to play and swing around the beat easily), or else giving her time to dwell on the very small melodic variations she adds in the first full sing-through of the song.

After the instrumental break she comes back in with a much bolder deviation from the melody throughout the whole of the last repeat verse and chorus. It's such a highly structured melody that she has to be careful in the way that she reinvents it, but she certainly does reinvent it for the first two lines coming in, throughout which she only hits two notes as written. She doesn't stray quite as far thereafter, often only jumping up four or five tones on a single note and then dropping quickly back into the standard melody line. The overall effect is one of sheer effortless musicality and gentle beauty – a very 'cool' jazz sound.

It's interesting to contrast this with her 'hotter' approach on *Lady Be Good*. Here she works very differently in her approach to this George and Ira Gershwin classic. Although she 'scats' and invents all around the track, she actually compresses the written melody line within the verse: instead of singing it through the way that it is actually written, she flattens a fairly rangy melody in the first few verse lines by centring on one note and playing gently around that central note through the line until the end. She adds extensive improvisation at the ends of lines and adds both notes and words in between the written verse lines. The track starts with a great sense of energy and you can almost feel that she is just allowing herself to warm up gently on the first two verses and middle-eight before she takes off for full flight as an 'instrumental' soloist midway through. She allows herself extraordinary play in the sounds she makes here and instead of the usual remarkable consistency of sung sound that we usually get when she is singing lyric (very consistent neutral thin- or thick-fold sounds, vibrato fades, easy onsets), we get much more compression in the finish, harder glottals and consonants, more falls off the note, and much wilder sounds.

At one point she adds extended creak or scratch into the tone, which is quite rare for her, but you just know that she's imitating sounds of other instrumental soloists (like Louis Armstrong) who brought a kind of gritty tonal colour to their instruments and had great influence on jazz vocalists. For me, these grittier more exciting sounds really bring her voice to life. The improvisation on this track is both inspiring and incredible and reminds us just why she is considered the finest jazz vocalist of all time. She had a remarkable command of musical structure and it isn't surprising that when Chick Webb (who was the leader of the first band Ella joined when she was a young woman) died, Ella led the band on her own for 3 years.

Despite the extraordinary effect of her scat singing in *Lady Be Good*, you still never get the sense that she raises the effort level of her singing too high. This is probably the most effort level you will hear from her, and yet it still isn't that high; her artistry lay precisely in the fact that she could do something this impressive (and this is difficult!) and make it sound as if it was just like a stroll in the park for her.

Peggy Lee, *The Best is Yet to Come* (1961)

Discovered by Benny Goodman when she was singing in Chicago, Peggy Lee replaced Helen Forrest as Goodman's lead vocalist for 2 years before moving on. She doesn't credit her years as a big band singer as having influenced her style as much as a discovery she felt she made while singing in a club in Palm Springs very early in her career. As the story goes, she was singing in her usual full, powerful vocal sound while all around her the audience was talking, drinking and generally ignoring the band and its vocalist. She decided to try something different and began singing in a very soft, intimate tone. Suddenly, the audience began to listen. The story may be apocryphal but the gentle minimalism of her vocal approach is one of her distinctive trademarks.

She makes this track (a surprisingly hard melody line to pitch correctly) sound so simple. This is really a composite of her style, that very staccato neutral thick fold in the mid-range which gives her real power when she wants it, which is often then married to the sweet melt into an aspirate voice quality – sexy and playful. She loves the microphone and has great intimacy with the listener because of this; she also has that bedrock requirement of jazz singing – absolutely perfect pitching. (In its various forms, jazz usually allows divergence away from the beat and the melody that only singers with extraordinary ears can really keep their place harmonically.)

She uses clean diction, very little vibrato and lots of quick compression on endings. There are nice changes of voice qualities, from belt to a whispery upper end with thin folds. At this point, she typifies the urban 'cool' sound that so many of the big band singers came to personify after the big band era had passed. She remains cool here, because she largely keeps the effort level very low, as if teasing with the power and then pulling right back. Even in the middle-eight where she begins to use her bigger belt sound, she caps each phrase with a very clipped finish and never goes in for the long sustained sound that would have raised her effort level here.

She finishes the song with a very cool, very low-effort-level sexy sound that just puts the whole thing together as a sophisticated reading. This is a jazz track, not because she has dazzling vocal improvisation or uses the voice like an instrument so much, but because she quietly impresses with absolutely solid musicianship and she allows that to be a more important feature than any immediate vocal 'colour'. She doesn't feel that she has to work at singing about love – like other, cool sophisticated city folk, she keeps her cards close to her chest. This is part of that jazz dichotomy: hot licks on the trumpet, cool licks from the vocalist.

Frank Sinatra, *In the Wee Small Hours of the Morning* (1955)

There are those who would argue that Sinatra is not a jazz singer; that his style is more accurately described as easy listening or middle of the road, but I think this misses so much about what he achieved as an artist. Sinatra began early with big bands, singing first with Harry James and then with Tommy Dorsey. His impressive sense of musicianship and 'swing' feel influenced everything he did as a singer. This track is vintage Sinatra – his style now has mellowed and matured – and I think this song typifies the way in which Sinatra 'masculinized' popular singing. Against singers like Bing Crosby or Perry Como (whose work always retained a lighter more 'crooned' sound), or Dick Haymes or Billy Eckstine (who employed a deeper, more resonant but still perceptively 'sung' sound), Sinatra's style seemed seriously male, very intimate, and although undoubtedly very satisfying musically and certainly 'sung' it always had a perceptively spoken feel about it. In other words, he was singing but never in a way that made you think first about his voice, instead, with Sinatra, you always felt as if you'd been dropped into a world of dream or heartache or love, and you had to hear what he was saying first. On second and third listening you begin to appreciate how he was saying it.

Although possessed of an amazing instrument, you can hear that he's adopted a kind of intimacy of style; like Peggy Lee, he clearly loves the microphone and caresses it in an extraordinary way. He doesn't always exploit the power of his voice. Instead here, in the little cracks and flaws of the voice, you hear the battle scars of a man whose love life has been tough – how else to explain the reluctant way in which he releases the sound of the word 'lonely'? He remains almost entirely in a neutral thick-fold sound and he employs very gentle note bends either up or down to ease us into the melody.

People so often talk about Sinatra's phrasing, but generally find it hard to articulate just exactly what they mean by that. I think you can hear it plainly in this track. He innately understands the way in which spoken phrasing is sometimes completely at odds with the often too-even rhythm imposed by musical structure and he's very smart about not letting that evenness destroy the more natural spoken rhythm of the words. A great example of this is the way he manipulates the 'sing-songy-ness' of a phrase like 'never ever' by closing very quickly on the final 'r' sound – we are immediately relieved of the cliché rhymed sound that results from dwelling on the 'eh' vowel sound. He does a similar thing at the end of this phrase with the word 'counting', where he cleverly lingers over the first syllable to prevent the whole of the line from sounding too evenly rhymed and thereby too 'artful' or contrived to contain the full heartbreak he means to convey here. These are small things, notable in one single phrase of the track, but they add up to just what it is that constitutes his brilliance.

He's creaking into some of his onsets and even allows a little scratched or creaked sustain in the voice towards the note finishes. He closes down the vowel sounds of the sustains very quickly so that even when he does sustain a pitch it never sounds 'sung' in the way it would if he remained open on an 'ooh' or 'aah' vowel sound. He often moves very smoothly from consonant to consonant with just a slight and vulnerable, fluttery vibrato to ease the transition. The great thing about his style is the way in which his extraordinary musicality, which makes everything move so smoothly, is at odds with the intimate and conversational sound that he achieves by closing his vowels so quickly and allowing those creaked and scratched sounds into a very clean diction.

The diction isn't overworked, it's just a bonus of finishing with the held consonant so often. He has a natural sense of how to finish even tough consonant sounds without overemphasizing them (listen to the way he gently insinuates the 'k' sound at the end of 'awake' in the first verse). As the track proceeds he grows cleverer with the placement of the phrase, almost never coming down on the beat but shifting just slightly ahead or behind the beat to allow a conversational rather than a sung rhythm to dominate the feel of performance. That was both the absolute wonder and the great secret of Sinatra's style at the height of his powers: he was singing to millions but it always feels as if he's talking to you.

Diana Krall, *Almost Blue* (2004)

In keeping with jazz style, the effort level here is really low; even though she often begins a phrase with a hard glottal or consonant sound and comes in with neutral thick fold, she usually quickly pulls back into a thin fold into aspirate sound and quick compressed, sometimes aspirated, often creaked finishes that add up to a very intimate sound. You get the sense that without a very good and sensitive microphone you wouldn't hear much of this performance live. She employs some unusual note bends, both up and down, which gives a very loose and languid feel to the piece. Her voice floats in a silky way over and around the small combo accompaniment, and is usually well behind the beat in her phrasing.

She particularly favours lengthening the sounds of words mid-phrase, which gives the track an interesting kind of 'stretched out' sound. She builds the song very subtly, rarely ever coming into full voice – particularly where most vocalists would go for the big sound, she draws back and adds just that bit more air or creak into the mix of the sound. She isn't flashy with improvisation and is perfectly happy to simply ease a phrase in or out with a few small additional notes or 'twiddles', and at no point does she ever really move or drive the song along the way that some great jazz singers do, but she's dead accurate in her pitching and overall the sound is incredibly sophisticated and intelligent. That, combined with things like a rather unexpected long, slow aspirate fall make the whole piece add up to a beautiful modern take on the gentle jazz vocal sound of singers like Peggy Lee or Julie London.

Jamie Cullum, *I Can't Get Started and I Get a Kick Out of You* (2010)

I Can't Get Started is Cullum's cover of a jazz standard, made famous originally in 1937 when Bunny Berigan began to use it as his theme song. In keeping with the Berigan classic, the star of the track is the horn. In Berigan's case it was his trumpet (a virtuoso performance that can still give you chills); on Cullum's track the star is the sax. He maintains a low energy level throughout, staying largely in a very spoken sound. There's a bit of creak to ease into phrases, and while he sustains some notes, it's mostly within the phrase rather than at the end. Most of his finishes either fall off or are quick compressions.

Despite the low effort level, his tendency here is not to back phrase, which you might expect, but to push most of the phrases just slightly ahead of the beat, which allows the sax player plenty of room throughout the track. There's a little melodic lift in the verse after the solo, and in the final 'What good does it do?' line. He finishes with final thin-fold notes held against a little blue accompaniment, and the whole track is a kind of laid-back tribute to heartbreak, which he apparently isn't going to glamorize for us here. For all the time given to the sax solo, it never comes near the excitement of the earlier Berigan track. Throughout the piece Cullum quietly demonstrates the absolute ease and confidence of his own musicality. It's a perfect 'cool' jazz track that suggests a kind of futility of effort.

I Get a Kick is Jamie in slightly hotter mode. He is playful and percussive in this track and his voice mirrors the sound of his piano in many ways with little or no sustain and quick explorations all around the central tune. It's all kind of jumpy and although it has incredible energy he never uses particularly high-energy vocal choices. Most of the song remains in neutral thick fold – he achieves the energy just through the quick, staccato delivery and the sense of humour and bounce that infuse the track. When you play piano this well, it must be hard to try to match the restless urgency of its sound with your voice, but Cullum gives it a game go here.

Summary

Jazz is a very broad church and at its most intimidating it includes vocalists with nearly superhuman powers of spontaneous musicality and accuracy, but in its more common form, jazz is the medium in which the artists, both instrumental and vocal, really work to achieve a kind of equality. The 'lead' sounds are usually equally divided between the singers and the players, and that requires a sort of common language in the overall approach to a song. The most common vocal qualities that define a jazz performance are:

1. Predominantly low effort or low perceived-effort level in performance, which often means lighter vocal qualities and/or less sustain
2. Generally very few (and sometimes no) changes of vocal quality within a song
3. Quick, often compressed or falling finishes
4. Great accuracy of pitching
5. Enough improvisational ability to allow the singer to adapt a song to fit within the musical world in which it is being performed
6. A strong rhythmic sense that allows the fundamental 'swing' or syncopation of the music to come alive
7. An easy sense of play and freedom in the delivery

Practice

Jazz is playful, and play takes courage. You really need to listen to jazz artists before you can find the courage, I think, to see just how far you can push things. It's helpful to spend time listening to jazz instrumentalists as well as jazz vocalists.

Once you've spent some time really listening, go to **Example 14 on the website** and listen to the accompaniment a few times. (The key may not be perfect, but C seems to fit general male/female ranges. Jazz style is extremely forgiving in terms of vocal quality, so don't worry if you're working a little higher or lower than usual – that could be helpful in terms of keeping your effort level low.)

Now try singing through a few times, but don't allow yourself to start a phrase right on the beat – come in either before or after the beat:

I sing because I'm happy

I sing because I'm free

His eye is on the sparrow

And I know he watches me.

Sing it through again, with your concentration in various areas.

First, try staying in predominantly one voice quality and keep sustains to an absolute minimum.

Try again, and this time compress or aspirate or fall off the notes as often as you can. Feel free to experiment with onsets, but keep them low effort. Keep working through your 'boredom threshold' with these exercises – you need to be so comfortable with the song that you can be really playful with it.

Practice (Continued)

Finally, try singing anything except the melody. It might help you to get someone else to sing the melody quietly with you, while you look for other possibilities. If you do this exercise, just tell yourself that you must try not to sing whatever the other person is singing.

You don't need to do any great extended improv on this, just gentle variations away from the melody will help you greatly to understand what all your possibilities are for extending and playing when you go back to singing the melody.

You might find that you do better working all of the exercises above with a (karaoke) backing track for a different song – one that you really like. Making an emotional connection with a song always gives your playfulness a little charge. If any of this came easily to you, you're probably a jazz 'natural'. If not, keep listening and keep experimenting. If this style is really foreign to you, make the effort to spend much more time listening. It will pay off in every other style you do feel comfortable in because listening and working with jazz style can really increase your sense of melodic and rhythmic confidence.

FURTHER LISTENING – JAZZ

Kurt Elling: *Nature Boy* (1997). You can feel his love of the unexpected in this track which is beautifully sung but also full of percussive and inventive touches. His improv towards the four-minute mark is really brave and much more like an instrument than a voice. He's so completely involved in the musical journey here that he doesn't worry at all when the voice goes a bit astray in terms of tone – strained and thin at times – it all just adds to the excitement.

(*Continued*)

FURTHER LISTENING – JAZZ (CONTINUED)

Tony Bennett & Amy Winehouse: *Body and Soul* (2011). While Bennett is from the kind of 'crooner' school of jazz singing (for my ear at least!) Winehouse masterfully proves her jazz credentials on *Body and Soul* with a performance that is a cross between Dinah Washington and Billie Holiday but put together in her own incredibly distinct way. For me, *I Heard Love is Blind* is Winehouse's best clearly jazz-inspired track – it's both musical and playful. She's great at moving a phrase all around the ground beat and she does that with real confidence here.

Cassandra Wilson: *Time After Time* (1999). On a beautiful and blue version of Cyndi Lauper's classic, Wilson turns in an understated and skilled performance. Listen carefully to how she weaves her melody in and around what's happening in the instrumental track. It's a master class in subtle but interesting phrase placement.

Eliane Elias: *That Old Feeling* (2013). Brazilian jazz pianist and singer, Elias includes this track on her tribute to Chet Baker. The easy, accurate, quick-attack vocal work and the general bounce of the track is an infectious sort of 'virtuoso cocktail'.

Al Jarreau: *Midnight Sun* (Live with Metropole Orkest, 2012). Jarreau is so bold here, he is absolutely unconcerned with consistent tone and he explores the whole of his range. He moves all around this incredibly intricate melody with great accuracy and it's a risky endeavour. Just listen closely to how many vocal qualities he runs through here!

Country

In 1949, the editors at *Billboard*, then as now the American music industry's most important trade magazine, announced a change in the nomenclature they would use to label

> different genres. Henceforth, what had previously been classified as . . . 'folk' music would henceforth be called 'Country and Western'.[8]

In the same moment that 'race' records were reclassified as rhythm and blues, records that had been selling as folk were also rebranded. From a contemporary perspective it may seem a bit strange, since we probably wouldn't see folk and country as similar categories now. In this section I'll be looking at country as a genre and not including western, which was a distinct style of its own, and actually much more of a pop genre. Western really grew in combination with transplanted dust bowl farmers from Texas and Oklahoma who found themselves in California around the same time that early cowboy films were coming out of Hollywood. Singing cowboys like Gene Autry and Roy Rogers were Hollywood stars and certainly never lived as cowboys. In a sense it was a kind of 'made-up' style – some of it (especially in its southwest shuffle or western swing incarnation) quite wonderful, but country in its early phase really was a much more organic thing.

Like early blues singers, seminal country artists like Jimmie Rodgers, Hank Williams and Loretta Lynn genuinely lived the lives they sang about. They had a number of similarities with blues artists despite the wide differences in style. Country music focuses on the same kind of subject matter that blues does but in a generally much less defiant way. Where blues singers often found ways to bring humour and a kind of determination to survive the worst in both their lyrics and their performances, the country artists often wholeheartedly give way to their despair, particularly in the ballad form. Country songs can be a sustained exercise in really allowing that despair to work itself through musically.

---

[8]Miller, James *Almost Grown: The Rise of Rock* (London: William Heinemann Ltd, 1999), p. 44.

In many ways, early country music was the white version of the blues. It evolved from its early folk roots through influences from early jazz and blues styles but nevertheless remained for some time stubbornly *un*refined as a genre and pitched its appeal to a poor rural (Southern) white working-class audience. Like the blues, country based its appeal in authentic experience, in hardship, in living off the land, in survival, but somehow country always did so in a more theatrical sense. Its themes were similar to those of blues music and centred around the everyday tragedies of love, loss and hard work. It also features the common consolations of love, sex and drinking, but it did so much more, I would argue, through a sense of the singer as an almost theatrical (or melodramatic) character.

As with early blues, most of early country was acoustic guitar-based and composed of simple chord patterns, but its overriding distinction – and the distinction that it was socially forced to maintain – was that country was a white musical form. This meant that against the rise of popular music and the widespread availability of radio music shows in the early decades of the twentieth century, country artists were facing (whether consciously or not) a unique difficulty: how to create an identifiably white musical style/sound through a body of music that had so many similarities to what was already a well-established body of black musical sounds.[9] Of course in this situation radio only forced the issue: if the listener couldn't see whether the singer was white or black, then the listener had to try to discern the colour difference simply through the sound of the singer's voice. Despite the

[9]In *Faking It: The Quest for Authenticity in Popular Music* (London: Faber, 2007), authors Hugh Barker and Juval Taylor make the point that the early popular music scene itself was not wholly segregated – there were black and white musicians who played together – but it suited the record companies to promote a segregated market.

many similarities in background and musical form, when you listen now to early blues and to early country singers, their stylistic differences are marked.

At the most basic level, you can hear an accent in the singing that neatly identifies the genre. Country singers nearly always employ a detectable southern drawl, and that drawl itself has a kind of twang in the tone of it and a 'bend' in the melody of it – both of which heavily influence style in country singing. Despite the many fusion forms of contemporary country singing, there are some clear traits that run straight through from Jimmie Rodgers to Kenny Chesney, or from Patsy Cline through to Deana Carter.

On the whole I don't often encounter singers who want to work on this style – pop, rock, gospel and jazz being the areas most singers want to explore – but the style has been so influential in rock music and has produced artists of such distinction that I always include it when I'm teaching vocal style and singers have always found pleasure (if unexpectedly!) in experimenting with it.

Hank Williams, *Your Cheatin' Heart* and *Hey, Good Lookin'* (1951)

Hank Williams was perhaps the greatest of the early country 'icons' and I think much of what distinguishes country sound is clearly evident in his voice in these two seminal tracks. A raw, nasal twang, and a direct, unfussy delivery typified his style. In *Your Cheatin' Heart*, his heavy reliance on the flip onset pushes the ear right up into the sound, creating the opposite effect of the downward inflection of blues delivery. You can hear the influence of early country 'yodelers' like Rodgers in the sound that he uses on this track and he uses that yodel extensively in tracks like *Lovesick Blues*. The tone is 'unschooled' and almost painfully raw sometimes, but still has a 'sung' sound – in other words, it's musical and exploits the sustain of sound. This creates a very different sound from the 'spoken' delivery and rumble of so many blues artists. Sustains are longer and while vibrato is rare, Williams tends to finish his long phrases with a heavily bent note attack on (you can hear this particularly on the word 'me' in *Hey Good Lookin'*) a lengthy sustain with no vibrato, that finishes in a little fall off the note. Longer sustains mid-phrase contribute to the more 'sung' feeling of his songs, yet the unrefined tone still manages to create what so many of the blues singers did: the sense that the listener is hearing a kind of primal emotional sound from an artist who has lived through much and who values that experience over any kind of fancy 'artistry'.

In *Hey Good Lookin'*, Williams' bright, twangy sound seems to capture wonderfully the optimism and good-time feel of his lyric, which sets the scene with great detail: the hot rod Ford and the two-dollar bill that Williams uses to entice the unknown woman were the dreams of a common man and his vocal performance is common in the very best sense – there is absolutely nothing sophisticated or premeditated about it. He does nothing to beautify the hillbilly identifiers of his nasal, drawling sound, and the effect is almost like looking through a camera lens at a scene that most of us now have never seen anywhere except perhaps on film, but in Williams' time, no doubt, the match of sound to experience would have had real resonance with his audience, and that audience would have responded to the raw honesty of his work.

There are many 'flaws' detectable in this track: his sustains employ a certain generosity of pitch, and sometimes he works them hard enough to push a bit of scratchiness in the sound. His tone releases are almost entirely rather wayward falls from the note – not elegant in any sense. On the whole, he employs less flip in his sound here (either in onset or in glide between notes) than he does, for example, in *Your Cheatin' Heart*, where the flip and a more gentle, darker sustain with mild vibrato brings a bit of relief to the long, relentless nasal twang sustains of this song. Despite these 'flaws' and the admission that at its most hard and focused point, Williams's twang is probably the opposite of vocal beauty, I still respond at once to what I find irresistibly life-affirming and exuberant in the performance.

Perhaps more than that, in this track I see a perfect match of form and content. Somehow, *Hey, Good Lookin'*, as a song, makes life seem inviting. The pleasures Williams sings about are both easy and immediate. Lyrics about free soda pop and dancing might seem absurdly innocent to a contemporary audience, but Williams creates a compelling sort of philosophy from these simple things. Combined with the raw sincerity of Williams's performance, the whole song seems to make life sound uncomplicated and pleasure sound accessible to anyone.

Despite some similarities in both blues and country styles, there seems no doubt that Hank Williams's voice is the voice of a white man. It has the thin nasality of certain white Southern dialects and I am willing to bet that no one in the Southern states at the time of Williams's recordings would have come to any other conclusion. Country audiences were not looking for anything other than 'ordinary' folks singing of 'ordinary' life and experiences, and to some extent early country artists, from Minnie Pearl to Ernest Tubbs, seemed to feel obligated to present a non-glamorous image to accompany this non-glamorized vocal style.

The general suspicion of these audiences was that anything too sophisticated was bound to be dishonest in some way, but this notion was never without its tensions: from 'rhinestone cowboys' to 'big hair', country music has tended to fashion its own version of acceptable glamour. Unlike the change that one could trace in the blues-to-jazz crossover artists like Billie Holiday or Ethel Waters (where increasingly sophisticated audiences demanded increasingly sophisticated music), country musicians perhaps found themselves drawn to slicker presentations in sequins and heavy emotion, but the musical simplicity and 'authenticity' (however melodramatically manufactured!) of the country sound remains a touchstone of this style.

Tammy Wynette, *D.I.V.O.R.C.E.* (1968)

Tammy Wynette's *D.I.V.O.R.C.E.* is a much later track than Hank Williams's *Hey Good Lookin'*. As such, although it employs stylistic elements found in early country, it was produced at the point where I believe country songs had commonly moved from the raw emotional dramas of Hank Williams's *I'm So Lonesome I Could Cry* or Patsy Cline's *Crazy*, into full-blown melodrama. Like so many country songs (*Did I Shave My Legs for This?*, *Drop Kick Me, Jesus, Through The Goalposts Of Life*, *Get Your Tongue Out of My Mouth, I'm Kissing You Goodbye*), a comic title belies a soap-opera content and delivery. *D.I.V.O.R.C.E.* is a good example of the aforementioned tendency towards theatricality, and the overplayed sentimentality of Tammy Wynette's vocal choices here move an already pretty soppy song into the territory of kitsch. Indeed, the song is considered by many to be a camp classic.

I think it's important to stress that I don't necessarily think this is a bad thing. Melodrama/campness may or may not be to your taste, but most vocalists know that there are times when a bit of carefully judged vocal 'over-egging' can have a real impact, and *D.I.V.O.R.C.E.* is quite a pudding. The lyrics are, in themselves, so contrived that it's doubtful whether anyone would want to try this song with a middle-ground sort of delivery. It's an all or nothing proposition, and Wynette's voice is perfectly placed to make the whole commitment.

Because it is pure storytelling, Wynette is careful about diction. Generally, country singers are careful about diction because so many of the songs are reliant on the listener's ability to understand the tale they tell. From great songs like Marty Robbins's *El Paso* to Dolly Parton's *Coat of Many Colors*, this is a genre that has always rewarded a good yarn. *D.I.V.O.R.C.E.* is an old-fashioned tear-jerker that employs some straightforward emotional techniques. Wynette's overall aim is to invite the listener to share/believe in her pain. It's a somewhat strange experience, though, since she makes only a few vocal choices and sticks rather rigidly to them. This removes the sense of spontaneity from the performance (a spontaneity that blues and gospel trade heavily in) and perhaps this is what gives the performance a rather theatrical feel.

Throughout the song her delivery has regularity. Phrases are weighted quite evenly and for the most part placement is like clockwork. Occasionally you can hear a slight back phrasing at work in the verse, but it's rare and the chorus phrases are always delivered right on the beat. As the song progresses the 'D.I.V.O.R.C.E.' lyric works in a rather bizarre counter-time against the backing track which reinforces the 'right-on-the-beat' feel of the performance. The overriding vocal choice of the track is a fairly quick flip onset and short but definite upward bends in the note attack which, combined with a vulnerable-sounding thin-fold tone (which is the only vocal quality detectable in the piece) and a series of quick, compressed releases, makes the whole performance sound like the imitation of a crying woman. The important word here, I suppose, is 'imitation' because at no point (at least in a close listening) does it feel as if the crying could be real, the whole track feels too closely regulated for that, but the combination of an artful impression of crying and the sentimentality of lyric seemed to prove a very potent combination for country fans as this was a huge hit for Tammy Wynette and remains a 'classic' of the genre. That little cry or catch in the voice has remained an important part of country style – it lends an immediate (if, again, theatrical) sense of heartbreak to the listener.

The effort level is relatively low – both perceived and true. This is another factor which prevents us from experiencing the song as something raw or direct, and in that sense Wynette differs here from many country artists, who tend to prefer the exact middle ground when it comes to effort level: neither low nor extremely high. This middle-ground effort level is a consistent trait of country and one that strongly distinguishes it from blues and gospel. Nearly every complementary element of style can be used by the country singer to create an emotional effect, but that emotion doesn't seem to spring from raw unmediated energy. For example, *Hey Good Lookin'* is a relatively high effort for a country song, yet compared to most gospel or blues numbers, it's a low-key affair.

There would be any number of ways to read the effects of the low or middling effort coupled with high emotion in country classics, like Dolly Parton's version of *I Will Always Love You* (where the effort level itself does much to distinguish her version from Whitney Houston's soaring, massive effort on the same song), but for me they generally add up to a kind of unabashed vulnerability. Unlike the kind of pain or vulnerability of the blues singer, country singers don't always convince me that they're going to make it through this latest crisis. In this context, pain and suffering can become epic – even noble. Of course, not all country songs are about suffering, but the upbeat country sound often has far fewer distinguishing stylistic elements than the tear-soaked country ballad, which is why, I think, so many of the most memorable country songs are the ballads.

We're at the point, of course, where response to stylistic choices remains stubbornly subjective. Your response to these songs may be completely different, or perhaps, like me, country music wouldn't ordinarily be your first choice when listening to music, but there is much to learn from the boldness of such artists and the greatest challenge for any vocalist is to make their choices well – the more you have to choose from, the greater the possibilities.

Miranda Lambert, *Mama's Broken Heart* (2013)

This is a terrifically quirky song about a mother's tough-love advice on heartbreak. Lambert does a roaring trade with songs about women who are just slightly unhinged, as *Crazy Ex-Girlfriend* and *Gunpowder and Lead* will attest. From the heaved sigh at the very start of the track you can sense Lambert's lack of patience with her mother's utilitarian and unsympathetic directions about how to handle being dumped: 'Go and fix your make-up, girl, it's just a break up'. Lambert's twangy little sound, with nice mid-phrase note bends and flip finishes against an insistent if fairly thin backing track, gives this just the defiant sound she wants as she argues that this is her own heartbreak and not her mother's. She manages that defiance with a low effort level throughout the song, and that is the result of her refusal to make this performance pretty. She doesn't hold a note and her diction is incredibly clean – you get every word. It's a catchy hook that stays in your head long after you have listened to it, and as 'pop country', the whole affair would sink under a heavier vocal sound. Lambert seems to know just how to balance humour with melodrama and this recording is a great example of that. It also demonstrates so well the way that country songs give singers a lot of scope for story and character in their work – we can almost see her mama.

Blake Shelton, *Who Are You When I'm Not Looking*, (2010)

Shelton was born in Oklahoma and moved to Nashville as a teenager to pursue his music, yet for all that his brand of country has a distinctly pop sound, and he uses the easiest elements of country sound: mid-level effort, a nice vocal tone, a lot of creak sound, a comfortable nasal twang and a lot of slow upward note bend. It all adds up to an honest 'Southern gentleman' sound that works for this song about a man who is thinking that the beautiful woman he loves is just too good to be true. He's careful about the effort level because the sound he wants to create here is a conversational one. He's also careful about the sustain – it's enough to give the song a 'sung' sound but he keeps the length fairly minimal. Where he holds the ends of a line ('I want to know' on the chorus) he's careful to fade without vibrato so that the line sort of melts away but doesn't sound self-consciously sung or pretty. Shelton quite neatly sums up here the middle-of-the-road, comfortable country sound that traces its line through artists like Charlie Rich and Ray Price. It's fairly bland stuff that doesn't confront or surprise, and it doesn't tell much of a story. It's a simple, straightforward country love song and Shelton isn't a great country artist but he's certainly a commercially successful one.

Summary

Country music in its early phase was not a crossover genre. The rare crossover hits were the exception that proved the rule. These days, of course, it can sometimes be quite a challenge to distinguish country singers from pop singers, since there has been such a great fusion within the sound, but overall, the strong stylistic tendencies of its early days remain influential in country music still, and if you're interested in exploring this style, find a song that you feel real affinity for (preferably one with a good story!) and then work through it, observing the following common country singing characteristics:

1. A heavy reliance on heavier vocal qualities (belt, twang, neutral thick fold), although these qualities are generally employed in a middle-range effort level rather than a high effort level (which, if used, would probably result in a rock sound).

2 A tendency towards very even phrase weighting and placement – syncopation or improvisation is rare in this style.

3 There tends to be very little variation of vocal quality in country, so keep your vocal quality consistent. The majority of songs are sung in neutral thick fold with a middling effort, and although belt is used, it is rarely a high-effort-level belt.

4 Most country songs have a very strong, 'sung' sound – long sustains are common, as is vibrato, although it is often combined with a compressed finish rather than a fade (which would make the sound more refined and less gutsy). Country singers don't always attempt to 'sweeten' the sound.

5 There isn't a lot of play in dynamics or sung volume levels – songs don't tend to build to a high point or go from a scream to a whisper. It's a very consistent style in terms of both tone and effort all the way through a song.

6 There is limited use of the different elements of style. Onsets tend to be the most varied part of the country sound but even here there is not a wide variation. Stick to fairly hard glottals and simultaneous onsets (coming in right on the beat of course!) and flip or creak.

7 Even contemporary country singers still tend to sing with a heavy Southern American accent, which gives a natural upward bend in the note attack and a rather twangy sound, even when in neutral thick fold.

8 Songs tend to be delivered with a kind of melodramatic intensity, so you need to make sure that you've chosen a song with lyrics that you can put real feeling behind.

COUNTRY – FURTHER LISTENING

Tim McGraw: *Live Like You Were Dying* (2004). McGraw isn't a particularly remarkable singer, but he has that perfectly honest sound that country rewards. This is a smart song because it speaks to all the country preoccupations: the melodrama of a man dying and a sentimental list of good things to do before you go. There aren't a lot of style elements here – the story is the driving force of the song. He employs some gentle country-style note bends, but this track reminds me of the way that pop country relies a lot on arrangement and instrumentation to distinguish its genre. If McGraw sang this to a solo piano, it might simply sound like a cabaret or musical theatre song.

Dwight Yoakam: *Guitars, Cadillacs* (1986). This is a surprisingly 'old school' sound for a song that was a hit in 1986. The overly twangy guitar opening (clearly reflecting the lyric), slide solo and 'old-timey' fiddle seem to be employed in a sort of postmodern way here, but Yoakam is an interesting artist whose diverse influences (rock and pop) can be seen throughout his work. His gentle flip-and-twang style matches the overall production well. This song is both a tribute and a parody of the Nashville scene and the lyrics about guitars, Cadillacs and hillbilly music being the only thing that keeps him holding on after having his heart shattered by the woman he's singing to are pure country hokum.

Loretta Lynn: *You Ain't Woman Enough* (1991). This is one of Lynn's biggest hits and she has such a naturally powerful voice, that you can feel how tough it is for her to stay in the mid-range dynamic that country style demands. She manages it, though – if largely through just keeping her sustains really short and compressing all her finishes. She tells a great story of a woman who refuses to relinquish her man. She personifies the artless, straightforward country storytelling style.

Willie Nelson: *Blue Eyes Crying in the Rain* (1975). Nelson has a homely sort of voice that has warmth despite its nasality. This low-tech production makes the most of what I think Nelson does best: simple, honest melodies with a no-frills production. Nelson's vocal sound, like many of the earliest country artists, is incredibly simple and doggedly 'unschooled'.

Rock

It could be said that in many ways rock 'n' roll began when the hard distinctions between black and white music began to dissolve. That doesn't mean that the segregated market didn't continue as it does now, but it does mean that the early rock artists were happy to blend blues, country and hillbilly styles to form a high-energy fusion sound (often referred to early on as jump blues) that revolutionized the music industry. Of all the styles we've looked at so far, rock is the most difficult to categorize because it *is* such a fusion. It's also probably the most impossible to prescribe practice for (I will not even try!) because historically, it isn't so much a form as an energy. It takes the rawness of blues, the playfulness of jazz, the melodrama of country and extreme high energy of gospel and then sort of explodes over a highly amplified musical backing. What made it so distinct, despite the fact that it is a genuinely derivative form, is most apparent in the very early works, so I'll start with a few of the classics before going on to look at more contemporary works.

Elvis Presley, *Don't Be Cruel* and *Heartbreak Hotel* (1956)

Situated at the perfect junction between blues, hillbilly and country music, the overall energy and drive of Elvis's music lifted it stylistically away from anything that had gone on before his first recordings and appearances. Because he was white and because he was working in a guitar/bass musical accompaniment, Presley was initially marketed as a country singer. One of his very first appearances was on the Grand Ole Opry, where he sang *Blue Moon of Kentucky*, but like so many white Southern artists of his time, he'd spent much time listening to and being influenced by black blues artists:

> I'd play along with the radio or phonograph. We were a religious family going around to sing together at camp meetings

> and revivals, and I'd take my guitar with us when I could. I also dug the real low-down Mississippi singers, mostly Big Bill Broonzy and [Arthur] Big Boy Crudup, although they would scold me at home for listening to them.[10]

He had even attended a local black Baptist church where he was no doubt influenced by gospel music. Given these influences, he represented a challenge for DJs and marketing people alike. At the first sign of success with *That's All Right*, Sam Phillips (legendary owner of Sun Records, where Elvis recorded his first works) recalled the problems of having found such a unique artist, when one disc jockey told him that Presley 'was so country he shouldn't be played after 5 a.m.' while the country DJs 'said he was too black for them'.[11] Phillips quickly arranged a radio interview with his young singer, and the DJ asking the questions made sure that he worked in a question that would allow Elvis to state that he had attended the whites-only Humes High School, just so that the listeners would be in no doubt about his racial identity.

But his voice was particularly flexible and unique, and when you go back to listen to some of his early classics, it's clear why he was such a compelling mystery. Although white artists covering songs by black artists was nothing new at this time, the difficulty in classifying his sound, and the extraordinary playfulness in his vocal approach (along with the bizarre nervous tics of his early stage performances which he learnt to exaggerate to induce squeals from delighted audiences), made him stand out as a pioneer of a new kind of music.

In a piece like *Don't Be Cruel* you can hear that he's fearlessly exploring – and there's so much going on. His confidence has grown in the years between the early Sun recordings and

---

[10]Elvis Presley, quoted in Peter Guralnick, *Feel Like Going Home* (Edinburgh: Canongate Publishers, 2003), p. 172/3.
[11]Guralnick, *Feel like Going Home*, p. 173.

these two tracks, and he's really come into what is so unique and exciting in his sound. There's a definite percussive edge to the note delivery and attack. His diction ranges wildly from clean and crisp to a strange sort of contrived slur. He employs a whole range of onsets here from hard glottal to flip to aspirate. His finishes are extreme compressions, which gives the track a wonderful percussive rather than 'sung' sound in the delivery. There's no flow at all to the line – he leaves that to the Jordanaires, who 'bop-bop' or croon away in the background. This highly clipped delivery feels very much as if it all happens in the throat – he's glottal stopping all the way to keep that extreme compression jumpy and alive, and sometimes adds a quick catch in the throat that sounds rather like a very compressed flip.

His improvs are strange affairs, mostly a few oddly negotiated sliding up-and-down sounds at the beginning of phrases. He uses audible breath and a few aspirate finishes to give this a slight sense of high effort although the true-effort level is rather middling. He stays in neutral thick fold with only occasional jumps up into a single note in thin fold or the occasional exaggerated cry quality in places like the repeat 'thinking of' lyric. He uses a bit of fluttery vibrato just occasionally, which lends a little vulnerability to an otherwise very upbeat, edgy delivery, and his phrase weight is very even here as he works against the tightly rhythmic backing in the verses.

Heartbreak Hotel is still more extraordinary in the range of stylistic elements he employs. Although it is a ballad, he's so bold in his exploration that it stands well away from the straighter and duller ballad sounds he settled down with once his career was more advanced. There is more sustain and vibrato here, as you would expect with a ballad, but the vibrato is fast and fluttery which lends a sense of pain and vulnerability to sound. The sheer number of vocal quality changes and stylistic flourishes lend the song a high perceived-effort level. He throws the energy heavily at the top of each verse and then, as he lets the clean diction and attack melt into a cry quality towards the finish of the verse (on the 'so lonely') that suggests a kind of emotional breakdown. Presley was a master of using the cry quality to great effect and he combines it here with creak, aspiration and percussion to give it real power. That sound itself is then further subverted by the playful and percussive sounds in the chorus that recall the defiance of the best of blues ebullience.

Because there is such a lot of stylistic exploration and vocal quality change going on, the dynamics of the song vary wildly from the high-energy twang of the verse openings to the mumbled play of the choruses. His approach is highly theatrical, but convincing for all that. Because of the spontaneous feel of the piece and the outrageous vocal choices he's making, this song never descends into camp but instead feels honest and raw – just right for a rock ballad. He could not have lent these recordings such style had he not had great energy and courage in exploring – that energy and courage, along with a kind of defiance in the face of what might constitute 'legitimate' singing is what gives rock vocal its definition.

Little Richard, *Tutti Frutti* (1956)

The story of this recording is legend: Little Richard, whose stage persona was incredibly flamboyant and energetic, found himself completely unable to bring these qualities into the recording studio, where he was working on a dull slow ballad called *Lonesome and Blue*. Disillusioned, both producer and artist took a break and during lunch at a local club, Little Richard jumped up on the bandstand and began singing one of his more outrageous live concert songs. The original lyrics were far too racy to record so they were rewritten in an afternoon by a local songwriter and they went back into the studio to record *Tutti Frutti*. The track sums up so much of why he was and remains an extraordinary influence in the rock vocal sound. He was heavily influenced by artists like

Louis Jordan and Ruth Brown, particularly in terms of energy and that massively pushed release sound that occurs so often in tracks like *Tutti Frutti*.

Perhaps the greatest distinction of his sound is the energy. No matter what he's doing, the perceived-effort level is always incredibly high. There's absolutely nothing that he does that a voice teacher would approve of. There's no trace of 'good' singing here: it's pure raw energy and joy. In the early verses, he's simple – he keeps the sustains short and uses mostly a constricted voice quality to achieve the sound of raw energy. This kind of rumbled sound, while similar to Louis Armstrong's, did not have the same permanent quality as Armstrong's voice. With Richard, it was clear that this constricted sound was a choice and if you listen to other tracks recorded in the same year (e.g. *Slippin' and Slidin'*) you can hear that when he chooses to sing without it, he has a warm sandy tone similar to Sam Cooke's.

He weights both the opening and finishes of his phrases, although not consistently. He often simply doesn't really bother to complete some phrases and he employs almost no sustain. He compresses finishes without falling off the note and indeed will often push the note ending up with great energy and volume. Where a gospel release often ends with a hard exhalation of air, Little Richard pushes that exhalation into a high short scream. It's an extraordinary sound that seems to suggest that nothing can really contain his energy as it spills out far beyond the end of the phrase. His improvs tend to be through a highly energized 'whooo' falsetto sound – a sound that many subsequent rock singers employed. He didn't bring much more than raw unmediated energy to market but that alone made him highly distinct from the 'pop' male vocalists of the day like Pat Boone. His refusal to follow the rules in singing style influenced a great many artists to come, from James Brown and Otis Redding to Paul McCartney, whose work in many places emulated Little Richard's kind of 'primal scream' sound.

The Beatles, *Don't Let Me Down* (1969, remastered 2003)

Great rock ballads are hard to find. This is because the vocalist needs to find a balance between the raw passion of the rock form and the kind of natural tendency to sweeten vocal sound in a slower tempo. *Don't Let Me Down* manages that balance brilliantly I think, because it never surrenders its defiant sound. This is a track with a fascinating history and it gives us a lot of scope to explore the relationship between vocal sound and recording techniques. Written by John Lennon and sung by Lennon and McCartney, this rock ballad was said to be a kind of angst-ridden love song to Yoko Ono, penned by Lennon. Tensions within the band were high at the end of the 1960s and the *Let It Be* album went through some strange revisions. Both George Martin and Glyn Johns worked as producers at various points, and when things got particularly difficult, Phil Spector was brought in to do a final mix/master/producing job. Years later, McCartney, who was never pleased with Spector's symphonic rendering of *The Long and Winding Road*, re-released the work in a *Let it Be . . . Naked* version, which was essentially a collection of the pre-Spector sessions, mastered for CD rather than vinyl, and released in 2003. According to McCartney, the original intention of the album was to return to their earlier rock sound, and presumably Spector's orchestral reworking took the album some distance from that original intention.

I want to start by listening to the isolated vocal track (which you can find here: http://www.youtube.com/watch?v=X_1b0nZONes). I stumbled across this quite by accident when looking for something else and I was struck by a few things. The first is the incredible power, intensity and rawness of this performance, both from Lennon and McCartney. The track features growling, raspy, and rather flat sounds from Lennon, and a raw power in high range from McCartney. In the film version performance, George Harrison also sings on the 'don't let me down' line, but here Lennon carries that solo in the beginning. In the tradition of great rock singing, there is no attempt to beautify the sound. Particularly in the chorus sections, the whole thing grows wilder as the track progresses with McCartney on some spectacular 'soprano' riffs towards the end. There's a bit of sustain in the finish in the first verse, but once we get to the power of 'don't let me down', it's all compressions and falling off the note. The phrases are heavily weighted towards the front and Lennon is particularly given to falling away from a phrase. There's something incredibly 'unsung' from him in the 'she done me good' verse. McCartney twiddles about in thin-fold upper range towards the end in a really effective counterpoint to Lennon's hard-glottal-onset 'ow' screams, and the overall honesty of the track achieves just what a great rock vocal performance always does: a strong level of belief in the listener and a sense that the vocalist is happily exposing raw-nerve emotion in the service of their art.

The striking thing, for me, was that I remembered the full original 1969/70 track from the *Let it Be* album and didn't recall that the track had the raw kind of rock power ballad feel that these isolated vocals had. (You can find the original here: http://www.youtube.com/watch?v=EB9tqgdCt5I.) It's quite a subdued affair in comparison with the 'isolated vocal' version. That's partly because in this early Spector mix there's more of a 'reverb blend', which dampens the vocal sound considerably and makes the bass, cymbals and keyboard feel as if they sit quite high in the mix. The tempo is also appreciably slower here than in the isolated version. I think this is why, in its early form, I never quite appreciated the edgy power that Lennon and McCartney actually achieved here.

In the *Let it Be . . . Naked* version, the dampening effect of the reverb is lifted considerably and the tempo is a bit faster. (You can find it here: http://www.youtube.com/watch?v=K0IT-PxONNw&list=PL9D5407132C3EA699 at about the 21:40 mark). The vocal sound is much higher in the mix here and retains much more of the brutal energy you can hear on the isolated track. It's fascinating to compare the tracks and it became very clear to me in doing so just why McCartney wanted to release this 'naked' version so many years later.

Jon Bon Jovi, *Livin' on a Prayer* (1986)

This is another isolated track analysis (you can find it here: http://www.youtube.com/watch?v=dYA6SwQholI). While I realize that YouTube doesn't offer the finest sound quality for us, it does have an amazing range of isolated vocal performances; when it comes to rock style, this is really useful. Rock is a bit like the old big bands where vocal performance is concerned, in that the voice is only one of many big sounds that make up the experience and that means a vocalist can get a bit overwhelmed by the force of the instrumental backing sometimes. Where the old big band singers solved this largely by sticking to sweeter, straighter amplified sounds, and working in a subtle way around the ground beat, rock vocalists tend to take on the band in a bold fight to the finish where energy and volume are concerned, and that makes the isolated track analysis so useful for us. It gives us the chance to really hear the passion and brilliance of Jon Bon Jovi's performance on this rock classic, without the distraction of the band.

The energy it takes to fashion a performance like this is very evident in the listening here, and what is also evident is that Bon Jovi's sustained constriction in many areas of the song are a choice. In other words, we're not hearing a damaged voice – we're hearing a very hardy vocal instrument that has learnt how to work constriction to his advantage. As ever, I worry about endorsing this because many singing teachers would be aghast at the sounds Bon Jovi makes, but what makes it clear that this is his choice is the difference you can hear in a phrase like 'Baby it's okay / someday' (around the 1:49 mark), where you can hear that as he goes up into the 'okay' he loses the fully constricted sound and just belts at high chest end, following with an aspirate sound on 'someday'. Through much of this you can hear that the overall scratchy, constricted sound is largely the effect of the energy he comes in with and that he uses it most often on short phrases, in the lower part of the range where, presumably, the constriction isn't as difficult to sustain. As the tune goes higher 'oh-oh, living on a prayer', the sound gets cleaner and the 'livin' on a prayer' at the high end (near the 2:35 mark) is remarkably 'clean' and clear.

Once he kicks into really high gear after the long solo silence, it's really fascinating to hear so closely the blend of scratch/constricted sounds and clean/clear sound that he uses. Because the belt is so powerful, whichever way he uses it, it has massive emotional power. Of course, not all singers can sustain this kind of hard usage and Bon Jovi himself didn't always work this hard, but he's still recording and he still sounds strong. You can hear that in his latest album, *What About Now* (2013). He doesn't exploit that high range much, and his sound has definitely mellowed, but he's still rocking and the voice is still in good shape.

Arctic Monkeys, *I Bet You Look Good on the Dance Floor* (2005)

Alex Turner has a voice that feels as if it's come through a straight line that originated in John Lennon's sound, took a quick detour through Oasis and exploded into this extraordinary indie track that seemed to redefine the whole rock landscape when it emerged. This track works well in context and wouldn't reward an 'isolated vocal' listening the way others do. Turner makes the most of a speech quality delivery that manages to do something fairly rare in rock style: to really highlight the lyric. The song is the product of Turner's lively intelligence and his references to Duran Duran, Shakespeare and Orwell are just too much fun to miss, especially as it all adds up to a kind of hopelessly inept attempt to pull on the dance floor and manages to undercut the driving confidence of the guitars with a massive whack of teen nerdiness and desire.

Rather like Lennon, Turner has a slightly nasal sound, but rarely ever comes out of a straight speech-quality tone. His diction is fairly clean and on the whole there's little vocal quality change. As the track progresses his breath becomes much more audible (you can really hear the gasp just before he heads for the final 'I'll bet that you look good on the dance floor'), and as he gears up into the finish, while all his finishes are compressed, the finishes in the final four lines of the songs almost feel pushed as he throws energy into the delivery. There's just the hint of creak compression in the final '1984s' and in the very last line there's a small amount of constriction in the final 'from 1984'. The track has such drive and the gun-shot drums move the whole thing at a pace that doesn't allow a singer much time or breath, so it isn't surprising that the choices here are limited, but what is surprising is the strength of the diction and how clearly the lyric stands out against everything else happening in the track. Turner doesn't bother with being beautiful as a singer but you really sense that he values the story he has to tell here.

Judas Priest, *Metal Gods* (1980, remastered 2001) and *Painkiller* (1990)

I confess to a real love of heavy metal – it's honest and unapologetic and reminds me of a lot of hot, sweaty summers in a garage in Southern California, screaming away with musicians of dubious quality. It will probably always be a big part of the soundtrack of my youth and I'm sure (I hope!) I'm not alone. This is a typical sound for the metal form of rock – heavy, buzzy repetitive guitar riffs against a relentlessly straightforward bass and drum background. If one wanted to make a real argument about rock being the musical form of Modernism, I think heavy metal rock would be Exhibit A. In so many ways, its purpose is to disrupt our expectations, to shock us, to defy anything aesthetic, safe or 'beautiful' and simply to push music to its limits in terms of expression.

Rob Halford's voice is a bit of a wonder – not so much for its work on *Metal Gods*, which (with a few exceptions) isn't particularly impressive in terms of range, but more so for its longevity. Halford started recording in the 1970s and he's still going strong. His remarkable range has inspired many people and if you have the patience, there's a whole segment on YouTube that is incredibly detailed and includes many, many clips of Halford's voice doing remarkable things.[12] He has extraordinary power in his upper range and is absolutely fearless about using it with an amazing amount of sustained constriction. If you want to do a close study of his sound at the upper end, you might want to listen to the sometimes isolated vocal on *Painkiller* here, which doesn't start until about 30 seconds in and also includes a long guitar solo midway through: http://www.youtube.com/watch?v=FhH7wFpcqvI. But when Halford lets loose, the guitars drop out and you can get a real sense of the kind of visceral passion he has. The best part is hearing him make a quick but very obvious transition out of the constricted metal vocal sound on this track at 5:43 and hold a long, clear note for a full 20 seconds that reminds you of just what a beautiful voice he has when he chooses to use it in this way.

In *Metal Gods* he uses a lot of belt, constriction and scratch and most of his finishes are compressed or falling. There's little use of vibrato here, and little change of voice quality, although there are surprising moments such as a quick drop into a very legit and clean-sounding belt with vibrato on 'knowing we'd be found'. It's almost as if Halford wants to remind us that he could sing this song 'beautifully' if he wanted to, but the overall lyric about a machine takeover of the world and the loss of the 'human' is too critical to really sing about. So instead, we get the sound of metal everywhere – from the heavy guitars, to the crunching sounds that finish the track – and all of it is matched beautifully by the rather robotic and metallic sound

[12]You can find this at: http://www.youtube.com/watch?v=z8Xz9WFOt4c, and there are copious notes on his range posted along with this compilation video.

of Halford's passionate and urgent sound. He doesn't pull the phrase around at all; the delivery is very even and right on the beat. He doesn't really play with the weight of the phrase; each line feels evenly weighted, with great energy on the attack and great energy in the finish. Overall the sound paints a kind of scary vision of the dystopian machine-ruled future that he's warning us about – Halford's singing is self-consciously robotic here.

Summary

Rock, like blues, is a style that doesn't reward a 'sung' sound. It needs a more immediate, straight-from-the-heart kind of sound that may come in a whisper or may come in a scream, but however it is delivered we want to be absolutely certain that the singer is holding nothing back. Because of this, we're not primarily concerned with the beauty of tone, although a great number of good rock singers like Freddie Mercury or Bono happen to have great tone as well as passion.

Rock singers rarely work without a heavily amplified and percussive accompaniment, so it can be quite difficult to attempt practice in this style without a band working alongside you, but if you can find some backing tracks and blast them on high volume, you'll have something to use as you start working through the most common elements of rock style, which are:

1. Predominantly thick-fold vocal qualities: neutral thick fold, belt or twang. Changes from one vocal quality to another tend to be abrupt rather than 'artfully' negotiated.
2. Voice quality changes are often kept to a minimum.
3. Consistently high effort level in the performance, both true and perceived.
4. Sustains or fades of any kind are relatively uncommon – most finishes are compressed, falling or variations on pushed or gospel releases.

5 A wide variety of onsets is employed, although the high-effort onsets – flip, glottal, constricted or rumbled onsets – are most common.

6 A fearless exploration of sound in performance, which frequently means the use of some constricted or 'dangerous' qualities that, by sheer effort, convince us of the singer's raw passion and energy.

This last element is, of course, negotiable by the singer; as we've noted, many voices can sustain very little use of these 'dangerous' qualities, but the first five common elements of this style will certainly see you through if you couple them with a great passion for whatever song you're singing – that will be really important when you're trying to find the abandon needed for this style.

FURTHER LISTENING – ROCK

Chris Cornell: *Billie Jean* (2007). This is a remarkable cover of the Michael Jackson classic, reinvented as a bluesy rock ballad that really makes you hear the torment of the song anew. Cornell brings great passion to his tortured denial of 'the kid'. You can hear that Cornell occasionally allows a bit of vibrato here on the sustains, but he compresses his finishes neatly, with the volume turned right up to the end. Working through thick fold, belt and the high effort level this isn't beautiful – it's too important for that.

Rolling Stones: *Down the Road Apiece* (1965). This is a superb version (by way of Chuck Berry) of Don Raye's 'roadside boogie' done by a particularly perceptive young white English singer who did manage to go on to greater things. The early Rolling Stone tracks are always so amazing to revisit, not only for the excitement of the sound (which still jumps out at you some 50 years later) but also for the way that Jagger so completely embraced the sound and style of a music happening thousands of miles away from him. Jagger never does anything in a 'singerly' way – the tone is a thin, twangy belt. He generally falls off a note and he knows just when to add a bit of grit/scratch to give the right, rough texture to the whole thing.

(*Continued*)

FURTHER LISTENING – ROCK (CONTINUED)

Deap Vally: *Baby I Call Hell* (2013). Rock needs more women singers and here Lindsey Troy shows exactly why. Right from the start she begins with incredible energy, and the twang/belt sound combined with a bit of constriction and some extreme pushed finishes work so well against the fuzzy guitar riffs. She's really brave about exploring sound and the lyric is pure anti-romance. The whole thing is defiant and anthemic, just the way a good rock song should be. She's a real master of the pushed or flip offset and you can hear this in *Walk of Shame* (http://www.youtube.com/watch?v=D6FVh0e1qns).

Nirvana: *Where Did You Sleep Last Night* (1993: this is the 'unplugged' version, which you can find here: https://www.youtube.com/watch?v=9pb8iLS18wo). You might wonder, when you start listening to Cobain's version of this traditional folk song, why I've classified this as a rock ballad – particularly when the song is most associated with celebrated blues singer, Huddie Ledbetter, who recorded it seven times. Cobain starts with a kind of quiet, almost folky feel, but as the track progresses he kicks the whole thing up with a most extraordinary intensity. Extremely high effort level, constriction, compressed and pushed finishes move this into pure rock territory and give the song a kind of dangerous and very unnerving feel.

Pop

Pop: a genre of popular music which originated in its modern form in the 1950s, deriving from rock and roll . . . the main goal is usually that of being pleasurable to listen to, rather than having much artistic value . . .[13]

---

[13]Definition, courtesy of Wikipedia: http://www.en.wikipedia.org/wiki/Pop_music

Because we've looked at some very early examples of style in popular music, it seems logical to conclude with a look at contemporary pop, which is a fusion of all these styles, but if it is difficult to define jazz or blues, it is that much more difficult to define pop. As we can see in the definition of pop above, it has come to stand as a genre in its own right but of course its borders are hotly contested. This is the one style I feel I don't need to add a 'further listening' section to, since most of what we hear on a daily basis falls into the pop category.

There is a tendency to think of pop singers as bland and a bit disposable – great voices are rarely thought of as pop voices. There's nothing wrong at all with Madonna's voice or Jennifer Lopez's, but you wouldn't mistake them for Tina Turner or Amy Winehouse. In fact, great voices don't make particularly good pop singers, as Barbra Streisand neatly proved in her few unsuccessful forays into pop music. That might be because good pop music is really usually much more about the song than it is about the singer. This is also why so many pop singers come and go quickly. The rare few who do sustain a career have to work extremely hard to bring the focus onto themselves as performing personalities.

This was, of course, the great irony of a show like 'Pop Idol' – most 'idols' in music have not been pop singers – Elvis Presley was many things but he was not a pop singer. Otis Redding, Mick Jagger, Bruce Springsteen or James Brown all took their influences from a variety of sources, but in the end you wouldn't call any of them pop singers.

Great pop songs, on the other hand, tend to have real staying power. The whole purpose of the pop song is to be memorable, not generally for great/profound lyrics or complex, compelling harmonic structure (although some do achieve this), but in much simpler terms; their repetitive structure and accessible tunes get stuck in your head. The best pop songs produced by pop writing teams like Stock, Aitken and Waterman would not be well served by a great singer – an outstanding voice would obstruct the song's ability to get right inside your head. Consequently, the simple melody/lyric line and Kylie

Minogue's light, easy voice singing about being so lucky, lucky, lucky was just the right combination. In an earlier era of pop singing, Burt Bacharach and Hal David found a similar muse in Dionne Warwick, whose easy musicality combined with a low perceived-effort level proved just right for getting a pop song like *Do You Know the Way to San Jose* or *I'll Never Fall in Love Again* 'hooked' into our memories.

Pop draws on all styles and presents them in a 'lite' version. This is only possible when singing voice and material are themselves lightweight. That doesn't mean unskilled; whatever else one might think of Stock, Aitken and Waterman or Kylie Minogue, they are highly skilled practitioners. You can feel that the songs are carefully crafted and there is usually skill involved in the singing. We are concerned with 'craft' when it comes to pop, and it is not a category that rewards raw honesty or lack of 'art'.

But when both song and voice are remarkable, we're usually out of the pop category, no matter how much mass appeal a recording may have. Perhaps considering the career of a group like the Beach Boys makes this point. In their early 'Surf 'n' Hot Rod' recordings, the sound of their traditional close harmonies and easy, swooping melodies made great pop music – it had an emotional appeal which was charming and shallow, and the easy vocal sound allowed us to focus on the catchy fantasy tunes about being a teenager in Southern California. But as the writing and the lyrics grew more profound, and as the voices and the productions grew more complex and sophisticated they became almost unclassifiable. Songs like *Surf's Up* challenged all the work that they'd done in their first decade and came, for many, to signify a loss of the innocence that had infused their early pop sound. Suddenly, Beach Boy or not, Brian Wilson was in the more challenging territory of musical modernism.

Pop music has a long history, of course, so even our responses to it have to be seen in historical contexts. I am aware that a lot of singers see pop music as a genre that appeals to the pre-teen or young teenage market and many singers actively dislike the whole commercial pop genre and want to find ways to distinguish their sound from it. But whatever you think of pop in its most commercial form, from my point of view it is probably the hardest style of all to teach.

I think there are a number of reasons for this but high on the list would be the amount of skill and ease a singer has to have to do it successfully. From the vocal point of view in many ways pop is closer to jazz than it is to rock. It has a kind of 'swing', but it isn't the highly sophisticated rhythmic thing that swing can sometimes be in jazz. It certainly requires that a singer know how to move around a ground beat comfortably, to improvise with ease (even though not necessarily with great extension), to have extremely good pitch, to be able to shape a phrase so that it has a certain flexibility and sinuousness to it, to understand melodic line but not to get caught up in singing it too 'straight', to understand the fundamentals of producing a good tone (in that traditional aesthetic sense) but not to sound schooled, to have an easy command of a number of elements of style and to be able to employ most of them effortlessly. In other words, it's extremely demanding but must be perceived as effortless. And while there are many things about this that can be taught, some things are quite difficult.

Even trying to articulate what I mean when I say above that the shape of a phrase needs to have 'a certain sinuousness to it' makes me aware of the paucity of language in trying to describe musical effect at times, but most people who have ever tried to sing/learn/teach pop music from sheet music will know exactly what I mean. Sometimes that flexibility or sinuousness comes from the build of a creak or aspirate onset into a full vocal quality with a light bend that glides effortless into the next note and melts into an aspirate finish that falls with a light downward bend – pop style often has a lot of dynamic variation within a phrase. Sometimes it's about the way in which small melodic additions or grace notes are negotiated with some mild swing that makes the singer's glide between the notes feel just that slight bit uneven and gives the little melodic lift some elegance. Sometimes it's about negotiating voice quality changes with craft and ease and other times it's about making those 'gear changes' abruptly, as part of the overall effort picture. All this can make it very difficult to help the young singer who has been practising in choral music or on musical theatre numbers with a voice teacher all their lives suddenly understand how to make a song like Daniel Powter's *Bad Day* or Natasha Bedingfield's *Unwritten* really come alive vocally.

Pat Boone, *Tutti Frutti* (1956)

It's almost cruel to resurrect this track, although there's a kind of compelling awfulness to it. I don't think I'm out of line in suggesting that this record probably marks the moment when pop as a genre was born. Boone's cover was the record company's attempt to score a hit with a 'race record' and as such it thoroughly personifies the pop tendency to render a 'lite' version of other genres. The quick cover version by white artists of a hit 'race record' was standard practice in the early 1950s and many black artists like Big Joe Turner (*Rock Around the Clock*) were sadly trumped in the money stakes by blander white artists like Bill Haley.

Pat Boone was often called upon to record cover versions of hit 'race records', and along with *Tutti Frutti* he had hits with a number of other songs originally sung by black artists, including Fats Domino's *Ain't That a Shame*, Ivory Joe Hunter's *I Almost Lost My Mind*, and Big Joe Turner's *Chains of Love*. Boone's remakes of these great songs aren't really even R&B or rock 'lite' – they are just 'lite'. I've included it, however, because I think it not only has some historical interest in terms of vocal style, it is also particularly demonstrative of what kind of terrible consequences follow when an artist just can't adapt their style to their material. But be warned: it's awful!

Where Little Richard's original recording was an inspired piece of impassioned expression, this production relies on the bland sound of Pat Boone's voice, which gives us time to focus on the song itself. This turns out to be a high-risk strategy in the case of *Tutti Frutti*, because the song is not strong enough to stand on its own. The lyrics are insipid unless delivered with a great energy and a sexually charged innuendo.

It's hard not to feel that Boone is a bit embarrassed at being caught so spectacularly off his usual middle-of-the-road pop ballad turf. He is incapable of approaching the song with the kind of explosive energy that made Little Richard's version so memorable. Boone does not make any attempt to alter his usual style apart from trying to compress his finishes and stick rigidly to a kind of speech voice quality. On the occasional 'whoo' sounds he is so uncomfortable with the improv that he misses his pitch every time. If you listen to Boone in his natural milieu (easy listening pop ballads like *April Love*) you can actually admire his kind of smoothness. He always employs a very 'sung' sound – it's as pleasant as can be, if never remarkable at all. He swings easily between neutral thick- and thin-fold sounds, never working outside of the low-effort-level range. He usually exhibits a kind of bland fluidity, but *Tutti Frutti* just baffles him completely and the listening experience is an embarrassing one – a bit like hearing your granny try an Eminem cover.

Britney Spears, *Toxic* (2004) and Gwen Stefani, *What You Waiting For?* (2004)

Pop seems to break down into a number of categories, but to my ear the most distinguishable are the pop dance and pop ballad. These two tracks are both good examples of the really modern twist on pop dance sound – a sound that probably had its beginnings in Little Eva's *Locomotion* or Chubby Checker's *The Twist*. Pop dance songs usually rely more on instrumental 'hooks' or unusual production than on sung hooks. With *Locomotion* it was the driving saxophone line and with *The Twist* it was the repetitive 'around and around' chorus and the great dance groove of the track. You can hear that as a postmodern version of this kind of pop, *Toxic*, while wearing all manner of 'street-cred' style elements, is nevertheless a no-holds-barred big pop production that sells an instrumental hook in the strings line. It's so overproduced that Britney (and indeed the melody) barely gets a look in. When she does sing, there's not a lot of room for her, she's almost crowded out by that string line and a heavy synth bass sound, so she really makes the best of her opportunities. She runs through a lot stylistically and although there's really no chance for her to stray from the melody at all, she works hard to give all the phrases some shape and interest with distinctive onsets and mild bends in note attacks mid-phrase. With few exceptions (opening verse), the voice has been recorded many times over and fed through electronic filters and when she does sing she wisely keeps it very simple although she provides variation in the effort level throughout.

She begins in a kind of twangy thin fold with both voiced and unvoiced creak onsets. She follows with a thin-fold/aspirate mix and then waits until the 'toxic' chorus to really come into the voice, and in these sections alone do we really hear a nice neutral thick-fold sound. She switches with ease between these thin- and thick-fold qualities and she has great ease in the really high note sounds that come in about midway, but we never get any high-effort-level qualities. The high effort we hear comes entirely from the instrumental track. We get many different sounds from her, which makes the vocal a great match to the ambitious amount of sound overall. The creak-into-whisper is Britney's stock in trade and as a sound it goes well with her cultivated sex-kitten image. It's a really clever production – designed to get us dancing and if you can't hum the tune afterwards, you recognize the string line melodic hook immediately. All the breaks are given over to strange instrumental invention and towards the end a strangely 1960s sounding guitar twang. There's little room for sustain here and nothing whatever, apart from her love of creak onset and creak finish (particularly at the end of the song), to distinguish her voice so she exploits that sound. Like all good pop dance numbers we respond to the song (and here, the production) much more than we respond to the voice, and there's no particular emotional pull for the listener.

Like *Toxic*, Gwen Stefani's *What you Waiting For?* is a very heavy production with so much going on that it's surprising how much Stefani manages to pack in, in terms of style choices. The song's hook revolves around the clock metaphor and apart from the heavy 'tick-tock' choruses, the whole track moves forwards relentlessly in keeping with the message of time both pressing and running out on us. This pace nearly dictates the even phrase placement throughout, and some of the phrases come in so neatly on top of one another that you know the recording process involved some 'cut and paste'. Sustain is rare here, and when she does use it, it's very brief. Stylistically, the most interesting thing about this recording is the quick and skilful changes of voice quality. Within the first 50 seconds she goes through at least five qualities. The first four lines are the only gently 'sung' sounds in the piece, using unvoiced creak onsets, a slightly twangy thin fold and aspirate onsets to create a kind of contemplative mood. This is followed (after the clock sounds) with a seven-line verse that features:

1. very twangy thin-fold sound and flip onsets
2. neutral thick fold that has a slight cry quality mixed in
3. neutral thin fold
4. neutral thick fold and
5. a high, fluttery thin fold with quick vibrato.

There is little sustain in the verse, phrase placement is even and the finishes are largely compressed. Note attack features slight bend throughout, which helps to keep some sense of musicality going throughout this rushed and layered first section. By the time we've made it through the piece, we've gone through quite a list of stylistic choices which, along with the overall pace and production of the piece feel rather dizzying. It's hard to say what the song adds up to overall – perhaps just a successful attempt to give stress a dance groove? The lyrics aren't impressive and the set of the lyric to what melody line can be heard is often rather clumsy, but with its catchy tick-tock hook, the song has real appeal in that classic dance pop way, and Stefani's performance is both clever and perfectly matched to the varied sounds in the track.

Robbie Williams, *She's the One* (1998)

She's the One is a well-crafted pop ballad that suits Williams's voice well. The lyrics are relatively inane – never a bad thing in a pop song – especially if the melodic 'hook' is memorable. He has much more voice than you actually hear here; he's deliberately mixing quite a lot of aspirate quality in the verses, which he keeps light. He finishes his phrases with either compression or a mild bend and then jumps quickly up a semi-tone and half down to ease out of the line. There's little sustain in these opening verses. He hardens the tone just slightly in the middle-eight, which sounds a bit twangier and gives this driving middle section a little bite, but the great majority of the song is delivered with a low effort level. He uses only these two voice qualities for the song and the switch between the qualities is not extreme. The phrases are very evenly weighted, and there's nothing remarkable about the shape of the phrases. There's very little improvisation until the end and even then, the melodic variations are slight and repetitive. He ups the effort level in this final section with some mild vocal constriction to give the piece more sincere rock sound, but he never really relinquishes control enough to make this late move convincing. This allows the song, rather than the vocalist, to be centre of our attention. Perhaps the overall emotional effect of the recording is enhanced if you have some knowledge of the Robbie Williams persona (like the few really superstar pop singers, Williams has been smart about building his public image), and you feel attracted to it as so many of his fans are, but in truth, nearly any good singer could make a hit of this song if given adequate airplay; it's an easy-going memorable piece, but it certainly doesn't have a strong emotional pull because it sounds like the calculated hit that it is. It would take either a great and/or unique voice – I can just about hear what Rod Stewart could do with it – to transform this song into something that might evoke a heartfelt emotional response.

Justin Bieber, *All Around the World* (Acoustic) and *Fall* (2013)

These two songs are good examples of Bieber's tuneful and savvy way of giving simple melodies/lyrics some life. Typically for a light pop singer, Bieber uses many style elements. There are some nice examples of aspirate, glottal, twang and creak sounds here. He uses audible breath in places to up the perceived-effort level and he's very skilful at moving a phrase around so that he can add interest to even the very repetitive parts of the songs. He's not a big 'riff and run' guy, but he has just enough small twiddles and extensions to make his sound contemporary and fresh. Both these tracks feature just Bieber and some restless guitars, and the recording really gives you the chance to hear the way that he moves through the many different vocal qualities. His kind of intimate, moaning sound here on both songs probably gives his target market a thrill. Whatever you think of Bieber, in vocal terms these are pretty accomplished gentle pop tracks and I think they illustrate the way in which this style is hard to teach. Everything here is just slightly 'tweaked', nothing is straight or 'legit', and the vocal tone is very pleasing. The vocal qualities change up a lot, all the onsets and offsets are mixed and the sounds have great variety. The phrase weight remains even, the overall effort level never really rises beyond the middling, and it's a very 'sung' sound.

Leona Lewis, *Run* (2007) and The Script, *The Man Who Can't Be Moved* (2008)

Leona Lewis's cover of Snow Patrol's *Run* is a fairly sombre affair. Lewis is the queen of the mid-phrase and offset flip. She begins here with a fairly aspirate and careful sound. You can hear a flip from thick to thin fold throughout the song but particularly in the 'light up, light up' sections. She has a rather slow and wide vibrato which, when combined with the very light vocal qualities she uses throughout most of the track gives a very vulnerable feel to the whole piece. She uses a gospel release every now and then, but the controlled and careful approach here doesn't really exploit the sound for power. Lewis probably should be an R&B singer, but she doesn't bring that kind of energy to things. Once the chorus joins her for the big finish, she remains quite enamoured of her flip technique, which means she must flip into thin fold, and only in the very last chorus of the song does she abandon her flip long enough to build some gutsy sound, but she quickly undoes it all with a breathy and tentative couple of 'ooohs' that leave the track right where it started – wistful, gentle, uncertain. The song itself is incredibly catchy, and despite (or perhaps because of) its ambiguity, it remains with you.

Danny O'Donoghue brings an engaging if gentle style to *The Man Who Can't Be Moved* and right from outset there's the sense of a little more effort happening. He's in neutral thick-fold sound, and he uses a fast-vib-into-compression finish to most of the early phrases. There's a lot of note bend here, and he moves the phrases forwards in the opening verses, which gives a kind of urgency to the performance. You can hear the difference clearly when he comes into the chorus where he comes in very straight on the downbeat right the way through; it gives the choruses an almost robotic evenness, and consequently the free phrasing in the verses is very welcome when it comes. In the verses after the first chorus he's back-phrasing most of the time, and he has a lovely 'looseness' about his sound that floats easily in and around the ground beat. It fact, it's the easy sustains, softened occasionally by small flips into thin-fold sound that make the whole song feel kind of buoyant, despite its heartbreak theme. You never get the sense that there's great effort here, but you do feel how very musical he is and how tuneful. While it's not a performance that grabs you, it's such a catchy song that it really stays with you.

Summary

All this emphasis on production/song rather than voice may make pop singing sound easy, but as mentioned earlier, I find it one of the hardest styles of all to teach. It requires a number of things that can be difficult to isolate and describe, consequently it's particularly difficult to feel like you can get a handle on the style. There is a wide range of artists who fall into the pop category, but I think they all share certain style qualities:

1. An overall 'sung' sound – pop singers tend to have *good* voices (which means pleasant timbre and tone, good pitch, flexibility, accuracy), which are almost never *unique* voices.
2. While there is a wide range of stylistic elements employed in pop music, those elements are usually employed to create a kind of middling effort level. This means that while the really high-effort-level voice qualities (belt, twang) are employed in pop, the neutral qualities are vastly more dominant.
3. The onsets and releases generally employed are of the low- to mid-effort-level variety: flip, simultaneous, aspirate, creak. Vibrato fades are common in pop music and they do much to give pop that really 'sung' sound.

4. Improvisation is almost always evident but it is rarely of the extended jazz or gospel type. When you do hear pop singers who employ extended improvisational patterns, the listening experience is usually one more closely associated to rhythm and blues (albeit a kind of R&B 'lite', rather like the Leona Lewis song). Pop improv consists more often of small additions to the front or back of a phrase, often very quick, usually no more than just a couple of additional notes.
5. Phrase placement is often very even, but also often just behind or ahead of the beat. There is never great play or variation in placement of the kind you would hear in jazz vocal, but neither is the 'easy' looseness of pop well-served by coming in right on the downbeat too often, unless it's a dance pop tune.
6. There is a sinuousness and ease to the shape of phrases, often created through dynamic variations within a phrase, well-judged – usually gentle – note bends, variation in onsets and finishes and a lot of small melodic 'adjustments'. These adjustments are not really like improvisation, since they usually serve to just 'ease' a straight melody line and give it a little more shape.

I've learnt that it's much easier to approach teaching pop style if a singer has spent time working on blues, jazz and gospel first. Because these earlier styles are so much easier to delineate in terms of the elements that make them up, they allow a singer who has spent some time working through them to subsequently explore those elements in the lighter way that pop demands. Work on blues should give you a good sense of how to occasionally find the raw, more spoken sounds that are sometimes used by braver pop artists like Stefani. Work on jazz style can go a long way towards finding that sinuous, flexible sound through play of phrase placement and improvisation.

Work on gospel style should lend some ease and confidence in the lighter kind of pop version of R&B numbers and also give some increased confidence in extended improvisation. If you've worked your way through all these areas with real dedication, you will ultimately find pop style coming rather naturally, as long as you make sure your effort level stays fairly middling and your tone is pleasant throughout.

CHAPTER FIVE

Practice, performance, artistry and finding your own style

For me, Bob Dylan and Patti Smith, just to mention two, are superb singers by any measure I could ever care about — expressivity, surprise, soul, grain, interpretive wit, angle of vision. Those two folks, a handful of others: their soul-burps are, for me, the soul-burps of the gods. *The beauty of the singer's voice touches us in a place that's as personal as the place from which that voice has issued. If one of the weird things about singers is the ecstasy of surrender they inspire, another weird thing is the debunking response a singer can arouse once we've recovered our senses. It's as if they've fooled us into loving them, diddled our hard-wiring, located a vulnerability we thought we'd long ago armored over.*

Falling in love with a singer is like being a teenager every time it happens.[1]

–JONATHAN LETHEM

Forget your perfect offering/there is a crack in everything/that's how the light gets in. . .

–LEONARD COHEN

In the years since this book was first published, I've done many workshops based on the material here, and in most of these I always seem to be faced with two questions at the end of the sessions. The first is something along the lines of: 'How do I connect the analysis of all the elements of style presented here with the actual practice of performance?' The second is always put in different ways, but basically it can be boiled down to this: 'What do I do about my vocal "problems"?'

Answering these two questions – which are quite complex – always takes a bit of time, largely because for every singer the answers are unique, but I do think there are some things that can help everyone who loves singing and wants to be more expressive/exciting/engaging in their practice.

Be dedicated

All musicians – either formally trained or not – have to practise. A lot of the work done in practice will never directly be a part of what that musician does in performance, but all of it will

---

[1]This is from an Introduction to *Rolling Stone* magazine's 100 Greatest Singers and you can find it at: http://www.rollingstone.com/music/lists/100-greatest-singers-of-all-time-19691231

inform the performance. Think in terms of the endless scales that piano players do when they're first learning to play. The piano player isn't going to play scales in a performance, they simply strengthen the player's ability to feel comfortable in any key, and all that practice work will have given the player a kind of ease and fluidity of expression. Of course, scales aren't the only thing the piano player has to work on, they're only a part of the whole picture, which combines experience, hours of practice, building repertoire and making a lot of mistakes.

Singers don't always feel like they have to put that kind of time into their practice, but I actually think they do. Even if you're gifted with an amazing voice, it takes many years of work to learn how to use it tastefully, how to be expressive and how to find a style that really works for you. I hear many singers, and I sang professionally for many years, and I know the difference between a confident performer and one who hasn't had much practice, but perhaps more importantly, I know the challenges of getting started.

To gain confidence, you need to practise, but unlike many other activities I think singing practice is greatly aided by working alongside others. When I first started I worked on my own, singing and playing guitar. I learnt a lot that way, but I learnt much more as soon as I joined other musicians. Some of them were at about my level, some were much better and some were worse. That didn't matter too much; what mattered was learning to listen, learning what sounded good and what didn't, what worked and why. I always advise singers to work with others if they can, but there's a lot that you can do by yourself, and working your way through this book is one good solo activity.

Music is easy to source these days, so go through all the examples here and listen closely. The more you listen, and the wider the range of what you listen to, the stronger your opinions will be about what makes a great performance and what doesn't. Listen to everything here, even the stuff you think you don't like. Analyse the sounds you're hearing, and listen for everything: onsets, voice qualities, phrase placement, effort level, etc. Get a feel for what really sounds good to you or for what really moves you. Music isn't easy to analyse in emotional terms; you can almost always talk about the way a singer uses a given element of style, but you can't always explain why you find something moving. That's why listening with your heart as well as your head is so important.

Be musical

There's an old joke that describes drummers and vocalists as people who like to hang out with musicians. Joke or not, it's often true that until you get quite a few years' experience you're probably unlikely to be as knowledgeable about musical form, theory and structure as your keyboard or guitar player is. Unless, that is, you play an instrument yourself. You don't have to learn to read music – I made a living for many years just accompanying myself on guitar, and I can't read music – but the longer I played the better I got at hearing things. I was never a great guitar player but I played long enough to understand when a chord progression wasn't right and I worked in enough groups to know how to 'stack' a harmony, and those things give you confidence. I can still be intimidated by great musicians, who really know what they're talking about, but I learnt to trust my ear and I think much of that had to do with playing guitar – however mediocre I was. If you used to play an instrument and you've stopped, pick it up again. In the long run it will absolutely increase your musical confidence and that can only help your singing performance.

It will also help if you write songs. When I mention this to singers, very often I hear some form of defence: either 'I'm not a songwriter, I'm a singer' or 'I've never written and I would not know where to start'. So before you reach for either of those defences, let me be clear: I'm not suggesting that you be a good songwriter (although you'll never know if you are until you try). I'm just suggesting that you start writing. Only know three chords on the guitar? That's okay – the list of hit songs with only three chords is impressive. Just start writing. The point is not to create a hit song. If you sit down to write a song you will immediately start thinking about the basics of song writing – structure, melody, lyric – and I promise that whatever time you can put into this exercise will help you as much as it may frustrate you. The reason it helps so much is that you will start listening to music in a different way, you'll start seeing music in a more active/doing way and you'll begin to listen in terms of how the writer(s) worked, how they structured the song, why it does or does not work for you. All of that will increase your confidence in musical terms. If you stick with it long enough you're bound to write something interesting. Be creative. Be free. Don't judge too early, just let things develop. Start with ideas that mean something to you. Start with the things that make you passionate. If you go completely blank the minute you start, leaf through a book of good photographs or look at some paintings, or read a poet who inspires you. People respect singers who write, and if you can collaborate with other musicians on something that is better still.

Be curious

It's almost impossible to say what makes us respond the way that we do to voices. Apart from the obvious things that we know are hardwired in our response to sounds (our response to a baby's cry, for example), we all know the frustration of trying to explain our musical passions to people who simply don't share them. I can listen to Roy Orbison sing *Mama* and burst into tears, but I've seen people laugh. Kate Bush leaves me cold but I know deeply musical people (whose tastes I usually admire) swear that she is wonderful. If we don't have a 'science' of musical taste, we do at least have an abundance of voices to explore. That exploration will never be classifiable or quantifiable, but it will always add to the sum of our musical knowledge and might surprise us.

You probably know your own taste well but make sure you remain curious enough about sounds/music/artists who work outside the boundaries that you usually work/listen within. If you have a good look through your music collection and realize that most of the songs there were recorded within the last decade, it's time to take yourself on a journey to discover voices that have been recorded over the last century. If you find that most of your songs are R&B and pop songs, then it's time to awaken your curiosity and expand your references; find out what it is that makes country music so powerful for the people who love it, find out why early blues recordings have inspired so many great rock musicians. Listen. Imitate. Try out. Discard, if you want, but not before you've really worked your way through to an understanding of what the artist was trying to do.

Stay curious even when you feel sure of your musical direction. It's the way you keep yourself and your music alive and progressing.

Be brave

Along with all that listening, do the practice exercises in this book. They might sound strange or even horrible but until you learn to get comfortable with making some strange noises you'll never really come to know the full range of sound that your voice is capable of. Stop judging those sounds; just let them happen. Of course no one thinks, in the middle of a performance, 'I think I'll try a creak offset here'; in performance you're only thinking about how to connect with your audience and how to make a song come alive, but if you've spent time practising that creak offset, and learning how it gives an enigmatic vulnerability to your sound, you'll have it in your arsenal of vocal 'weapons' when the time is right for it, and simply go to it at the right time without thinking.

At first, just practise as many of the elements of style that we've gone through here as you can manage. Don't worry about the ones you can't do, they may come in time and even if you can't do them you can keep trying. I can't finish a phrase like Caleb Followill but that doesn't stop me from trying! This 'out of context' practice will seem a little mechanical, just as all the exercises in chapters 2, 3 and 4 did. That doesn't matter, all you want to do is get used to making sounds you might not think to make. If you get used to these sounds you'll find that from time to time when you're performing, they'll come to you.

Don't worry at first about whether you're sounding good or 'right' or like anyone else, just experiment without judging yourself. Go back and listen to some really brave sound artists, and let them inspire you. You can add these to your list, if you find yourself worrying about being 'right' or 'beautiful':

Screamin' Jay Hawkins: *I Put A Spell on You* (1956). If this doesn't make you laugh and at the same time wish you could have seen him live, I'll be amazed. He's completely over the top, whatever he does, and never complicates anything by worrying about whether it will sound 'good'.

Tom Jones: *Soul of A Man* (2012). Starting with the strange rumble coming up from the very cellar of Jones's range in the opening line, this entire track is a brave and truly masterful performance. Jones's whole gospel project was very publicly doubted by his own record company but a close listen to this atmospheric and heartfelt cover of Blind Willie Johnson's classic makes you realize why the gamble absolutely paid off. It gives you chills and for all of Jones's past form as 'rock crooner', you can feel that the singing is stripped right back here, and what is left is the soul of a man.

(*Continued*)

Eartha Kitt: *I Wanna Be Evil* and *I'd Rather be Burned as a Witch* (1953). You can always count on Eartha Kitt to give a full-on theatrical performance and she's just so wonderful on both of these tracks. She has a voice probably best described as 'cute' – it's small, twangy and full of very fast vibrato but she uses all that to just enjoy telling the story of a woman who's in the mood to make a little trouble.

Bette Midler: *The Story of Nanette/Alabama Song/Drinking Again* etc. (Live at Last, 1977). Midler is absolutely fearless about exploring all the sounds she can make in service of telling a story or creating a character. This live track feels as if she's trying out all the different kinds of sounds she can make and she runs in typical style from the ridiculous to the absolutely sublime.

Tom Waits: *Ruby Arm's* (1990). He sounds incredibly rough in this recording about a man stealing out in the early morning, and there's nothing at all 'tuneful' about his voice, but somehow against a strangely sort of 'cinematic' backing track the whole thing adds up to heartbreak. It's not beautiful – it's too moving for that.

Sly and the Family Stone: *If You Want me to Stay* (1973). This 'stripped down' drum-and-bass production features Sly himself on a funny and passionate performance of a man who seems to be at his wit's end to convince his lover that he isn't going to change. His fearless exploration of many unusual sounds makes this track incredibly memorable.

Bob Dylan: *Gotta Serve Somebody* (1979). Dylan is not a great singer in any traditional sense but I like the way he approaches this with a sense of abandon – he makes a lot of interesting noises here that work perfectly to get his song across and he does it with his usual sense of abandon. You just know that Dylan doesn't care whether you like it or not.

Big Maybelle: *One Monkey Don't Stop no Show* (1955). I love this track. She manages to be both aggressive and laidback and with one song she lets you know that she is not to be messed with – ever! She was the kind of singer who knew how to get her story across and whether she's singing about 'Hairdressin' Women' or no-good, rotten men, you can feel that it's the story and the experience that matters to her. She doesn't care whether she sounds good or not – she's here to tell you the truth. And the truth isn't always pretty. . .

Ida Maria: *Oh My God* (2008). This so beautifully captures the sound of a woman on the edge of a breakdown. There's nothing whatever 'sung' about it. Starting with a flat spoken sound she goes on to lay the whole of her neurotic story out for us – building up to something absolutely wild and infectious by the end. Mesmerizing.

Wyclef Jean: *Knockin' on Heaven's Door* (2003). This is a heartfelt cover of Dylan's classic, firmly placed in Jean's own neighbourhood. He makes a lot of interesting sounds here and you can just feel that what matters to him is the gravity of the song and his passionate plea to put down the guns.

Be you

Performance – especially when you're starting out – is a challenging thing. Not simply because the kinds of gigs most people play when they're starting out aren't exactly ideal (in terms of venues, sound systems or audiences) but also because it takes quite a long time to find a way to be comfortable on stage. Most singers I know say that they felt like they didn't really get the hang of how to handle an audience or how to organize a set, or how to really relax and explore when they were singing until they'd been at it for about 5 years. Every performance will bring its own challenges and there's really no handbook for how to start gigging, but I've learnt that you can never go too far wrong by just hanging on to who you are and what makes you passionate.

That sounds simple, but in fact it isn't, especially when you're first starting you tend to worry about sounding good, about sounding right or – as often as not – about sounding like Adele, or Bruno Mars, or whoever it is you love. That's okay, Tom Jones began by trying to sound like Otis Redding and Paul McCartney began by trying to sound like Little Richard, but some singers can get quite hung up in the 'comparison' game. All artists begin by imitating, and the best ones know that stealing good ideas from great artists who came before you is absolutely part of the development process.

But if you worry too much about sounding like a singer you admire you'll not only create obstacles on the way to finding your own style, but you're also quite likely to become a bit anxious about the sound you're producing. The only way to cope with that anxiety is to give up worrying. If you can't sound good, sound unique. Sound extraordinary. Sound passionate. Sound *un*like the singer(s) you love, or sound like two of them at the same time. But most of all trust your own passion and sound like you – for better or for worse. Stop focusing all your concern on the way you sound and focus more on what you mean when you sing. The more you listen to your own sound (and judge it either good or bad), the less anyone else will. It's a hard irony of this business but you only start to grow when you stop listening to yourself, look your audience in the eye and tell them what you have to say/sing.

Singers are like drug addicts; they become addicted to the 'drug' of their own sound. Give it up now. Don't get hooked. Get serious about moving people; serious about communicating; serious about really knowing what your lyrics mean and in making your audience go on an emotional sound journey with you. Listen to the musicians you're working with; listen to what your guitar player is doing and what your keyboard player is doing. If you're lucky enough to be working with really talented musicians let them inspire you, and try to inspire them with what you do. I've watched so many singers who have never really listened to the musicians they're working with. That's like having a fine car and then walking everywhere.

Be an artist

Dylan did with singing what Brando did with acting. He busted through the artifice to get to the art. Both of them tore down the prissy rules laid down by the schoolmarms of their craft, broke through the fourth wall, got in the audience's face and said, "I dare you to think I'm kidding."

–BONO[2]

When I'm auditioning people for television shows I have the chance to really listen, in a concentrated way, to discover what I can hear in the relationship between a person and their voice. I've learnt a lot in doing this kind of work for so many years. I often wonder how I'd fare at one of these auditions – they're focused on a certain kind of sound and what they're looking for is almost certainly a contradiction. These shows demand a great voice that has real versatility (if you make it to live rounds you'll be singing many different styles); they require that the singer has confidence in performing (but of course they're going to be judged at every step); and they don't generally reward things like stubbornness, single-minded focus, or individual artistic vision, but of course, these are exactly what a singing artist needs.

---

[2] *Rolling Stone*, 27 November 2008.

You might feel at this moment that you don't think of yourself as an artist, but if not, why not? This is probably the point at which we get right down to the question: why do you sing? What do you want to get from it? In a general sense there are easy answers to these questions: people sing naturally, in every society, in every culture; music is a massive part of what makes us human. Singing brings us comfort, it (literally) heals us; it can give us a sense of who we are. While nearly all of us – for better or for worse! – sing, there are some of us for whom singing and music is the passion of our lives, and if singing is the great passion of your life, then you need to take responsibility for the artistry of your work.

That should bring us right back to being stubborn, having a singled-minded focus, and an artistic vision. Read, think, listen, practise, demand a lot from yourself, but in the midst of it all, know what you like. Be open to new ideas, new sounds and unexpected pleasures: it's always important to listen and experience a wide range of musical sounds, those experiences should always be part of creating your sense of what you like, and what you value in performance. But even in the early phases of this, follow your instincts in terms of what really makes you 'tick' musically. This might sound paradoxical – be open-minded, and be single-minded – but it isn't. The open-minded part is what makes you grow as an artist – it allows you to listen and appreciate sounds that move you in surprising ways. The single-minded part is what always brings you back to your own practice, and to your own commitment in experimenting, putting together things from a wide variety of sources, and in communicating what's in your heart and soul.

The challenging part is to let go of need. There's only one thing that you can say with certainty about art: it should challenge our expectations. You can't really create it unless you're willing to give up the need to please. No one can really teach artistry. You have to learn it. Some people never achieve it, but no one ever regrets the time they spend pursuing it.

Some questions to help you start thinking about your musical artistry:

1. What is the purpose of 'rules' when it comes to singing? How would you sing if there were none?
2. Many people agree that failure is the key to all innovation. If they're right, why would you ever be afraid of being wrong?
3. Who do you envision when you're singing? Who are you singing to? How does your sound change when the person you imagine you're singing to changes?
4. What is the link between pleasure and art when you're working?
5. Can you learn to say 'yes' to it all: jazz, country, gospel, indie, rock, pop, good voices, strange voices, etc.? Why does being open to everything at first matter so much?
6. Why do you care what other people think?
7. Is passion all you've got? Is that enough? How do you define talent?
8. When are you most creative? When are you happiest making sounds?
9. Do you ever have to decide between being 'good' and being 'original'?

Let go

Most singers worry about the same technical things: they want more range, they want more power, they want better sound at the extreme ends of their range – especially at the top end – they want more stamina and they want better/prettier/rougher/*different* tone. Along with these things many singers I've worked with want to be able to do big, flashy improvs or just be able to create a powerhouse performance of some kind.

I know the importance of hankering after these things and I know that when singers focus on what they perceive to be their 'inabilities' they can often lose confidence, but at the same time I believe that these worries often stem from thinking that our voice should sound like someone else's. If you look at the list on the previous page (I want more range, more power, more improv ability etc.), you will realize that I'm right. When we're looking at words like more and better and prettier – all of those words carry an implicit comparison I think. Prettier than what? Better than what? I'm not for a moment suggesting that singers shouldn't want to improve – of course they should – but make sure that when you're working towards making things better, you're only comparing that to what you sound like now. So when you say you want your voice to sound better, make sure the unspoken part of that sentence is: better than *my* voice is now.

If the unspoken part of that sentence is 'I want my voice to sound better than Beyoncé's', you're probably headed into heartbreak territory. Let go of comparing yourself with other singers. I'd love to sing like Beyoncé. That would be fun. But I don't. I sing like me. And that has worked for me for many years. My point is this: be all about improving; be all about getting better, taking bigger risks, pushing yourself to practise more and listen more; demand more of yourself in terms of what you have to communicate, but don't compare yourself to anyone in all that work. Imitate, but don't regret. Steal from the best, but make it all filter naturally through your own unique sound. Play, experiment, fail, but don't judge any of it except in terms of what you can take away that feels right, feels better, makes you happy.

And in the meantime, contemplate the way that great, confident artists have always managed to transform their limitations into their signature – that is where style comes from. If you need convincing, let's go through that list again and figure out just how you turn 'problems' into artistry.

I want to have more range

Most singers already have more range than they think. Sometimes we don't like the sound we make in our upper register or on our very highest notes, and that means we concentrate our sound in the areas where we feel best. That often means that we think we have less range than we actually do. Still, there are some stubborn things about range, I've always wished that I could sing a high C. I'll never manage that – my voice isn't constructed that way; I have a range of about two-and-a-half octaves. It's rare that I use that in any single song. Most singers have at the very least about one-and-a-half octaves. So before you start worrying about your range, take some time to look at what singers can do with about one-and-half octaves.

Laura Mvula: *She* (2013). She uses exactly one octave here. Chilling and exciting and relatively low-energy, Mvula's sound is hard to describe, but she stays fairly comfortably in the jazz-style range – brilliant, accurate pitching; quick, compressed or sometimes pushed finishes; flashes of flip and aspiration in the onsets; and a musicality that aims to place the vocal in the context of an overall sonic experience rather than the kind of 'solo singer' sound of most R&B or gospel singers (whose styles clearly influence her work).

(*Continued*)

Susan Tedeschi: *Angel From Montgomery/Sugaree* (https://www.youtube.com/watch?v=ZrSK-0-MQ8s). Grit and heart make this Tedeschi cover of John Prine's classic really work. She never strays out of the (D-to-D) octave but there is something compelling and honest in her sound that I find really works for this desperate song about a working woman who can feel her life is just slipping by her.

Vaya Con Dios: *At the Parallel* (1992). Dani Klein offers up a master class in 'cinematic' music – everything she does here evokes a time, a place, an atmosphere that takes us right inside the stultifying bar where 'nothing ever changes' and gets right inside of the head of the chain-smoking dreamer who hopes that the girl in the leather coat wants him. Klein makes the most of moving phrases just gently behind or ahead of the ground beat that somehow captures the dreaminess and ennui of *The Parallel.* And all this within a single octave.

Lyle Lovett: *She's Already Made up her Mind* (1992). This moody track evokes the moment when a woman tells a man that she's decided to leave. There's nothing dramatic here – the whole track catches the feel of an announcement that is beyond discussion. Everything about the slow build and Lovett's trademark 'raggedy' voice suggests the helplessness of a man faced with a decision he can't alter. It's a track that doesn't use more than an octave to make its atmosphere and its heartache clear to the listener.

k.d. lang: *Hallelujah* (http://www.youtube.com/watch?v=nKrkEOlyJo8). With little more than an octave, and no vocal acrobatics Lang brings home one of the most original and compelling versions of this song I've ever heard. She brings that hallmark depth of tone (she always tempts me to describe her sound like a good wine: woody, musky, full-bodied, with strong, sweet, honeyed finish) and extraordinary taste in terms of where and how she places a phrase just one side or the other of the ground beat, and how she employs long note bends, and that absolute mastery of sustain. She makes brave choices about ignoring the melody altogether here at some points and does more with a couple of monotone bars than some singers can do with a whole song. Listen to the use of breath before coming to the second chorus – absolutely magical. With just minor uses of the flip-and-creak onset this is a definitive performance made through simple but hugely musical choices – you know her heart is wholly engaged here.

R.E.M.: *Losing my Religion* (1991). And then there are those for whom an entire octave would feel like a luxury: here Michael Stipe makes just half an octave go a long way towards painting the picture of a man who is both obsessed and a little paranoid. He sings simply, just putting across a poetic lyric about the way that we lose our confidence around people we're obsessed with – simultaneously worrying about saying too much; about not saying enough, and slowly drowning within our own inability to make something positive happen. The way in which the song's simple sort of 'round' keeps returning captures the essence of obsession in its very structure.

Otis Redding: *Dock of the Bay* (1967). This was Otis's last recording and catches him in a surprisingly reflective mood. Its plaintive and unusually wistful sound took on a kind of pathos after his death in a plane crash just a short time later. You can hear something slightly tentative in his voice here – he remains within an octave, working in neutral, low-effort sounds most of the time, and never comes near his usual high-energy vocal approach. The slow flutter of his vibrato gives a melancholy tinge to the proceedings. The whole track sounds like Otis's meditation on mortality and his restraint gives it a profound feel that it would never have had otherwise.

I want to have more power

If you listened to the examples on the previous pages, you'll probably already appreciate that a great vocal performance doesn't need a lot of power. Of course, in the right place, with the right song, great power can be thrilling. Most singers can develop more power in their voices by engaging more muscle, adding a little twang to their sound, and slowly building up their stamina for singing in belt quality, but for voices that are naturally on the quiet side, there's little to gain in driving the voice for power all the time. Save the power moments for when they'll really count in terms of your expression and learn to love the way that a quieter voice can really work a lyric.

Tom Odell: *I Think it's Going to Rain Today* (2013). Odell is brave about keeping things quiet and his cover of Randy Newman's enigmatic song is moody and intimate. He rightly senses that too much power or volume would get in the way of telling this particular story and his studied restraint allows the piece to really get under your skin. He comes into a bit more power as the track progresses, but he adds the gritty texture of sustained creak/scratch to suggest the loneliness and the pain of the piece and brings the whole thing back down to the level of a kind of still observation of a lifeless world around him.

Jeff Buckley: *Just Like A Woman* (2003, live at Sin-*é*). He does occasionally raise the volume here, but what's so interesting about this track is that Buckley's instincts are almost the opposite of most singers; rather than really use power on the big moments, he backs right off into his quieter, more vulnerable sounds. You can tell that where he's feeling the most in this track, especially towards the end, he brings the thought quietly back into himself and tightens the sound down into something that just kind of melts into softness. His voice is incredibly expressive and yet it isn't beautiful, it isn't faultless. Here he demonstrates just how powerful it can be to go from a shout back into a whisper.

Billie Holiday: *Strange Fruit* (1939). At her best, Holiday was never a power singer; what she brought to market was her unusual tone, and a deeply musical sensibility. This is an unnerving and quiet piece – perhaps because in its day it was a challenging piece of politics and many stations refused to air the recording. You get the sense here that Holiday wanted people to catch every lyric, and although it was almost too important to sing about, it was only because it *was* sung that it could get any airing at all. Haunting, melancholy and brave.

Antony and the Johnsons: *Crazy in Love* (2009). Antony Hegarty's extraordinary, fluttery and vulnerable sound set against an atmospheric orchestration takes this reinvention of Beyonce's song into the most unexpected territory. Johnson is anything but a 'power' singer, but his sound is unique and emotive. This is ethereal and inspired.

Smokey Robinson: *Being With You* (1981). Smokey's voice was one of the most influential of the twentieth century but was always a study in delicate, silky aspirate sounds that could float beautifully over any track. He had a kind of sinuousness and sophistication that marked out the Motown sound, which was geared towards wooing a white audience. There's nothing threatening in Robinson's sound and he never used power at all in his vocal choices, but the voice is so smooth and distinctive that you could never mistake him for anyone else.

I don't like my 'head' voice

I can't say that I'm surprised by the fact that so many singers don't like the thinner sound of their upper register. When I started singing I knew very well that what audiences seemed to respond to most was just the sheer volume I could produce. For so many years, I spent most of my singing time in my thick-fold, twang and belt range, and sort of treated the whole of my upper register as an unwanted guest. As I gained experience I began to realize that there was a wealth of expressive possibility in those lighter, airier sounds and I began to explore (rather tentatively at first) what I could do with that part of my range.

I still hear many singers who favour their loud voice to the point of creating a real imbalance in their overall sound. Often, when auditioning singers, I hear colleagues describe these kinds of voices as 'club singers'. When you hear these voices you can tell that the singer has spent many years belting out songs in an attempt to sing over noisy crowds at clubs or events, and they tend to grow increasingly husky. Once a singer's focus is trained on just being heard, all the delicacy in terms of expression is completely sacrificed to volume, and unless they really battle to retain a strong sense of what they're trying to communicate, they become a bit trapped. Ignoring all the vocal possibilities in their more delicate sounds, they just start reproducing volume. I played enough 'beer bars' in my younger days to know exactly how that trap works.

Then there are some singers who have spent time with more traditional vocal coaches, who see their purpose as trying to 'smooth out' the sound throughout the register, balancing the power and tone from those lower more powerful notes to the higher, thinner ones so that the whole voice has consistency. In 'legit' singing circles, this is one of the main goals of all that training. But does it make any sense in the world of popular singing?

Nerina Pallot: *Idaho* - Live (2005). This is a great performance from an outstanding musician. Pallot unashamedly jumps registers here, with no regard whatever to 'smoothing out' the sound. In letting that big difference between 'chest' and 'head' voice stand, she displays the beauty to be found in the kind of thin, airy 'head' voice that often troubles voice teachers and lesser artists who worry that their high notes have to have power or else have to have the same sound as the lower register. The simplicity of the thin-fold vocal sound against a very restless piano works tiny miracles here and the raw honesty of the song is beautifully served by Pallot's decision not to worry too much about the sound of those high notes.

Michael McDonald: *I Can Let Go Now* (1982). This little ballad of loss is beautifully rendered by McDonald, whose voice already sounds vulnerable. He doesn't really use much power at all and the intimacy of the performance is boosted by the honest and artless way in which he doesn't employ muscle or support even in the very highest parts of the song.

PJ Harvey: *The Devil* (2007). This is a haunting kind of gothic fantasy piece and Harvey rightly senses that it needs a strangely ethereal opening to get us into the mood of understanding the extreme state of a young woman whose desires are overwhelming her, but who is not likely to find answers in the usual places. So we need to hear a voice that isn't going in the usual places – here she makes the most of the thinnest kind of 'head' voice sound you can imagine and creates a wonderfully atmospheric track.

(*Continued*)

Billy Joel: *Leave a Tender Moment Alone* (1984). One of Joel's greatest songs, he jumps into his 'head' voice artlessly here and that ends up adding to the honesty of his lyric. It's all about a man who knows he's getting it wrong – telling jokes at the wrong moment, finding it impossible to relax, just generally overthinking the whole thing. The sort of blatantly thin sound he uses on the high notes mirrors his anxiety somehow, and keeps it honest. The overall feel of the song would have lost so much if he'd decided to sing those high notes 'powerfully' or in a well-produced 'legit' tenor sound.

I want to do big flashy improv

If you take a look at all the song examples I've included in this section, you'll realize that I've purposely included singers and performances that were nearly devoid of improv. Perhaps more than at any time I can remember, singers seem to think that the worth of a singer is determined by their ability to 'riff and run'. The trend of 'over-singing' seems to be everywhere and it is as often criticized as it is praised.

When we do auditions for 'The Voice' I often have the same conversation with the other vocal experts on the panel and it always centres around the question of why, when we've just heard someone whose audition featured extended melodic riffing, we don't feel like we know anything about the vocalist. Often, when I'm faced with that kind of audition, I ask the singer to just sing the melody for me in the simplest way possible. The surprising thing is how often they can't do that. So I've learnt much in watching singers who add endless frills and decoration to their sound – those additions quite often mask the fact that the singer can't actually sustain a note in tune. As you can imagine, then, a lot of improv makes me nervous.

But perhaps the big question, when it comes to how and why singers want to have this ability, is this: what does improv add to a performance? When does it really work? When is it actually enhancing our emotional engagement with a song, and when is it simply vocal acrobatics that have more to do with a kind of exhibitionism than with honest communication? I know that these questions require subjective answers – what works for me might not for you; what I think is a train-wreck might be your delight – but I'll risk it. These examples might help you when you're worrying about wanting to be able to do more in terms of improv, if only because it will get you thinking about what purpose it serves and whether it matters at all.

Destiny's Child: *Emotion* (2001). I'll be honest. I blame this song for a lot of bad auditions I see. When I listen to this version of the Bee Gees's pop hit, I have absolutely no sense of what they're singing about, or whether it matters at all. The lead voice wanders endlessly as if more interested in exploring her own range than thinking about what the song has to say. Admittedly, these lyrics are not going to win the Nobel Prize for literature but the song is about someone 'tied up in sorrow' and 'lost in my soul'. Surely it deserves at least some passing respect for the heartache it's based on. The vocal wandering gets more random as the track progresses and by the time we reach the 2:00 mark, the exploration becomes almost completely disconnected from the melody and you can't help wondering why they didn't just write their own song instead of 'singing over' this one.

Luther Vandross: *A House is Not a Home* (1981). This was the song that made a lot of people notice Vandross and it is a bold revision of the Bacharach/David song that had been a hit for Dionne Warwick. I would understand anyone thinking this is 'over-sung' and all too much, but for me it works. Maybe because there's never a moment when I doubt that Vandross knows what an empty room feels like

(*Continued*)

and there's never a moment when I think he loses track of what's at stake here. You never miss a lyric and you get, completely, that he's heartbroken. Perhaps it's simply the fact that he never really drives a lot of power through those extended melodic additions – it's all gentle hurt and hopefulness. Throughout all his improvised additions he never loses respect for the beautiful melody that Bacharach wrote.

Christina Aguilera: *Star-Spangled Banner* (http://www.youtube.com/watch?v=b94aBPC5T-E). Christina Aguilera is often cited as one of the worst offenders in the 'oversinging' category and this track shows you exactly why. The US National Anthem is fairly regularly tortured by guest singers, but even by past less-than-ideal performances, Aguilera is way off the mark here. She's so busy riffing, she doesn't even seem to be able to remember the lyrics. The fact is, the anthem is tough enough to sing even if you just sing the melody as written, as it demands a pretty confident octave and a half. Aguilera might have taken a lesson from Whitney Houston's 1991 performance (http://www.youtube.com/watch?v=6wvG5JQA5og), where Houston allows herself some melodic freedom, but never misjudges the importance of the lyric – particularly when a post 9/11 Superbowl was responding to a hyper-patriotic vibe.

Christina Aguilera: *Candy Man* (2007). This fabulous reworking of the Andrews Sisters sound takes Aguilera into really interesting territory. She works the close harmonies beautifully and the track is so full of passion, humour and energy that her vocal additions all around and over the top of the harmonies add just the right touch to get you into the whole flirtatious feel of the song. Aguilera is often one of the great offenders for those who can't take the 'riff and run' approach, but here, anchored by the chunky harmonic grounding of the song, the riffs feel fresh, liberating and exhilarating.

Mariah Carey: *Emotions* (1991). I'm sure that when one has a reported five octaves to explore, it's quite tempting to explore them all! If you're in the mood to hear some amazing vocal acrobatics over a synthy dance track this is just the ticket but as a piece of singing I can't imagine anyone feeling moved by this. The title – for me – ends up being incredibly ironic, since 'emotions' seem to have nothing whatever to do with this clear exhibition piece. As a kind of vocal 'wonder' this is interesting but Carey's freakishly big range and extended melisma have enticed many people into some fairly fruitless habits of 'over-singing' just for the sake of it.

Whatever your own take on melodic improv, everyone knows that a little ability to 'ease' and play around with a melody can help put your mark on a cover version, and sometimes make a style statement but I think singers who come to me and want to know how they can learn to do extended improvisational riffs are probably asking the wrong question. The right question is always 'How can I communicate better?' or 'How can I move people with my singing/my artistry?' because unless you can start there, you'll never know when or how to use improvisation.

Original or not?

When you're writing your own music your own style will emerge, but when you're doing cover versions (which is where most singers start) it can take some time to figure out just how to put your own stamp on things. There's an art to doing a great cover song and that usually centres on finding songs that really fit with your voice and your style, although often the great cover version is about reinventing a song in a way that makes us hear it in an entirely fresh way. You can be fairly brave about exploring things as long as your version demonstrates what you do well.

The key is to really get inside a song and try to understand what makes it work. If you can do that you'll have a good idea whether your style fits well with the song you're looking at. The thing to keep in mind is that (with rare exception) you don't want to do a song the way that the original artist did; that inevitably draws comparison between yourself and the original artist, and in most cases you'll come off looking worse.

Spend some time researching and listening to cover songs (every artist does them at some point) because that research will help you build your own taste. One way to really sharpen your artistic judgement is to listen to a single song recorded by many artists. This exercise is fascinating and it helps you to focus on the way that every song brings some integrity and some kind of emotional observation with it, which is a combination of its specific point of view, its original performance, and its lyrics. The melody might be good or bad, the lyrics may be thin and clichéd or richly poetic and ambiguous, but they always give you a starting point. Once you listen to a number of cover versions you begin to discover what really makes a song work. And what doesn't.

Nirvana: *Smells Like Teen Spirit* (1991). Cobain's provocative track was seen by many as a kind of cross between punk rage and alienation and became the anthem of the Seattle underground music scene. The lyrics are, in themselves, somewhat meaningless, but have a kind of frightening brilliance set against a pure 'garage band' sound, particularly in the chorus, where the 'here we are now/ entertain us' demand (coupled with the opening lyric about loading up on guns) feels particularly unsettling, and (rather like old posters of Malcolm McDowell in *A Clockwork Orange*) carry the whiff of feral, predatory male youth. The song has often been cited as one of the greatest rock songs of all time and it came in at number nine on *Rolling Stone*'s '500 Greatest Songs of All Time' list.

Songs this iconic are tough to cover, but that doesn't stop people trying.

The Good

Tori Amos (1992). Slowing the track right down, and spurred on by a restless piano exploration, Amos's slurred, often aspirated, generally tentative vocal translates the lyrical ambiguity into something evocative, invitational and incredibly intimate. The song loses its head-banger anthemic feel here and instead makes the most of its teenage-tinged angst.

Robert Glasper (2012). Running the vocal through Vocoder effects, and layering a sophisticated jazz sensibility over the whole track, this reinvention takes Nirvana's song into incredibly strange, techno, moody territory that is as musically ambiguous as the lyric. By the time you reach the end you might be in an arcade on a boardwalk or a dimly lit cocktail bar in Manhattan, but wherever you end up, you realize that Glasper has given the piece new life as an unexpectedly successful soul/jazz/hip-hop experiment.

The Bad

Miley Cyrus (https://www.youtube.com/watch?v=95OzzIl6dj4). It's almost cruel to direct your attention to this. Cyrus's perfectly serviceable country/pop sound works a treat on things like *The Climb* or *Party in the USA* but she doesn't manage what Amos and Glasper do, which is to adapt the piece to their own style and then allow us to hear it in a new way. Consequently we get a pretty embarrassing 'karaoke' Cyrus here, whose fairly tortured rock posturing reminds me of watching my parents dance when I was younger. . .

(*Continued*)

The Ugly

Paul Anka (2005). This will probably inspire you to reassess Miley Cyrus and decide that her take isn't so bad after all. Whatever could have convinced Anka – a veteran songwriter and successful 1950s pop crooner – to re-envision this song as a big-band number is something probably best left shrouded in mystery. If ever there was an example of 'cover-song-train-wreck', this has got to be it. It's a clear demonstration of why reinventing a song in your own style (which is what Amos and Glasper do so successfully) is not always a good idea.

On throwing out the rule book

I suppose it's time to confess my greatest worry about writing a book like this. Rules. Categories. Genres. They're all ways of organizing knowledge, and sometimes that organization is really useful but all artists know their limits and the best ones spend their lives defying them. If you go back and look at that list I referred to earlier, which was published in *Rolling Stone* in 2008, the number of voices that follow the rules or stick to categories is slim. To finish up here, I've found some tracks that remind me just how exquisite and liberating it can be to defy the rules and just bring your passion to the work.

Ray Charles: *Georgia on My Mind* (1960). The flaws make it all work. Charles's voice was a warm, honeyed, gritty affair and he had such trust in the way he used it that he knew even the 'mistakes' were valuable. This is a beautifully 'sung through' track, but you sense that he was keen not to allow it to be too clean. I'm always put off by the syrupy sound of his backing singers, but there is something compelling in the contrast between their clean, hokey kind of schooled sound, and his insistence on keeping things just a little raw in the lead vocal. Have a close listen to this track around the 3:07 mark when he's singing 'on my mind'. A lesser artist would have cleaned this line up – it creaks, falters and nearly fails – but it completely captures you and convinces you of the sweet pain it is to keep thinking of his lost Georgia.

Laura Nyro: *Lonely Women* (1968). This is Nyro's incredibly moving portrait of the agony of lonely women; the women that 'no one hurries home' to. Nyro rightly recognized that a sweet sung sound would never get all this pain across. She exploits sustain in the sound but never tidies up the ends of phrases; she either compresses, creaks or falls off the phrase which makes even the most sustained notes here sound rather like the sax that runs throughout the track. There's a craggy, inartistic sound to the big notes, which come across somewhere between a wail and a stab. She takes the final notes up into her high thin-fold register and on the finishing note she doesn't quite hold the sound together, so her voice just 'fails'. Like Ray Charles, she knew when to leave failure alone – the reedy, inconsistently held note here sums up in sound the thin, dry life she's singing about.

(*Continued*)

Joni Mitchell: *Both Sides Now* (2003). This is Mitchell's cover of her own earlier big hit. Perhaps no voice in modern recording has degenerated quite so much as Mitchell's. From the sinewy and sinuous folk soprano of her younger years, that could float effortlessly through even the toughest melodic inventions, she is reduced to a husky, vibrato-laboured alto with little power for sustain. This track should remind us sadly of the glories of her earlier work, but it doesn't. Instead here she is, flaws on show, struggling against a massively orchestrated production and hobbled by the most tentative phrasing, still teaching us what it is, finally, to discover the way that life and love just elude our grasp at every point. Brave and haunting.

Joe Cocker: *You Are So Beautiful To Me* (1974). Repetitive melody. Slushy lyrics. A strangulated voice and an upper register that damn near fails him altogether at the end – it's hard to say why so many people find this track moving, but over two million hits on Spotify says that they do. There's a kind of desperation and a raw honesty about it that gives this 'flawed' work an undeniable power.

Johnny Cash and Bob Dylan: *The Girl from the North Country* (1969). There's so much wrong here that I barely know where to start. Neither has much of a voice and Dylan sounds particularly odd here – a bit like Kermit the Frog. The harmonies, such as they are, range from shaky to downright out of tune, but somehow for me (and over a million other listeners on Spotify) this warts-and-all track from two legends singing a wistful song of lost love has pathos and meaning.

Judy Garland: *Somewhere Over the Rainbow* (http://www.youtube.com/watch?v=ss49euDqwHA). This footage from her television special in 1955 shows Garland at the end of a 'little tramp' sequence, hence the make-up. If you can remember the smooth rendition of *Over the Rainbow* that she performed in the film, then this will sound very choppy, slightly desperate and at times rather raw. But that, I think is the point. Here we see Garland, 16 years later and we can 'hear' how much of life she's experienced. At times it's as if we're watching her battle every emotional demon in her life. But somewhere, in those final moments, she seems to make the decision that she's going to survive. And at that moment it doesn't matter whether or not the tone is beautiful, the pitch is perfect, or if the whole performance is a bit wobbly. All that matters is that for a moment, she allowed us to see so clearly into her heart.

Amy Winehouse: *Take the Box/In My Bed* (http://www.youtube.com/watch?v=nEG0t-oW2NQ). This is a rare early recording of Amy and she looks and sounds amazing. There's much to admire here. I love the way she so restlessly explores all the sound she can make, and just never worries about the tone being full or resonant or consistent – she just explores, risks and works her voice like an instrument. She's accompanying herself here and you can really hear the jazz influence in her style, both in terms of how she plays and how she sings. Over the whole clip she works through a lot of different voice qualities, moving between belt, 'baby' twang, rumble, a kind of throaty 'cry' sound, and she also uses a surprisingly high thin-fold sound here which she abandoned entirely in her later performances. You can also hear her trademark glottal-stop glides, soft diction, and an almost complete lack of finish to any lyric. But what really stands out here is just what a talented jazz artist she was. She has such an amazing depth of musicality about her and this video shows just why, although you can hear the influence of so many blues and jazz singers before her, there's never really been anyone quite like her.

Leonard Cohen: *Anthem* (Live in London, 2009). He's not a singer in any conventional sense, he's an artist with passionate conviction and a poetic soul. Cohen writes amazing songs and they work just as

(*Continued*)

well in his raspy, mystical performances as they do when beautiful voices take them on:

'Forget your perfect offering/there is a crack in everything/that's how the light gets in.'

We're back where we started and somehow it sums up what I hope this last chapter has been all about.

APPENDIX

This section formed part of the first edition, and while the interview is now over 10 years old, there are still questions here that I've not seen addressed elsewhere. Because it was done specifically for the book, I've decided to include it here for those who are coming to this work for the first time. McCartney's appearances have not slowed down since this interview – if anything, at the age of 71, he is as busy as ever.

Interview with Sir Paul McCartney

Perhaps the most versatile popular singer of all time, Paul McCartney's career is now into its fifth decade, and his voice is as strong as ever. There are few singers who perform with quite his abandon and bravery who can say as much. In preparation for this book, I wanted to find someone whose career has stood that test of time, and whose voice is still (despite the demanding and extended work he has put it through) in great shape. It strikes me that he is part of a generation of singers (Rod Stewart, Tina Turner, Tom Jones, Mick Jagger, et al) who began singing in the late 1950s/early 1960s and are still going strong. Singers of an earlier generation didn't have the chance to sustain their careers in the spotlight in quite this same way and it's hard to say if many singers of this generation will have that chance. But it isn't only the resilience and longevity of his career that should be of interest to us – he is also able to inhabit style in a remarkably flexible way, while still retaining everything about his sound that is unique.

Early in The Beatles's career he was singing songs as diverse as *Long Tall Sally* (a cover of Little Richard's Rock hit) and *Til There Was You* (a sentimental Broadway ballad from Meredith Wilson's *The Music Man*). He still regularly switches effortlessly between his trademark rock ballad sound (*Michelle*, *Yesterday*, *The Long and Winding Road*, *Eleanor Rigby*) and his hard rock voice (*I'm Down*, *Jet*, *I Want to Hold Your Hand*, *Got to Get you into My Life*, *Back in the USSR*) and that other, sort of middle-of-the-road sound that seems to have grown out of British music hall (*When I'm Sixty-Four*, *Penny Lane*.)

Perhaps nowhere else is his versatility so evident as in two of his later albums: Flaming Pie (1997) and Run, Devil Run (1999). The first was seen by many as the most musically satisfying and complex work he has done since the demise of The Beatles, and the second was a particular challenge that he decided to set for himself in covering a handful of relatively obscure early rock songs.

In the following interview I wanted to try to get to the heart of how he sees himself as a vocalist and to see if I couldn't get him to reflect a little on what makes his voice so versatile and how he has managed (in a way that so many others haven't) to retain both the quality and the range of his voice throughout such a long career. Like many practitioners, his first response is always to say that he doesn't reflect on things – he simply does them. We met at his offices in Soho, London, and in the course of our afternoon I was surprised at how much he had to say (despite his repeated insistence that he doesn't think about such things!) about vocal confidence, about the relationship between confidence and sound, between writing and style, between mimicry and finding your own sound, and about singing and playing while performing. He talked much about how listening played such an important part in his own vocal development, about the continued curiosity he has in listening to other artists and about the breadth of his own evolving musical tastes and knowledge.

Perhaps the thing that struck me most during the interview was that although he is deeply suspicious of analysis, his own natural analytical bent was always evident. I think in many ways his style has grown out of much thinking, listening, imitating and analysing. But as he would insist – a great performance comes when you can let all of that go and just concentrate on what you want to communicate with the song.

The interview

Singing has much to do with confidence and I think for most singers there comes a moment when they actually find the confidence to think that they can think of themselves as a singer – or that they find the confidence to sing in public. Can you tell me when you think you first realised you were a singer?

I guess when I was a young kid. I used to sing along with records. I could hold a tune and I think that's when I realised. It wasn't so much when I was in school; it was more at home, singing along with records or the television.

Was there a particular moment when somebody validated you for doing that – did someone actually say something like "your voice is nice" or did you come into your own sense of confidence about singing?

I think it was always in my own head. And I suppose getting a record contract was the first validation.

And what about family – any musical influences?

Family – yeah, my dad would be the one. He would teach us harmony and things. He would say, "That's the harmony to that" and he would probably have said, "Well, you haven't got a bad voice" but he would never give me too much praise – he was frightened of me getting big headed.

You've always had a versatile voice and I've always thought of you as the 'hard rock' singer of The Beatles – you probably do know that a number of voice teachers might counsel you quite strongly against making some of the noises you make when you sing?

Yeah – I'm sure.

And they might say that you could damage your voice doing some of the things you do.

Yeah . . . and you shouldn't smoke either! I used to smoke Senior Service without [filter] tips *and* sing Little Richard.

What was your habit – what would you say was the highest number of cigarettes you would smoke in a day?

Forty a day. But the great thing about rock and roll is that none of us know anything about singing or else we probably couldn't do half of what we do. I don't know anything about singing at all. I didn't take lessons – I just knew people I liked and I would attempt to mimic them, just like a monkey would in the jungle.

So you were starting with imitation.

Yeah. I think everyone does. I started with imitation, definitely. I started with Elvis Presley – for me, if I sing ballads I think I'm Elvis Presley. Not so much these days – these days I think I'm Paul McCartney! But I used to think I was being Elvis Presley and if I sang high, raucous stuff I thought I was being Little Richard.

I'd like to come back to some of the influences, but I wonder if you could tell me first if you've ever had any vocal problems – any difficulties with recurring hoarseness, or loss of range or anything like that?

No. Well – once. Once when we were in the middle of a tour and I hadn't had any time to recover. I didn't really need to recover – I mean, with The Beatles it didn't seem to make much demand because we had shorter sets – we only did half hour sets which seems ludicrously short now and if we were angry we only **did twenty-five** minutes! And there were two singers – well three singers, but mainly two of us, so in half an hour I only had maximum a quarter of an hour's work per night and if George and Ringo both did a song it was even less than that. And so I never really had any problems to speak of. Now, it's two hours a set and generally speaking I'm the main vocalist, because generally speaking most people want to hear me singing instead of the other guys in the band. The last tour we did, Hamish from the Average White Band, he would do one number and help me on the vocals but I was still singing for two hours. Which is more than a two hour opera or musical because at least they've got other characters! But I've found that in doing the show, the main thing I've had to do is realise how long it would take me to recover. And I started to realise that what I should mainly do is have a day off in between shows. In The Beatles there were no problems because I had all these others singers – well, mainly John. But it was short sets and in the actual Beatles concerts there were never more than about twenty minutes of singing. In the Hamburg stuff we did, occasionally we did long hours but again, it was shared with the other guys. So the most difficult time for the voice has been more recently because along with longer sets and being the only one singing, I'm older. But in actual fact, I don't know enough to be worried. So for instance, on the last tour I would do a sound check, which would be about an hour's length and then have a few hours off and then do a two hour show. So it's about three hours singing a day with a couple of hours off in between and in fact it's all okay as long as I took a day off afterward. I would be all raring to go on the day afterward. The biggest problem I've found is talking after a successful gig – I'd be talking away – "Yeah, it was great, yeah, have a drink, yeah, I loved the way that went, oh did you see that person on the ground", etc. etc., and that was what did my voice in – it wasn't so much the singing – it was the sort of late night partying and talking a lot about how much fun we had. So I used have to sort of say, "Okay you talk – I'll just say yeah or whatever".

When you lost the voice for a little while how long did it last?

It was actually very short – it was in Pittsburgh – and it was only one day and we still did the show, so it wasn't actually like I lost my voice.

And that's the longest you've ever lost your voice or had severe hoarseness?

Yeah.

No illnesses?

No.

Have you ever had your voice "scoped"?

No. You know, I'm not that fussed. I just feel like I've been blessed with a gift and I don't want to look at it that much – it's like, you know, it just might vaporise? It might just disappear the more I find out about it so I don't really look too much. I just enjoy it.

Have you ever had any training of any kind?

No. I'm self trained.

Have you ever noticed changes in sound, like the tone "scratching" a bit or any change in the actual range that you can sing in?

Normally my voice sounds just like I want it to. To this point – touch wood – it seems to be just what I want it to be. I think it's a lot to do with practice and I'm pretty confident, which is due my success and I have practiced a lot. All those Beatle tours – Hamburg was every day, some days **for eight** hours, most days for three or four, but always everyday. Playing and singing became second nature. So I think that helps me now to this day. If I would show up and do the Cavern we would have one quick rehearsal on the day at the Cavern and I would just go straight on.

And that was two hours?

Cavern? No that was shorter. But the biggest difficulty was in Pittsburgh. I arrived at the sound check and started to do a song that had some falsetto in it but I couldn't get up into that high range. I thought "Uh-oh, this is a bit difficult". So I kept on with the sound check, thinking it would just right itself, but it didn't. So I got two voice specialists around. One who just sort of took a look and didn't do much and I didn't think was any good. He just sort of looked at my larynx and said right, you've got a sore throat, mild laryngitis and here's a potion, which didn't really help much. And I had a back-up guy, who they said somebody else had used and had good effect with and he did a bit more ultrasonic treatment on the throat and he did visualisation: "Imagine there's a white light coming in the top of your head and it's coming around and down and surrounding your larynx and it's feeling better" – it was almost like a mild hypnosis kind of thing. And that had enough effect for me to say okay I'll try and do the show. But the funny bit was, we were in Pittsburgh and we'd played Detroit the night before. And my big opener to the show was always "Good evening people of New York!" or wherever we were – a cheap trick – and you're off on to the music. And this night I was actually thinking of nothing but my throat and I was on auto-pilot and I was thinking "will my throat hold out?" and I normally don't give it a thought. I was thinking too much about it. So we did our first number, I got by okay, I scraped through, now came the time for my big announcement, and we're in Pittsburgh, and you know what I'm going to say, and I said: "People of Detroit!" and there was a beat – no reaction at all – and I said "People of Detroit!" – still no reaction and I said "You are *not* people of Pittsburgh" and then they roared. But I was just distracted thinking about my throat.

Well, your endurance is impressive and you've obviously enjoyed great vocal health during your career. I wonder if we could talk about aesthetics a bit. I've been really interested in listening closely to some of the vocal choices you make – I've been listening a lot of Run Devil Run and Flaming Pie. In aesthetic terms, do you have icons in your head in terms of who is a "good" singer?

Well, it depends on what style. Elvis Presley, Little Richard in those kinds of styles. R&B, well, for this year it's Nat King Cole who is, for me, the greatest. I love him. But I also love Fred Astaire. So when I started up, Elvis Presley and Little Richard – or Jerry Lee Lewis, the more sort of manly, somewhere in the middle kind of voice. Or Fats Domino, Ray Charles for a completely different, unique and husky kind of R&B voice. Marvin Gaye just for a beautiful voice, Smokey Robinson for a kind of falsetto-type voice, Bob Dylan for a quirky, personality type of voice, unique kind of voice but for this year I'm listening to a lot of Nat King Cole [he does a great impression of Nat King Cole singing *When I Fall in Love*] I think it's just great – so controlled, so musical, and it's just so effortless. And a big sound for no effort, which I'm always impressed by. I think microphones like lack of effort. I think a microphone diaphragm, if you scream into it very loud it kind of closes down a bit. I know this from making records. So you get a smaller record even though you're singing louder, but if you go to a mic and sing softly it opens up a bit and you get a bigger record. I think that's part of Nat's secret – his mic technique.

And what, in your mind, is a "bad" voice?

Oh I don't know – just people who don't sing in tune really. Or with very, very wide vibrato. Sounds like starting a car up. I don't really think about bad voices – I just ignore them.

Could you categorise your voice?

I would categorise it as a "wide-ranging voice".

And is there not one particular style that you think you're most at home in – perhaps ballad singing or rock singing?

No – I like too many types of things – I'm a Gemini so I like a lot of different things. So I enjoy doing a rock and roll album and I enjoy doing ballads and then I don't think of *I'm*

Down as any better or worse than *Yesterday*. Although they're completely different styles.

In your head then you feel pretty free about what you're willing to try?

Very free.

Because what you do is quite rangy.

Well, see, I still don't know my range – that's an interesting point. Sometimes I think well, I wonder if I can get this? And it's only by trying it out loud – I've got to do it full tilt – it's got to be right out – that's the only way I know whether I can get something or not.

Do you have a sense that your range has changed as you've grown older?

I keep expecting it to – I don't actually think it has much.

Did your range grow at all in your early twenties or late twenties?

I don't know. I don't really remember. But I think I can get deeper notes now. But on a good night, it's still pretty much what it's always been.

Could we talk a bit about quite specific style things you do – I'm interested in how rarely you use vibrato and actually how often you do what I would call "legit" ballad singing. Legit ballad singing usually ends with a kind of vibrato fade that eases us out of the sustain. It's not something you do often – is that a conscious choice?

My kind of people don't like it. My tribe don't like vibrato – we think it's a fake – to cover up like it is in string playing, because you don't know exactly where the note is, so you "vib" either side of it. People like Jeff Lynn, who I work with really hates vibrato. Notice The Beatles didn't do much of it. We used pretty much good straight notes, because there's something honest about it.

Does that make sustain difficult sometimes? What you often do is to fall off a note, or to use a compressed note ending or occasionally what I call a creak finish. Interestingly you do very few creak onsets, which is unusual because most ballad singers do a lot of creak onsets.

Just makes me unique you see.

The most common things you use are what I would call compressed endings or falling off a note, which are rock style finishes. Does this have anything to do with mistrust of vibrato – do you think you are consciously suppressing it?

I think to be honest, I don't actually like thinking about singing when I'm doing it. Like a friend said to me once, if you're painting never think you're going to paint a masterpiece because it stymies you – you get nervous about this masterpiece you think you're going to paint. So to me everything I like is often a surprise – I like to surprise myself. So I don't really think when I'm singing. I try and just think about communicating with an audience or with a person who's listening to the record. For instance, people ask me, well, is it a head voice or a chest voice and I still don't know what that means and I don't want to know what it means. I'm sure I've got a head voice somewhere, or a chest voice, don't I? People say to me what bass strings do you use and I say "long shiny ones". I think I'm trying to get an emotion over to people, so I'm thinking more about an emotion because I think the more I think about singing when I'm doing it, the worse I sing. I think it's like riding a bike. In abstract thinking, the more thought you put into it – well, think of Jackson Pollock who used to just drop paint to remove himself from the process – so he'd throw the paint to remove himself. The sheer act of throwing the paint to create line or somebody like de Kooning here [pointing to painting on his wall]. If you *tried* to paint the way he does it would come out all wrong. I admire that kind of thing in singing. That famous director's line about "throw it away" or "have fun with it", I think that's what art's about.

Once you've prepared to a good reasonable stage then I think it's time to throw everything out of the window and then just go do it.

To be fair, though, you started at that point that many people don't. If you're a young singer just getting started and you don't naturally have the kind of versatility you've always enjoyed – you'll have to do a bit of thinking, won't you?

Yes – when you're learning, yes, you have to think. But once you've done your practice, your learning, you want to be at the point where you don't have to think about it.

If we go back to the ballad sounds on Flaming Pie – particularly Some Days *and* Calico Skies *– were you aware of the great difference in the ballad sound between these two songs, was that a very conscious thing do you think?*

No, not really.

Was the difference in the sound about an emotional choice then?

I think it comes when I write it. When I write a song I suit the voice to whatever I'm doing when I write it. When I was writing *Calico Skies* it was all based around that little riff. And I think I fell in with that. I was thinking that the riff was little-ish, so I needed a little sound in the voice. I made the voice sympathise with what the musical backing was.

In Run Devil Run there's some extraordinarily free improvisation – do you feel freer in a sense when you're doing cover versions of songs?

Yeah – I always envy people who cover my stuff because I always feel that I have to lay down the song properly as it should be. I then think it's kind of nice for people who come later. Because everyone knows the tune, say, of *Hey Jude*, so then Wilson Pickett can come along and sing something entirely different. When you listen to him, I mean those aren't my notes at all – that's not how *Hey Jude* goes. But we know what he's doing. And I can never have a go at that with my own songs because I'm the one who's got to tell the world how *Hey Jude* goes.

It's interesting to hear you say that – maybe that's related to your diction. You may be aware that even in the hard rock stuff, your diction is very clean. Much cleaner than most hard rock singers. And when you are doing someone else's song, maybe that's when you feel free to relax the diction a bit. On the Fats Domino song on Run Devil Run – Coquette *– you actually let the diction slide a little bit and you do some improv. Melodic improv is rare on your own stuff.*

Yeah – but there we know the tune. It's been laid down by so many so whoever comes after – after the one who had that job of laying down the tune, or drawing the map – those of us who come after in a way have a slightly freer job.

So if you'd been a singer who'd never written any of the songs you've sung, do you think you'd be a different singer?

Might be, yeah. Yeah, I could have got much more into what my voice is. For me my voice is just part of the whole thing. Just part of it all. The writing the song, the accompaniment, I mean – take a song like *Blackbird*, it's 50/50 accompaniment to vocal. That accompaniment is very important – *Blackbird* almost doesn't work if you just do chords to it. It's quite different. So to me that's a good thing. I think if I didn't play instruments, and didn't write, all my attention would just be on what my voice was and I'd start to think that I'd have to know about it more. I would maybe have to do a bit of work on it. And also attitude – I think some people who don't do it all develop attitudes. Like, I think, Liam Gallagher – I've only just realised he doesn't write stuff and I knew he didn't play an instrument, so I think for him developing some kind of performing attitude is important.

Perhaps that's part of what he has to sell – a kind of defiant "rock" attitude?

Yes – otherwise he'd just be standing there twiddling his thumbs all the time because the rest of us have got chords to think about while we sing. One of the things I like in Run Devil Run was that I played the bass part as I sang and that made me feel free.

That's interesting because I would have thought that you would feel less free trying sing while having to play bass. Would it not have been a freer thing to have sung over the top of the bass track you recorded earlier?

No – it's a freedom that is like not looking too hard at a thing while you're doing it. The more you look at it the more you tighten up. The more you think about a thing the more nervous you get. With Run Devil Run I was new to those songs – I don't think I'd actually sung any of them before. I knew them all but I hadn't sung them. And I just decided that I was going to do it pretty much always in the key that the original artist had sung it in – I think only one or two were different. And I did have just one moment of panic on the Sunday night before the Monday morning session – I thought not only do I not know if I can sing these songs or not but I also had been grieving for a year and hadn't sung for a year.

So you hadn't sung at all for a year before going into the studio?

Nothing for a whole year so on the Sunday night I thought, "This is gonna be interesting. If it's anything like Pavarotti, well, on the Monday morning I won't be able sing". Because I really hadn't done anything – not even warmed up for a whole year. So I had a moment's worry when I thought, "Wow, this really might not work, I might have to say 'sorry everybody, better go home'." But I knew I'd only booked a week in the studio so I thought well, that wouldn't be too bad. So that was a bit of panic and I knew I'd never sung these songs before so I thought I wonder if I can do it.

So did you warm up on the Monday morning?

No. So, then, the other thing was, ooh – I also don't know the bass parts to these – so I thought what a mine of information I am *not*. And I am going to meet up with these people [the session musicians] – two of whom I've not met before – and I'm going to meet them from 10 to 10:30 and we're going to start work at 10:30 and I've got two songs to do before lunch. So I thought this is interesting. And I just dove into it head first. Met the guys I didn't know, found we got on fine. Gave them a real quick idea of what we were going to do – I showed them the song. We started at 10:30 and I said does anyone know this song – it was a song called *Fabulous* that I'd heard on a fairground when I was a kid – and they all said no, so without a warm up I just said it goes like this. I showed them on guitar just the basic riff and sang and they all went, yeah, okay, we've got it, and I got on bass and we just recorded. And that was the way we did the whole week – there were no warm ups or anything it was just dive right in.

Is that something that you're used to doing? Do you usually warm up?

No. Not at all.

Can I ask when you're doing that hard rock sound – are you aware at all of what you're doing?

No – I used to say about doing Little Richard stuff, I used to say to myself I just have to jump out of the top of my head. That's as much as I know about it. It's no good doing Little Richard with a pinched little voice you actually have to go for it – I can't show you here, it would be too loud. It's like playing bagpipes – you can't play them indoors. To me you can't do it in a small room. To me, well, it's just a matter of jumping out of the top of my head really – it's something that I just know how to do.

And you're not aware of any extra tension or muscle work going on when you sing that way?

Not really, no. I just sort of know the voice that I do that was based on imitating Little Richard that I did when I was a teenager, when he first came out and I got what was my impression of Little Richard down. And if you listen to *Long Tall Sally* it is a pretty good impression of Little Richard. And then I started to get my own style. Something like *I'm Down* was a bit more me than Little Richard. But it definitely started off with mimicking. But once I had an imprint of like the mimic thing my head and body knew how to do it; knew what muscles to use – I just knew how to mimic that voice. I couldn't really begin to analyse it. It's as if I play a role and all the chops in the voice go with it.

After singing that kind of hard rock do you find it hard to go into a ballad sound?

I don't think so. I do that on stage and it's quite good – it's a relaxing sort of pacing thing. On stage I'll have two or three loud songs and naturally bring it down a bit just pacing both for the audience and for me. So it all seems to just happen quite naturally. In everything I do the word "primitive" is always very important. So, like I sail a boat; I've never had a boat lesson in my life but I'm not a bad sailor. And when I get out with the sail and the wind I think yeah – primitive man did this. I love that – it touches me. When I paint I think of cave paintings and when I sing it's the same way. I've never had a guitar lesson, I've never had a singing lesson, I've never had a bass lesson. I have had a piano lesson like everyone has – doing scales – but I hated it. I've had quite a few attempts at that during my life and I've always hated it. I think about singing lessons, well, it's all horses for courses, isn't it. Some people sound good when they've had lessons. But I have to say – all the people I've really admired have not had a lesson in their lives to my knowledge. That may just be something to do with my taste but I think that generally people who are really moving music on – say the early jazz musicians in New Orleans – these guys generally weren't taught.

So throughout the whole of your life you've never had a singing teacher talk with you or work with you in any way?

No.

Finally – and you've touched on this a bit – are you finding the speaking voice lowering or changing?

No. I'm a bit of a chameleon. Ringo said this to me once – he was explaining it to Barbara – he said "he's got thousands of voices". I've always been a mimic – I mimic characters. I do have a lot of characters in my head. And it's the same with singing I think – it's just an extension of all of that. I ring people up on the phone when I'm kidding around and they often don't think it's me.

But when you're just talking in your normal voice – no changes you can detect?

No. Accent has changed – I've lived down here now longer than I lived in Liverpool. But when I go back up there I pick up the accent. Or when I spend even a day in Ireland. But I just can't help it because I always want to belong. I want to communicate.

The thing about the tracks on Run Devil Run, at this point in your career, I mean, they sound like Long Tall Sally – you seem to still have all the voice now that you had twenty, thirty years ago.

That's why I don't want to think about it too much.

But of course that's why I do! I mean, what explains people like you? For those of us who teach singers, it would be interesting to know why some voices, like yours, last well despite the kind of singing you do, which many voice tutors might worry about. No warm ups, "jumping out of the top of your head" to sound like Little Richard – you just seem to have an amazingly resilient voice.

Maybe it's something to do with attitude. If in some way I'm happy or focused or really know what I want to sing. No – that's bollocks – with Run Devil Run I didn't really know what I wanted to sing. But my dad had a great expression – DIN, Do It Now – that's quite a good one. Just do it. And somehow often in that sheer fact of doing it you find out more about it. I've worked a lot live. And maybe it's to do with confidence – you would have confidence if you'd been in The Beatles!

SONG INDEX

INDEX